T0283437

The Jailer's Reckoning

The Jailer's Reckoning

How Mass Incarceration
Is Damaging America

Kevin B. Smith

ROWMAN & LITTLEFIELD
Lanham • Boulder • New York • London

Published by Rowman & Littlefield
An imprint of The Rowman & Littlefield Publishing Group, Inc.
4501 Forbes Boulevard, Suite 200, Lanham, Maryland 20706
www.rowman.com

86-90 Paul Street, London EC2A 4NE

Distributed by NATIONAL BOOK NETWORK

British Library Cataloguing in Publication Information Available

Library of Congress Cataloging-in-Publication Data

Names: Smith, Kevin B., 1963– author.
Title: The jailer's reckoning : how mass incarceration is damaging America / Kevin B. Smith, Leland and Dorothy Chair of Arts & Sciences, University of Nebraska-Lincoln.
Description: Lanham : Rowman & Littlefield, [2024] | Includes bibliographical references and index.
Identifiers: LCCN 2024026897 (print) | LCCN 2024026898 (ebook) | ISBN 9781538192382 (cloth ; alk. paper) | ISBN 9781538192399 (epub)
Subjects: LCSH: Imprisonment—United States. | Prisoners—United States. | Criminal justice, Administration of—United States.
Classification: LCC HV9471 .S633 2024 (print) | LCC HV9471 (ebook) | DDC 365/.973—dc23/eng/20240701
LC record available at https://lccn.loc.gov/2024026897
LC ebook record available at https://lccn.loc.gov/2024026898

♾️™ The paper used in this publication meets the minimum requirements of American National Standard for Information Sciences—Permanence of Paper for Printed Library Materials, ANSI/NISO Z39.48-1992.

Contents

Preface

The United States of America is an inconsistency wrapped in a difference inside a contradiction. Its official anthem declares it the home of the free and the brave, but it is also home to the largest prison population in the Western world. Despite its vocal championing of individual liberty, it locks up its own citizens at rates autocracies fear to replicate. It is an evangelist of democracy and human rights but strips the franchise—the most basic civil liberty—from millions of offenders who have served their time and returned to their lives.

Why did this happen? How did the United States become what one scholar has described as an "incarceration nation"?[1] That description is not hyperbole. At any given time, there are more than two million people sitting behind bars in the United States. Another five million are under some form of correctional supervision. Something like one in thirty American adults have served at least some time in prison, a figure that jumps to one in six for African Americans.[2] As you read this something like half of Americans will have direct or indirect (know someone, most likely a family member) experience of prison. How did we manage that? Why create a system of mass incarceration that entangles so many and disproportionately targets people of color? And, perhaps more importantly, what has that done to us? How is this historically unprecedented experiment in normalizing the carceral experience shaping the social, economic, and political life of the republic?

These are the questions this book attempts to answer. Underlying those answers is a long-term scholarly project anchored in reams of data analysis, but this is a book written for a broad, general audience rather than for academics alone. As what follows details, the costs of mass incarceration—what I'm terming the jailer's reckoning—is borne by everyone. Whether that price is worth paying is something we all have a stake in, and a primary goal of this book is to clarify those stakes—and their implications—to as many people as possible. I'm less interested in wowing anyone with my scholastic chops than in communicating with anyone willing to listen. Accordingly, I've swept the vast majority of the statistical detail underpinning claims and inferences in this book into an online methodological appendix (see here: rowman.com/ISBN/9781538192382). For the true and dedicated data geeks, that appendix includes directions to the publicly available data and code. The analytic detail, in other words, is there if you want it, but this is a book intended to be accessible to any interested reader, not just for those who fuss over esoteric statistical particulars.

I should also note at the outset what this book is not. It is not going to advocate for a particular partisan policy or scholarly or ideological position. In interrogating explanations favored by progressives, by conservatives, by journalists, by lawyers, and by various disciplinary flavors of scholars, I've found gaps aplenty. Whatever your position—lock 'em up, let 'em out, anything in between—it will not find universal support in the following pages. I am not trying to make a case here. I am trying to make sense of what we did, why we did it, and what it's done to us. And the emphasis is most definitely on the "we."

This project has, to put it mildly, been a while in the making—indeed, its roots precede my time as an academic. I spent a decent chunk of my years as a journalist covering police and crime beats, and I took some of those interests with me when I entered grad school to learn my trade as a comparative state politics scholar. In this capacity and fairly early in my career—this would be late 1990s, early 2000s—I published a study or two on state-level incarceration and crime. One of those studies still gets cited pretty frequently and over the years has prompted a series of conversations and emails—some coming wholly out of the blue—that, in so many words, say, "Hey, are you ever going to follow up on this? Why the heck do states lock so many people up? Is it really because of what this or that scholar/journalist/lawyer/guy next to me on a barstool has been saying?"[3] Even though I mostly morphed into a political psychologist a while ago, those questions kept coming and I never stopped thinking about them. They became a two-decade itch that resulted in the book you currently have in your hands.

Producing this book was far from a solo effort. Underlying what you are about to read is the toil of a couple of generations of research assistants. Before they went off to law school, Benajamin Schoenkin (Washington University) and Emily Johnson (Harvard) spent a non-trivial part of their undergraduate years doing some of the all-important grunt work, even though that labor would not bear fruit until after they had a juris doctorate and launched careers. Alison O'Toole, one of my PhD research assistants, went so deep into a review of the relevant scholarly literature one academic year I wasn't sure if she'd ever come back. Another of my PhD students, Clarisse Warren, not only put in a lot of research labor but also played a big role in helping to keep me organized—not a task for the fainthearted. I've been working on this project for so long that I fear I've forgotten and left out others who rightly should be included on this list, and for that accept any apologies owed. I alone am responsible for any mistakes, errors, flubs, or whoopsies you might spot in or on the following pages. Credit for any and everything readers determine is worthwhile is properly shared by whoever pitched in with the work along the way.

I'd also like to say big thanks to Michael Kerns, my editor at Rowman & Littlefield. I'll not go into details, but suffice to say a project aimed at a general audience that also has to hurdle a standard scholarly peer review process can result in a convoluted development process. Michael believed in this from the get-go, and this book wouldn't exist without him.

And as always, thanks to the fam—every damn one of them—who heroically declined to respond rationally to my repeated out-loud musings on the substance of this book over a years-long period. Encouragement, support, and love are not always earned, but always appreciated.

Chapter 1

A Million-Dollar Sandwich

*In which we discover a seventy-year lunch, that mass incarceration
is a state phenomenon, and how differences among states
might help explain why so many people are in prison.*

Sometime during the early afternoon of January 12, 2010, Larry Dayries walked into a Whole Foods in Austin, Texas, and picked up the most expensive tuna fish sandwich in history. Dayries paid nothing for lunch—he stiffed the deli counter—but that meal's ultimate cost easily runs to six figures. The tab started accumulating as soon as Lance Johnson, a Whole Foods loss prevention officer, saw Dayries giving two slices of sourdough spread with mayo and fish the old five-fingered discount. What happened next is disputed. Johnson said he followed Dayries outside, where Dayries proceeded to pull a knife and threaten him. Dayries said he did no such thing. He'd just absent-mindedly wandered out of the store when Johnson began harassing him. While the kerfuffle's specifics remain uncertain, there is no doubt Dayries was subsequently arrested and found guilty of aggravated robbery with a deadly weapon. His sentence? Seventy years. With good behavior, his earliest parole date is set for February 7, 2040. If he serves his entire sentence, he will get out of prison in 2080 when he will be 111 years old.[1]

With more than 200,000 inmates, Texas operates one of the largest prison systems in the world.[2] Those sorts of numbers bring economies of scale—per inmate Texas pays less for its penal operations than many states—but keeping people like Larry Dayries behind bars is unavoidably expensive. Estimates vary, but a rough projection for Texas is $22,000 per inmate per year.[3] If we take that as a reasonable annual baseline and assume away inflation and anything that might influence future per inmate costs, locking up Dayries will cost the state of Texas roughly $1.5 million if he serves his full sentence. If he gets out at his earliest parole date, it will "only" amount to about $750,000. Averaging those two extremes, Texans could easily cough up a million dollars to keep Dayries behind bars—for stealing a tuna fish sandwich.

Most reasonable people would agree keeping society safe from sandwich snatchers at such eye-watering cost doesn't make a whole lot of sense. Even granting full credence to Johnson's claim that Dayries menaced him with a knife, the cost-benefit sums of a seven-decade stretch for such offenses seem ridiculously out of whack. Dayries obviously loses his liberty and any shot at ever being a civically or economically productive member of free society, and free society pays through the nose to make that happen. You do not have to be a full-throated supporter of lunch counter larceny to conclude that's nuts. And that would include the people who locked up Larry Dayries.

Dayries received what amounts to a life sentence not just for pilfering a sandwich, or even for the violence he allegedly threatened in a follow-up confrontation. The proximate cause of Larry Dayries's seventy-year sentence was his past. According to the Texas Department of Criminal Justice, Dayries has a lengthy criminal record. Prior to walking into that Whole Foods, he'd already been convicted of burglary, armed robbery, and a string of thefts, and he served several prison terms as a result. In short, he was classified as a habitual criminal when he stood before a jury in the District Court of Travis County. In Texas, that's something you definitely do not want to be. Texas is one of twenty-eight states with what are colloquially known as three-strikes laws, which permit the state to impose tough—some might say draconian— sentences for repeat criminal offenders. The logic here is that if you make a habit of breaking the rules of society, then society is justified in tolerating only so much before it exiles you to a penal institution for an extended period. Possibly for life. The triviality of the offense triggering this sanction is less the issue than a chronic criminal history: A piffling offense to civil order can put you behind bars for a very, very long time if it is preceded by an established pattern of social predation. Even if you vehemently disagree with habitual offender policies and recoil at the injustice of brutal punishments for small-fry infractions, there's a certain tough-love rationality underpinning this argument.

Or maybe not. Maybe that argument is just cover for more malevolent motivations to deprive select people of their liberty. Dayries did not have just a history of criminal activity, he had an even longer history of mental health struggles and drug addiction.[4] He is also Black. As a society we sweep disproportionate numbers of all three groups into prison. Roughly two-thirds of people in prison have some sort of substance abuse disorder,[5] and in some state institutions between 15 to 30 percent of inmates are suffering from some sort of significant mental health issue.[6] The racial imbalance in prison populations is jaw dropping. Incarceration is a fate that singularly afflicts a single demographic group—Black people, and specifically Black males. Roughly 12 percent of Texas's population is Black while roughly a third of the people locked up in its prisons are Black, a disparity that scales nationally.[7] In the

United States, the lifetime actuarial probability of being incarcerated is estimated as roughly 30 percent for Black males. It is less than 5 percent for white males.[8] Dayries, in short, was playing some pretty poor odds when he walked into that Whole Foods and pinched a tuna fish sandwich.

What happened to Larry Dayries, then, is not a simple story of a punishment fitting or not fitting a crime. Tangled up in this narrative are questions of racial justice, public health, crime prevention, society's tolerance for rule breakers, where and when that sufferance should end, what happens once someone crosses the proverbial line, and much, much more. Dayries is just one subject among millions involuntarily participating in a forty-year experiment whose social, economic, and political impacts we only dimly understand. During that span the United States has deprived its citizens of their liberty at a clip unprecedented not just among liberal democracies, but at a rate calculated to make the most authoritarian regimes blush. In doing so it has created a massive underclass. As of 2010 an estimated 3 percent of the entire US population—15 percent of the Black population—had a prison record. Eight percent of the entire population—and a stunning 33 percent of the Black male population—had a felony record.[9] A felony conviction imposes constraints on a wide range of economic and social opportunity, and it can even lead to permanent political disenfranchisement, the loss of the basic democratic right to vote. Why? Why did we do this? Why did we become the world's biggest jailer? And, just as importantly, what has it done to us? How has having the world's biggest ex-prisoner population shaped us socially, economically, and politically? The object of this book is to seek answers to those questions. It is no easy task. As the case of Larry Dayries amply demonstrates, the system's severity and head-scratching consequences can readily be pointed out, but its complexity and absurdity can defy description, let alone explanation. Starting an investigation into the causes and consequences of the carceral state with a story of a stolen sandwich makes about as much sense as anything. A more systematic pursuit of answers to the questions at the heart of this book, however, first calls for an analytical map. Picking up that map leads us straight to a jailer with two faces.

THE TWO-FACED JAILER

The United States locks up a greater proportion of its citizens than any other country, and it's at a rate far above that of comparable liberal democracies. On a per capita basis, the United States incarcerates four times more people than Australia, five times more than the United Kingdom, six times more than Canada, and eight times more than Germany.[10] When it comes to depriving citizens of their liberty, the United States keeps company with the likes of

Russia, China, Rwanda, and El Salvador, authoritarian regimes with dubious commitments to human rights and countries with recent histories of violence, civil disorder, and repression. Estimates by the federal government's official criminal justice ledger jockeys—the Bureau of Justice Statistics—indicate the incarceration rate has been north of 600 inmates per 100,000 for decades. Those are astonishing numbers. By some estimates, by the early part of the twenty-first century something like 1 out of every 100 US residents was sitting in some sort of jail cell.[11] The numbers have since declined, but they still outstrip any comparable liberal democracy by a margin large enough to inject a painful irony to America as a self-described "land of the free." Of course, there's nothing new here. America's unprecedented commitment to locking up its own citizens is a familiar tale told countless times by scholars, journalists, politicians, and reform advocates. Here's the thing, though: That story is wrong.

In reality, the United States, as in the US government, tosses its citizens into the pokey at roughly the same rate as well-known criminal coddlers like Norway, Denmark, and Finland. At any given time in the past few years, there were something like 175,000 people locked up under federal jurisdiction.[12] In a nation of roughly 330 million, that works out to an incarceration rate in the ballpark of 50 inmates per 100,000 population.[13] Those numbers put the United States somewhere between Japan and Sweden, at the very bottom of World Incarceration League and a very long way from the oft-told tale of America's imprisonment exceptionalism. So, what's the story with the numbers? Is America a nation that uses incarceration rarely and judiciously, somewhere in line with the most liberal members of Northern Europe? Or is it a nation of harsh justice and severe punitiveness, herding people into involuntary confinement at rates that would make totalitarians blanche?

These are actually harder questions to answer than you might think. The reason is that unlike many of the countries it is often compared to, the United States does not have *a* criminal justice system. Instead, it has fifty-one of them: in addition to the federal system, every one of the fifty states operates an independent counterpart, each with its own criminal codes, law enforcement agencies, courts, and prisons. Most important for the purposes of this book, each of those systems is controlled by a sovereign political government with the legal authority to exercise considerable independence in deciding who gets locked up for what and for how long. Those political systems exercise that independence to the full. In America, your liberty—or even your life—may be forfeit not simply because of what you do, but where you do it. If Larry Dayries had run off with a lobster roll from a lunch counter in Maine it's unlikely that he'd be spending the rest of his life behind bars.

The fact is, we have a two-faced system—technically, you could argue a three-faced system—and the one with the real killer eyes is not the federal government but the governments of the fifty states. The vast majority of people behind bars fall into three distinct buckets. There are those under the jurisdiction of the Federal Bureau of Prisons, people convicted of federal crimes and serving time in federal institutions. They account for less than 10 percent of the two million–plus people locked up in any given year. A little less than 30 percent are in local jails. Some of these are serving time for misdemeanor offenses, but most—about half a million—have not been convicted of any crime, let alone sentenced for one. They simply couldn't make bail after an arrest and are just sitting in jail waiting for the system's gears to grind and figure out what to do with them. That raises its own set of questions about (in)justice, but they are beyond the scope of this book. It is the third category that is the focus here: those held under state jurisdiction in state prisons. They account for roughly 60 percent of all incarcerations in the United States, by some margin the lion's share of mass incarceration.[14] This is the jailer that swallows whole the likes of Larry Dayries.

Unlike the selective accounting that can be applied to the federal ledgers, there's no generous fiddling of the numbers that can make things look better at the state level. Collectively, state incarceration rates are roughly eight times higher than federal incarceration rates. Put the states into that World Incarceration League individually and they absolutely dominate the top of the table. While there is some movement among the leaders depending on the year and statistical source consulted, Louisiana, Oklahoma, and Mississippi consistently make the top five.[15] Georgia, Texas, Arizona, and a handful of others are not far behind, all peddling hard in the prison population peloton, all capable of making the periodic sprint to the front. In the last ten years—years when prison populations were flat or falling—at least ten states were locking people up at levels that were skating close to 1 percent of their population. It bears re-emphasizing that I'm trying to exclude federal incarcerations and people behind bars in local and county jails from these numbers—I'm looking only at those serving a minimum of a one-year sentence in state institutions. Across four recent decades (1978–2019), the peak annual incarceration rate of those falling into this latter category was 885 per 100,000 population. Louisiana achieved this dubious distinction in 2009.[16] The axiomatic principle of all that follows is that states are the best place to search for answers to why we have become the world's largest jailer and to understand what taking on that job has done to us socially, economically, and politically.

An important argument for this starting assumption is that while most states tend to have high incarceration rates compared to other countries, compared to each other they are all over the place. Florida locks up people at roughly twice the rate as New Jersey. Texas at roughly three times the rate of Minnesota. Louisiana at roughly four times the rate of Vermont. These relative differences among the states are remarkably stable across time. For more than a century, incarceration rates have tended to change synchronously, in other words, they head up or down at roughly the same time in most states. That suggests there are national forces that drive incarceration rates. Yet there's virtually no evidence that states have ever, or ever will, lock up people in roughly similar proportions. Pick any time period in the last 120 or so years and the incarceration rates might look very different, but the state rankings in the "World League" look awfully similar.[17] Whatever national-level forces are in play, they cannot explain these huge, persistent state-level variations.

A general sense of the variation in incarceration rates is conveyed in figure 1.1, which summarizes the distribution of annual incarceration rates for each state between 1978 and 2019. This is a boxplot, a type of chart designed to capture a range of summary statistics: (1) the range of values between upper and lower quartiles of the distribution. This range is represented by the "box" associated with each state—the wider the box, the greater the dispersion in incarceration rates over the forty-one-year period covered. (2) The minimum and maximum incarceration rates—these are the values indicated by the ends of the "whiskers" coming out of each box. Dots represent outliers, or data points that are unusually far away from all other values of the distribution and are placed beyond the whiskers. (3) The median, or the value that splits each state's forty-one annual incarceration rate observations into two equal halves—this is the vertical "stripe" in the middle of each box.

Figure 1.1 clearly shows the huge incarceration rate disparities between states. Between 1978 and 2019 Louisiana's *lowest* annual incarceration rate (top line) exceeded the *highest* incarceration rate recorded in Maine during the same time period. The median values of the highest five states are orders of magnitude higher than the five lowest states. The chart captures not just the variation between states but also within them. Louisiana's whiskers range from 179 all the way to 885, meaning its highest incarceration rate was about five times more than its lowest. This is why it has a "wide box"—its annual incarceration numbers are not just high, they are widely dispersed. In contrast, Maine's maximum incarceration rate was "only" twice as high as its minimum, and the range of values involved was much smaller from 51.7 and its highest at 152. Comparatively speaking, Maine is a "narrow box" state, its incarceration rates staying in much smaller range than the wide-box states.

What could explain these huge differences, both in the absolute levels of incarceration and changes in those levels? Differences in crime are an obvious guess, but a large body of scholarship has long since concluded that differences in criminal activity both between and within states is, at best, only a partial explanation.[18] Instead, the differences are argued to be more a product of dissimilarities in institutional setups, socio-demographics, diversity in the will of voters, and the consequences that naturally flow from variation

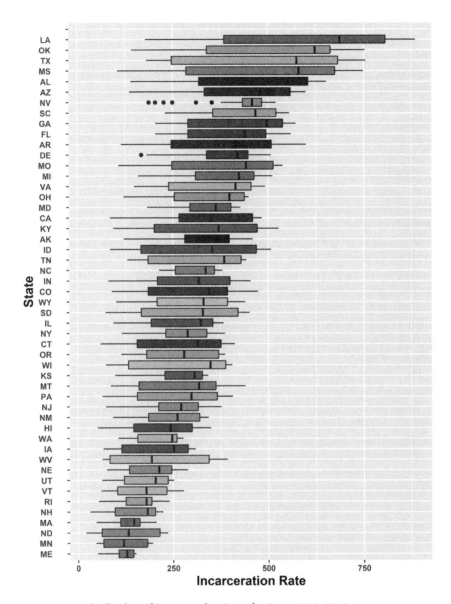

Figure 1.1.　Distribution of Incarceration Rates by State 1978–2019

between sovereign political systems. This is all addressed in detail later, but for now the key concept to underline is that the states are not alike. On a wide variety of measures—not just incarceration rates—differences among the states are large, substantive, and meaningful.

DIFFERENCES THAT MAKE A DIFFERENCE

The United States is a big, complex place and in practice an attempt to explain any element of its political, social, and economic makeup—certainly any causal aspects of its multidimensional criminal justice arrangements—requires ditching a lot of important nuance. That same complexity, however, also has advantages. True, there is no getting around the baffling, fragmented, and balkanized fact of the US political system. It contains overlapping and redundant processes, duplicative institutions, supernumerary decision makers, and bureaucratic choke points, and it routinely marches in different directions under the orders of assorted administrative buttinskis. The governing machinery is not only full of Rube Goldberg gears furiously spinning without actually seeming to drive anything; it is collectively piloted by a confederacy of adversaries. Officers on the bridge and swabs in the engine room not only routinely disagree on direction and speed, they frequently have no consensus on exactly what sort of machine they are operating. Metaphorically, they sit in everything from a rowboat to a spaceship. Dragging systematic comprehension out of all that is not a task for the faint of heart. Yet some of this same complexity also offers a critical explanatory lever. All political systems are confusing in their own way, but the United States uniquely compartmentalizes its confusion in a way that can actually contribute to clarity.

The majority of nation-states have unitary forms of government, political systems where a single, central government holds sovereign power. Regional or local governments—states, counties, whatever—are subordinate to that central government and can do only what the central government lets them. For more than 80 percent of countries on the planet this is the preferred way to run a nation's political railroad.[19] In contrast, the United States is one of only two dozen or so nation-states to have federal political systems (other examples include Australia, India, Brazil, Mexico, and Canada). This means national and regional governments are co-sovereigns, so the latter have the legal freedom to act independently of the central government in at least some policy arenas. In a federal system, central governments can (and do) try to influence how regional governments exercise their freedom, for example, by offering or withdrawing monetary support. The key thing differentiating a federal from a unitary system, though, is that a regional government can choose not to do what the central government wants it to do. In its constitutionally designated lane, regional government is in the driver's seat and, at least in theory, can drive as fast or slow as it likes. The United States is unique even among the handful of nations organized along federal lines in the sheer number of such governments it has stuffed into its political system. The fifty states represent close to double the number of sovereign regional governments in any other comparable federally organized nation.[20]

It's not just the number of states that's important, but the fact that they all exercise sovereign power in fact as well as in theory. To be sure, governance in the United States in many major policy areas is a state and federal amalgamation, a programmatic and management mélange making differences hard to discern. States nonetheless exercise real independent power, and what most people—including many scholars of American government—do not fully grasp is that state governments are fundamentally different forms of government than their federal counterpart. The federal government is a limited government, meaning it can exercise only the powers explicitly or implicitly granted to it by the US Constitution. States are very different. Technically they are governments with plenary powers, in other words they are *not* limited governments.[21] They do not need to consult the United States' or their own constitutions to seek legal authority to act. In effect, the federal government has to ask the constitution if it has permission to act. In contrast, the states have to ask if they are specifically prohibited from acting. That's more than a semantic difference. In 2024, if you sold weed in Colorado, you could have been running a legitimate business in complete compliance with state law. No chance of that next door in Nebraska—there you'd have been violating a range of criminal laws that could have put you behind bars, quite possibly for a very long time. That's a big difference.

The vast majority of the criminal law in the United States is independently formulated by states using the freedom granted by the Tenth Amendment. Arguments over what the states are free to do without federal interference have been raging for more than two hundred years and with luck will rage on for another two hundred.[22] Yet there's been general agreement from the beginning that dealing with crime is mainly the business of the states. The reason mass incarceration is mostly a phenomenon of the states is in no small part because the states write and enforce the vast majority of criminal law under the authority of their own constitutions. And they have gone about this in very different ways.

The states differ not just in how punitive to make their criminal justice systems. They are different in lots of other ways—geography, geology, topography, and weather are just a handful of examples. Almost by definition these things imply profound differences in how a wide range of policy issues will be prioritized and dealt with. The regulation of marine fisheries, for example, is not much of a concern in landlocked Nebraska. On the other hand, that's a big deal in Maine. Snow removal is never far from the minds of local government officials during winter in Wisconsin, but it practically never crosses the radar of their counterparts in Florida. All of this makes the states a unique laboratory for analyzing policy and political questions. They represent a large number of sovereign governments who are simultaneously readily comparable—they all must operate within the framework of the US Constitution—while also acting as highly independent policymakers. They differ on a huge variety of dimensions that almost certainly influence how that policymaking independence is exercised. From one perspective, that does indeed create a system that looks complicated, redundant, and spinning off in lots of different directions for lots of different reasons. From an explanatory point of view, though, it's a gold mine.

Which brings us back to the task at hand of figuring out why we lock so many people up and getting a handle on what that has done to us. One set of differences among the states can be examined to see if they predict other differences. Plenty of scholars have sought to exploit exactly that variance—I'm far from the first to argue that mass incarceration is fundamentally state-level phenomenon that can be best understood by looking at comparative patterns across states.[23] That variation, though, still has much to tell us, the patterns far from comprehensively examined, let alone fully understood. For example, scholars of state politics have long been fascinated with the concept of political culture, the idea that states have their own distinct, self-replicating communal beliefs on what government is and what it should (or should not) be used for. The best-known concept of state-level political culture is the framework formulated by political scientist Daniel Elazar in the 1960s. Elazar argued that states have distinct political cultures rooted in the religious and ethnic backgrounds of three distinctive waves of settlement that rolled out across America in more-or-less straight lines from East Coast to West Coast between the seventeenth and nineteenth centuries.[24]

The three basic types of political cultures identified by Elazar are moralistic, individualistic, and traditionalistic. Moralistic political cultures spring from the Puritans who settled the Northeast and their Yankee successors who, along with Scandinavians, Germans, and Eastern Europeans, settled across the north and the Great Plains. Reflecting their religiously anchored social origins, moralistic political cultures view government as a means to help build a better society, a vehicle to advance the communal good. Individualistic cultures are anchored in the English, Scottish, Irish, and German settlers who settled such states as New Jersey and Pennsylvania and moved West into Ohio and Indiana. These folks, Elazar argued, had distinctly different civic values than their compatriots to the north. They came to the United States in search of individual opportunity, not to faff around building religious utopias or communally idealized versions of the good society. This gave them a very different orientation to government, which was viewed essentially as an extension of the marketplace. Government was there to either help the individual get ahead or to get the hell out of that individual's way. Traditionalistic cultures are exclusively Southern and Southwestern, bounded by Virginia and Florida on the East Coast and extending across the nation's belly to Arizona. Political culture here views government through a lens of tradition, hierarchy, and class divisions; here government exists to defend and maintain the existing social order.

Elazar recognized that states would not necessarily be "pure" versions of these categories—he identified lots of states as mixes—but nonetheless argued that in each state one of these cultures would dominate, its core values institutionally embedded and passed on to succeeding generations who absorbed the civic beliefs and principles they marinated in. Elazar is far from the only scholar to advance an idea of culture as a "sticky" social phenomena, something planted in the communal soil by the ethnic and religious values of a settler population that becomes so rooted it continues to bloom in very different communities generations removed from their historical origins.[25] Still, scholars in the 1960s were initially pretty dubious about the validity of Elazar's concept of political culture, let alone its ability to help explain any meaningful questions about politics and public policy. Elazar's entire analysis was anchored in impressionistic historicism, mushy stuff to a generation of political scientists who were just starting to take the "science" part of political science seriously.

That changed in 1969 when Ira Sharkansky put numbers on Elazar's political culture classifications.[26] Sharkansky was somewhat skeptical about the notion of state political culture, but nonetheless he argued that if Elazar was right, it should be possible to create a unidimensional, numeric measure of state political culture. Sharkansky did exactly that and then set about seeing whether his spiffy new political culture index could predict anything of interest about politics and government at the state level. It did. Everything from voter turnout to tax effort to the size of state government to the generosity of welfare payments, and much, much more. And these were not piffling relationships. Some of the correlations topped .70 (a correlation ranges from -1.0 to +1.0, so the maximum absolute value is 1.0, and political scientists live in a world where robust correlations half that size precipitate much rehearsing of award acceptance speeches). The demise of Elazarian political culture's eye-popping explanatory horsepower has been forecast pretty much ever since Sharkansky quantified it. The argument is that as generations pass, mobility increases, and as virtual community replaces the actual thing, the clean edges of Elazar's classifications will gradually erode until they dissolve entirely in the solution of a nationally (perhaps even globally) homogenized culture. And, fair enough, Sharkansky's measure doesn't perform now quite as well as it did fifty years ago.[27] Even so, it still does a better job of explaining and predicting political and policy differences among the states than most other options. It is a difference that makes a difference.

With all that in mind, imagine a polity whose culture views a primary job of government as maintaining the social status quo, to protect and defend existing social hierarchy and divisions. A reasonable hypothesis is a government embedded in that culture is going to take a pretty dim view of people who threaten the status quo and its attendant rules and norms. Anyone on the lower end of the social strata who represents a vague or even mostly imagined threat to the existing social order should not expect much in the way of clemency if the jailer catches them hovering around the line of the law. Now imagine a culture where government is seen as a vehicle to improve society, as a means to benefit everyone in the commonweal. Comparatively speaking, is that government more likely to seek penitence rather than punishment from scofflaws, to show a little more clemency to the less privileged who break the rules, and generally be a little less inclined to deprive members of the community of their liberty?

Figure 1.2 puts this hypothesis to the test, showing the relationship between Sharkansky's quantitative measure of Elazar's state-level culture and state incarceration rates in 2010. Sharkansky's scale scores states on a continuous 1 to 9 index, with a 1 indicating a pure moralistic state, a 5 a pure individualistic state, a 9 as a pure traditionalistic state, and numbers in between those anchors represent states with mixed cultures. The pattern is visually pretty obvious. States with traditionalistic cultures have higher incarceration rates, and states with moralistic cultures have lower incarceration rates. In other words, exactly what we'd predict if temporally stable political cultures mapped by Elazar shaped criminal justice policy. That one measure

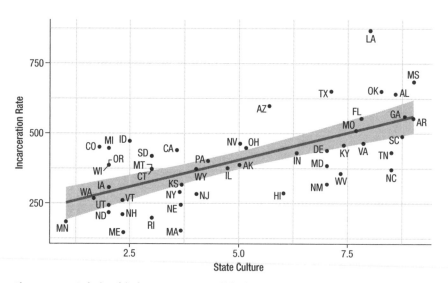

Figure 1.2. Relationship between State Political Culture and Incarceration Rates

can explain 45 percent—nearly half—of all the variance in 2010 state-level incarceration.[28] Again, that's a difference that makes a difference. And, just to ram the point home, *state political culture is almost wholly absent from existing scholarly attempts to explain state-level incarceration rates.*[29]

To anticipate some perfectly legitimate objections, I want to make clear I am *not* arguing that, end of story, the phenomenon of mass incarceration comes down to a matter of differences in political culture among the states. The key takeaway here is that if the objective is to try to explain why we lock up so many people and to try to understand what that has done to us politically, socially, and economically, the place to look for answers is the states. If we focus on states as the unit of analysis, we've got fifty independent governments who bear the primary legal authority to lock people up, who have exercised that power very differently, and also who differ on a lot of other things that might be reasonably expected to predict incarceration. Culture is simply one example of this. The fact that incarceration rates in 2010 can be so accurately predicted by a measure of culture conceived of forty years earlier certainly suggests the latter is capturing something important about the states that is linked to their criminal justice policies. To be sure, it is unlikely that culture alone explains incarceration. The tight culture-incarceration correlation more likely says something about states' relative receptivity to a larger political and social environment that pushes policymakers in a more punitive direction. More proximate political and social causal drivers might include poverty, ideology, partisan polarization, and, even levels of criminal activity. And, of course, race, which looms large over not just what happened to Larry Dayries but to any investigation of incarceration in the United States. It is all of these differences and more that provide the explanatory leverage for what follows. What else besides culture might predict incarceration? And do so in a way that makes causal sense? These are questions that can be (and have been) directly and empirically attacked using the states in exactly the same way as I just used culture to predict incarceration.

Yes, this is largely a correlational analytical strategy, and yes, appropriate cautions and caveats need to be recognized in drawing causal inferences from such an exercise. Clearly, correlation is not causation. That said, it's pretty hard to have the latter without the former. And until we can randomly assign states different crime levels, their electorates' particular attitudes and behaviors, and all the other variables that we'd have to experimentally manipulate to gain real traction on causality, it's mostly what we're stuck with. It means we have to proceed carefully and be particularly alert to questions of spuriousness—other explanations that might explain observed correlations—but it is no reason not to move forward at all.

STALKING THE JAILER

Why has the United States, among its liberal democratic contemporaries, engaged upon a decades-long effort to deprive vast numbers of its citizens of their liberty? What are the social, economic, and political implications of taking on the huge logistic and administrative burdens, not to mention the eye-watering expenses, associated with that policy project? Those are big, difficult-to-answer questions—in macro-level metaphorical terms, the aim of this book is nothing less than to understand where the jailer came from and what he has done to us. And as the sad case of Larry Dayries makes all too clear, the motivations, justification, and effects of the jailer are, to put it mildly, head scratching.

Nonetheless a path to getting those answers lies in leveraging exactly what plays a central role in making the underlying issues so complex—the fragmented nature of how America distributes legal authority over its criminal justice operations and organizes its political system. In the states we have not only a large number of comparable governments with enormous independence on matters of criminal justice but also political units with identifiable differences on everything from culture to the weather. Finding systematic patterns between those two broad sets of differences—differences in incarceration and differences in things that reasonably might be expected to cause states to be more or less aggressive in locking up its citizens—provides an analytical tool, a means to go looking for those answers. Still, having a compass and map are not much use if you do not have a destination, or at least a direction. Where do we go looking for explanations? Before we start taking advantage of the analytical possibilities of the states and search for patterns among their differences, it might be a good idea to first have at least a rough idea of what sorts of patterns we should be looking for.

Fortunately (or unfortunately, depending on perspective), we do not have to look far for suggestions. Indeed, if anything, we have a surfeit of theories claiming to explain the phenomenon of mass incarceration, most of which can already call on a raft of state-level scholarly studies to support—or cast doubt on—them. The real challenge is trying to sort through which, if any, are worth their analytical salt. Why are so many people in prison? Well, if we are trying to figure out why we make such profligate use of incarceration, it might be a good idea to first figure out what is incarceration's social purpose: what are prisons for? The answer to that turns out to be a highly contested subject, and where you come down in this debate points you to very different answers about why we have so many people sitting behind bars.

Chapter 2

Dungeons and Dickens

In which we follow the penal preoccupations of a famous novelist and a French aristocrat and find out what purpose prisons are supposed to serve.

In 1831, the French scholar Alexis de Tocqueville undertook an investigatory tour of America that resulted in a famous and still widely read book: *Democracy in America*.[1] This is justly remembered as one of the most perceptive analyses of the republic's civic character. Roughly a decade later the English novelist Charles Dickens undertook a similar excursion that produced a considerably less flattering picture of the United States: *American Notes for General Circulation*.[2] The same trip also provided partial inspiration for one of Dickens's lesser-known novels, *Martin Chuzzlewit*, which doesn't exactly paint Americans in a good light either. Among other things, it lacerates American hypocrisy regarding its proud self-image as a paragon of liberty while maintaining a brutal and oppressive system of racially based slavery.

De Tocqueville's book is a work of serious scholarship, mostly concerned with figuring out why representative democracy worked in America while it seemed to be having such a hard time getting going in Europe. There was something about America and Americans that allowed a sprawling, heterogeneous democratic republic to work. What was it? That was a really interesting puzzle for a French social scholar of the early nineteenth century given the struggle that *liberté, égalité, fraternité* sorts of arrangements were having back home. Dickens's *Notes*, on the other hand, was not much more than a tongue-in-cheek travelogue. Unlike de Tocqueville, Americans impressed Dickens not so much as the fascinating atoms of an emerging representative democratic body and more as an agglomeration of chisels and blowhards with bad manners and disgusting personal habits. In particular, he couldn't get over the expectorant norms of American men, who not only constantly chewed tobacco but also hawked the salivary products of their mastication pretty much everywhere. You might say de Tocqueville celebrated America's democratic grit while Dickens denigrated its nicotinic spit.

Though these two works are not linked in any obvious way, their inspiration and the reason for their authors' presence in America have something central in common: prisons. Indeed, for de Tocqueville, prisons were the only reason he crossed the Atlantic. De Tocqueville and his longtime frenemy Gustave de Beaumont received a commission from the French government to investigate and report on prisons in the United States.[3] Dickens, on the other hand, was in America mostly to see if he could persuade Americans to buy into the notion of international copyright. This was a new concept at the time and, given the huge numbers of unauthorized copies of his best sellers floating around, he thought it a swell idea.[4] He was disappointed in the American response to his attempts to spread the gospel of intellectual property rights, which was mostly to ignore him. And indulge in yet more spitting. Yet when he wasn't dodging saliva and failing to dissuade the locals from pirating his novels, Dickens fixed a good deal of his attention on prisons. According to at least one analysis, prisons were not only a dominant theme of *American Notes*, they occupied a greater proportion of that work than other subjects that attracted Dickens's interests, like the press and slavery.[5] Even without the motivation of an official commission, Dickens spent a remarkable amount of time poking around jails, talking to inmates, and questioning wardens and jailers.[6]

Why the interest in prisons? De Tocqueville and de Beaumont in an official capacity, and Dickens in a more personal way, were drawn to study prisons because at the time the United States was internationally known for its pioneering penal reforms. To an extent not matched anywhere else, America—or more accurately, a specific set of state governments in America—were experimenting with new approaches to incarceration. These included everything from using individual cells for prisoners, keeping the incarcerated in those cells for extended periods of solitary confinement, issuing them with standard clothing, and focusing on rehabilitation rather than punishment. All of these are familiar now as long-standing institutional norms of the criminal justice system, or at least as the basis of seemingly perennial debates over the norms that should define that system. At the time, though, a lot of this was new. This didn't just boil down to state governments doing some innovative R&D on what to do with people behind bars. There were broader philosophical issues at stake. The reforms were the product of some very bright minds attempting to come up with a systematic answer to this question: what are prisons for? The question is of central importance to this book. The fascination with American prisons demonstrated by de Beaumont, de Tocqueville, Dickens, and many others of the time was in no small part due to the belief that penal reformers in America had come up with a really interesting answer.

THE ORIGIN STORY OF PRISONS IN AMERICA

Prisons as we currently know them are largely a product of the reforming philosophy and institutions of early nineteenth-century America, the very things that attracted the interest of de Tocqueville and Dickens. Colonial America of the seventeenth and most of the eighteenth century really hadn't had much in the way of prisons at all. The population was mostly too small to justify the expense that prisons incurred, and even where they did exist, they bore little resemblance to the contemporary notion of such institutions. They were a sort of people warehouse with no segregation by gender, age, or crime. The notion that the natural outcome of a criminal conviction was to be incarcerated in a cell and let out only under the observation, supervision, and discipline of uniformed guards was not really a thing.

This is not to say that breaking the law didn't have consequences. In colonial times the theoretical underpinnings of crime and punishment were to a large extent rooted in the English Common Law and a Calvinistic conception of human nature. The latter held that people are naturally sinful, and the best way to keep them on the straight and narrow is to make breaking the rules very costly. Those costs were exacted mostly through corporal punishment, social ostracism and humiliation, or both. The former included whipping, beating, branding, and lopping off various parts of a malefactor's anatomy. As to the latter, scofflaws might find themselves being put in stocks, forced to engage in acts of public penance, or required to wear some public signifier of shame (for example a scarlet letter, a concept Nathaniel Hawthorne spun into a pretty good novel).[7] Capital punishment was also used for a wide variety of infractions, not just murder and rape, but for behaviors as varied as blasphemy and bestiality.

The prevailing philosophy of the day held that there were a set of divinely ordained social rules that everyone should abide by. The problem was that because people are naturally sinful, they have a hard time not giving in to temptation. So what do you do with those who went into a murderous rage, took up coercive ravishing as a means to satisfy their lust, stole their neighbor's livestock, or, even worse, got caught in the act shagging said livestock while sacrilegiously yelling the Lord's name in vain? You make an example of them. In addition to the biblical eye-for-an-eye justification, punishment also had a deliberate element of deterrence. Social ostracism and humiliation could exact a massive cost on individuals living in fairly small communities and send a persuasive message that breaking the community's rules simply was not worth the trouble. The local preacher might look dishy and be easily tempted, but one look at Hester Prynne sporting her scarlet letter would presumably be enough to discourage any further action on that front.

This is a philosophy that can work pretty well in terms of restraining rule breaking in small and cohesive communities that share a core set of behavioral norms. Shame and humiliation, after all, constitute a potent emotional brew that most find highly disagreeable and would prefer to avoid. Humans are intensely groupish, and a real possibility of being ostracized or even banished from your in-group is a powerful incentive to stay on the straight and narrow path. Likewise, public whippings and hangings also send a powerful message, specifically that emulating the behaviors of the lashed and the lynched is probably not a good idea. But what happens when society starts to get bigger and more heterogeneous, where norms and values start to diverge among social sub-groups, and these messages not only get more diffuse and diluted but become increasingly unmoored from their philosophical—primarily theological—justifications? Roughly speaking, that's where the United States was around the turn of the nineteenth century.[8]

Bright minds in the Old World like Jeremy Bentham and Cesare Beccaria had been pondering issues of crime and punishment for some time prior, and these ideas were picked up and expanded upon by the pioneers of American penal reform, people like Benjamin Rush, Thomas Eddy, and Caleb Lownes. Roughly speaking, their reform efforts were anchored in a less theological conception of human nature, one where criminals were seen as essentially rational agents. The operating assumption for some reformers was that people broke the law not because they were naturally sinful, but because they saw a decent probability that crime would pay. Others saw criminals not necessarily as individual free agents calculating the cost-benefit ratios of getting away with murder, but more as products of their environments. The rapid social change and fluidity of the first decades of the nineteenth century had led to a breakdown of social norms, where law-abiding communal influences were being replaced by environments that positively encouraged lawbreaking.[9] Deterrence was not enough for these folks, they needed to be reformed, to be persuaded (or forced) to adopt a set of values that would better match their individual choices with the common good. Bottom line, crime was increasingly seen as not just a case of someone giving into the temptation of their innate sinful nature, but as a product of risk-reward calculations about breaking rules and of behaviors conditioned and condoned by social environments that simply didn't have much in the way of collective norms restraining predatory behavior. From these philosophical foundations, penal reformers in America began rethinking the nature and purpose of prisons.

The genesis of the modern penitentiary is generally reckoned to be the Walnut Street Prison, in Philadelphia, Pennsylvania. What marked this as a new sort of institution was its adoption of cellular incarceration—separate cells for individual criminals—segregation between different sorts of inmates (e.g., segregation between debtors and criminals, as well as by gender), and the imposition of mandatory hard labor as punishment. Prisoners were issued uniforms, alcohol was banned, and inmates received a standard meal plan rather than bribing the guards for their supper.[10] While this all sounds standard to contemporary ears, if nothing else the familiar background stuff of a thousand movies, TV shows, and books, at the time of the early American republic they were all radical innovations. What's important to keep in mind here is that the Walnut Street Prison was specifically designed to punish, to deter, and to rehabilitate—these goals represented the *raison d'etre* of the new penal institutions. What those institutions promised was that if you break the law you'd lose your liberty, you'd be confined to a cell to ponder the nature of your transgressions, and your time out of cellular confinement would be put to productive purposes not only to pay your debt to society but also to inculcate the habits and rewards of hard work and discipline. Walnut Street was not simply a municipal one-off. It sprang from a 1790 law passed by the Pennsylvania state legislature that provided the legal foundation for a whole penal system rather than just a prison.

Walnut Street was actually a fairly small-scale experiment. It started out with just sixteen cells, and not every prisoner had one. The first two really modern penitentiaries were constructed in New York and Pennsylvania a few years later, both of them purpose-built to hold hundreds of prisoners in separate cells under easy observation of guards. These were Auburn (New York) and the Eastern State Penitentiary at Cherry Hill (Pennsylvania).[11] States being states, these had some significant differences and even at the time were recognized as representing distinct systems—the Pennsylvania System and the Auburn System. Dickens, and de Beaumont and de Tocqueville, saw the Quaker-inspired notion of solitary confinement at Cherry Hill, which in practice meant cutting people off from virtually all social contact and leaving them in a cell to meditate on changing their ways, as a dud. Rather than having the desired reformatory effect, being subject to extended periods of social isolation took an enormous psychological toll. Many inmates suffered from what de Beaumont and de Tocqueville termed "melancholy," and what we'd call depression. Rather than extended solitary confinement, a hybrid system emerged at Auburn that was widely adopted and modified by other states.[12] As de Beaumont and de Tocqueville put it, "the Auburn system, i.e. common labour (sic) during the day, with isolation during night, continued to obtain a preference: Massachusetts, Maryland, Tennessee, Kentucky and Maine have gradually adopted the Auburn plan."[13] Confinement to a cell, with designated time out for work, meals, or educational and recreational pursuits, remains a common characteristic of contemporary prisons.

In the early nineteenth century, then, there was a deliberate effort across a range of states to set up institutions specifically designed from the ground up to punish crime, deter crime, and reform offenders through the mechanisms of cellular confinement, regimented discipline, and hard work. These efforts—considered daringly innovative and progressive—were far from universal. In New Orleans, de Beaumont and de Tocqueville visited a prison where they "found men together with hogs in the midst of all odours (sic) and nuisances. In locking up the criminals, nobody thinks of rendering them better, but only of taming their malice: they are put in chains like ferocious beasts; and instead of being corrected, they are rendered brutal."[14] Indeed, the duo basically threw up their hands in despair at what they found in Southern states, where the system of criminal justice (or, rather, injustice) was ruthlessly deployed as a means to support slavery:

"We shall not speak of the Southern states, where slavery still exists; in every place where one half of the community is cruelly oppressed by the other, we must expect to find in the law of the oppressor; a weapon always ready to strike. . . . Punishment of death and stripes—these form the whole penal code for the slaves."[15]

Pennsylvania Quakers might be pushing their state legislature to think systematically and humanely about prisons and inmates and how best to use the power of confinement to deter crime and steer transgressors onto the straight and narrow. Other states, however, were clearly using their penal systems— such as they existed—as a means to help enforce a brutal social hierarchy. What they were doing was less about punishment, deterrence, or reform, and much more about imposing draconian social controls to serve political and economic interests that had little to do with a systematic and rational framework for addressing crime.

Even in the states embracing the new philosophy of prisons, economic and political interests sidetracked the focus of reform efforts. In the progressive penitentiaries of Pennsylvania and New York, prisoners were forced to work and their labor exploited for profit by prison administrators, which started to raise thorny questions about what the reform agenda was actually achieving. Philosophically, these penal reforms were grounded in serious attempts to grapple with the underlying causes of criminal behavior. Institutionally, though, there was a real question about whether the upshot of this good-intentioned effort was just a slightly more enlightened form of state slavery, something that crept uncomfortably close to the cruelties that horrified de Beaumont and de Tocqueville about penal systems in the South. And even without getting into full-blown serfdom and servitude, from the beginning there were those who also wondered whether the reforms amounted to mollycoddling. After all, why should criminals get a warm bed and a free meal ticket when honest workers watched their kids go to bed hungry?[16]

While the pros and the cons of such issues have been debated for two centuries, the systems pioneered by places like Eastern State and especially Auburn have become firmly institutionalized. Today we broadly accept without question that prisons are institutions purpose-built to deprive convicted criminals of their liberty by forcibly confining them to cells or dormitories, where their behavioral options—certainly their labor—can be closely observed and regulated by state authorities. Dickens and de Tocqueville found this all new and fascinating, and two centuries on, it is simply the way things are. So, this is what prisons are for, right? Well, maybe. But maybe not.

THE SOCIAL ORDER THEORY OF PRISON: BELIEFS AND REALITY

The central purposes of prisons, their basic theoretical or philosophical justifications and aims, are contained in the origin story of the modern penal system. Note the plural. From the get-go it was clear that however singularly focused reform efforts were in theory, in practice, prisons served no single social objective but a variety of goals being advocated (or co-opted) by a scrum of competing constituencies and interests. All of these goals, though, can be roughly lumped into two buckets. The first is to maintain social order and the second is to exercise social control over certain groups or demographics, or at least to use social control to serve a particular set of political, social, or economic interests. Let's first clarify the social order framework, which was the underlying philosophy that really drove the pioneering efforts discussed in the previous section.

The driving arguments here were not just about ensuring public safety but about upholding and defending a set of universal social norms. At their most idealistic, the early reformers were shooting to create institutions consciously designed to punish, deter, and rehabilitate in a way that reflected systematic deliberation on how to best address the social problem of criminal behavior. As de Beaumont and de Tocqueville put it, "What is the principal object of punishment in relation to him who suffers it? It is to give him the habits of society, and first to teach him to obey."[17] In other words, we lock people up to exact retribution for transgressions against civil order, to ensure those transgressions are not repeated during the period of confinement, and to make the incarceration experience unpleasant enough that offenders will think twice about disobeying the law again. In addition, we will also use confinement to encourage (or force) lawbreakers to accept and adopt the habits and norms of civil society with the aim of returning them to the community less likely to repeat the behavior that landed them in the jug in the first place. The idea was not to ensure a harsh social response to sinners, but to punish those who violated criminal laws laid down by the sovereign authority of the state, ensure that the punishment fit the crime, and, if at all possible, push people away from future criminal behavior.

It is important to note that the early reformers who initiated this agenda were not pie-eyed idealists. Far from it. Thomas Eddy, a Quaker who helped import some of the ideas of his Pennsylvania brethren to the early New York reform movement, referred to prison inmates as "wicked and depraved, capable of every atrocity, and ever plotting some means of violence and escape." Yet Eddy also urged prison administrators to "always be convinced of the possibility of their (inmates) amendment."[18] Even realism, though, was no defense against the practical difficulties of pursuing these aims in an unavoidably political environment. Given social attitudes toward criminals, the appropriate balance of punishment versus rehabilitation was inevitably the subject of disagreement, and control of prisons and their primary social purpose could quickly become political footballs. Eddy, for example, resigned his position as a prison administrator after political appointees and party politics made his reforming agenda untenable.[19] These political struggles not only reflected disagreements over the most appropriate distribution of effort and emphasis on punishment/deterrence versus rehabilitation but also bled out into broader issues such as prison labor and who controlled it and who profited from it. In other words, it was less about defending communal norms and more to do with lining particular pockets and advancing particular political interests.

The boundary where social order crosses over into social control can get fuzzy. Nonetheless, an underlying philosophical difference clearly separates the two. While its implementation might dissolve into messy political squabbles about society's right to enforce punishment versus its obligation to reform and rehabilitate, the bedrock first principle of the social order perspective is that prisons serve a set of primarily instrumental goals for society as a whole. Regardless of differences over the appropriate points of emphasis, at the core of the social order perspective is a belief prisons exist to ensure rule breakers get their "just desserts," to provide a credible threat to potential rule breakers that crossing the line exacts a high cost, and to transform social malefactors into good citizens. In other words, social order perspectives are squarely fixed on how society should best respond to the problem of crime.[20]

Beliefs about the purpose of prisons embedded into the social order perspective clearly struggled to navigate their way through various political and social obstacles even as they were being implemented. They nonetheless continue to shape our basic assumptions about what prisons are and what they are for. Evidence for this comes from a number of studies investigating public attitudes toward prisons that consistently find Americans espousing a set of firm social order beliefs about prisons. People clearly believe in the punitive nature of prisons, that criminals deserve to spend time behind bars, and that their incarceration definitely should not be a "country club" experience. These get-tough attitudes, though, are "mushy." For example, there are clear differences in attitudes toward violent versus non-violent offenses. Public opinion is pretty firm in wanting the former to be incarcerated, no questions asked. People are much more open to alternatives to prison—fines, probation, community service—for non-violent offenders. As long as they are convinced prisons are giving criminals the punishment they deserve, the public is also fairly supportive of programs aimed at rehabilitation.[21]

Ask people about the goals or priorities of prisons or the criminal justice system and what you'll likely get is a list of social order beliefs. For example, more than 90 percent of respondents to a 2014 survey of Wisconsin residents said public safety was either a very important or absolutely essential priority, and almost 90 percent said a key priority should be to ensure that people who committed crimes got the punishment they deserved. Roughly three-quarters also said that rehabilitating inmates and helping them become better members of society is also a very important or absolutely essential priority.[22] Similar attitudes are found in national surveys.[23] The philosophy that motivated reformers like Eddy and aroused the curiosity of the likes of de Tocqueville and Dickens seems two centuries on to be a broadly shared article of faith. What are prisons for? The answer to that question, at least in the sense of public opinion, is found in social order beliefs. Prisons exist to keep social order and protect public safety by punishing and deterring crime, and to a somewhat lesser extent by rehabilitating rule breakers into good citizens.

Faith and reality, though, are two different things. The social order perspective has a clear set of beliefs about what prisons are for, but do those beliefs actually reflect what's going on? To beat the proverbial dead horse one more time: from the social order perspective prisons exist to address the social problem of crime by punishing it, deterring it (or at least isolating ne'er-do-wells from polite society), and rehabilitating criminals into more law-abiding citizens. Let's bring some data to bear on these issues. Just how are prisons doing on those key objectives?

States being states, differences abound, but it's reasonable to conclude that the punishment side of things is being taken care of, at least if incarceration rates are any guide. Indeed, states seem to have gone a little overboard on this dimension. As already noted, some states lock up a lot more people than they used to while other states lock up their citizens at rates comparable to repressive authoritarian regimes. Is all this punishment a response to the social problem of crime as the social order perspective would expect? That's a frustratingly difficult question to answer. If you look at the correlation between violent crime and incarceration rates *between* states, the answer is a hard yes. If you look at the same relationship *within* states across time (or across time nationally), the answer becomes much more qualified.

Figure 2.1 graphs the relationship between incarceration and violent crime rates and incarceration rates for all fifty states at decade intervals from 1980 to 2010. Note that not all crime is reported to police, and violent crime

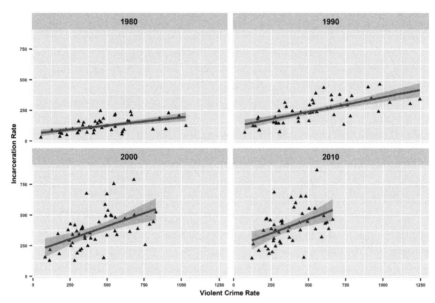

Figure 2.1. Relationship between Violent Crime and Incarceration Rates in 1980, 1990, 2000, and 2010.

Note: These estimates are based on straightforward OLS regression analysis where incarceration rate is the dependent variable and crime rate is the independent variable.

is specifically defined here as offenses in the following categories that are known to authorities: murder, non-negligent homicide, forcible rape, robbery, and aggravated assault. If we use 1980 as a baseline, two things immediately jump out from these charts. First, violent crime rates—the points along the x-axis—make a noticeable shift to the right in 1990 then shuffle to the left pretty sharply in 2000 and 2010. This reflects a general pattern of increasing crime rates through the 1980s and a general pattern of decreasing crime rates thereafter. Second, and perhaps more importantly, the overall relationship consistently gets stronger. Look at the line capturing the general linear relationship in each chart—it gets steadily steeper as you move from decade to decade. So, looking at the relationship between these two variables for each of the fifty states, violent crime rates become a stronger predictor of state-level incarceration rates in later years. In other words, these data seem to be telling us that incarceration rates jumped as a response to the central concern of the social order argument—crime. In 1980 it took roughly 10 additional violent crimes per 100,000 to see one more person locked up. By 2010 it took only 2.[24] So, score one for the social order argument? Prisons exist to deal with the social problem of crime and that's exactly what they have been used for? Clearly not.

For one thing, limiting an analysis to the relationship between two variables can be extremely misleading—it fails to account for alternative, potentially more powerful predictors of incarceration. For another, we need to remember that we've been looking at these relationships cross-sectionally, that is, examining differences only *between* states. What happens if we look at that same relationship across time *within* states? Rather than using fifty state observations in a given year to estimate the impact of crime on incarceration, what happens if we use, say, forty or so years of annual observations for a single state?

Figure 2.2 plots incarceration rates (top row) and crime rates (bottom row) annually from 1978 to 2014 in three different states, Delaware, Oregon, and Louisiana. These three were chosen to represent the different relationships that can occur within states. You can get a sense of those differences by comparing each graph with the one below it. In Delaware crime rates and incarceration rates tracked each other reasonably well over these decades, at least in the sense that the linear relationship between crime and incarceration across time looks pretty similar. In Oregon, it's a totally different story: incarceration and crime trends went off in completely different directions with violent crime nosediving while incarceration rates marched upward. Louisiana follows another pattern. Incarceration rates went up in a pretty linear fashion. Crime rates followed the same pattern until the early 1990s but then fell precipitously. In summary, across time the relationship between incarceration and crime was positive in Delaware, negative in Oregon, initially positive and then negative in Louisiana. What's driving these different stories is clearly crime. If you look at the top row, incarceration rates uniformly went up (note, though, that while the trend is similar the levels are very different—Delaware's incarceration rate peaks around 500 per

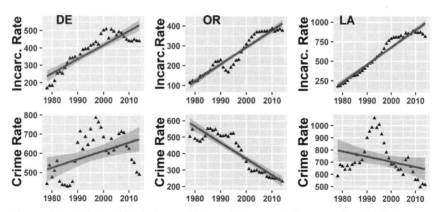

Figure 2.2 Relationship between Violent Crime and Incarceration in Delaware, Oregon, and Louisiana

100,000 population, Oregon's under 400, and Louisiana's nearly double that). Crime rates did not. While they started to decrease at different times in each state, decrease they did.

While within-state general trends can be harder to parse, it's fair to say that in most states, crime was pretty high in the late 1970s/early 1980s and the exponential growth in incarceration was triggered in some way at the same time or shortly after. Some years after that—the timing varies somewhat by state—crime went down and incarceration just kept going up. That growth finally flattened in the early part of the twenty-first century and even declined somewhat, though these decreases came at a considerably milder velocity than the drop in crime rates that preceded them. By now there are two or three decades of academic research on the diminishing correlation between crime and incarceration rates. At least some of that research suggests the relationship did indeed turn negative at some point, with high incarceration increasingly associated with lower crime—the pattern exemplified by Oregon in figure 2.2.

The consistent story told by figure 2.1 and figure 2.2 is that states became more punitive. There is a persistent pattern of being tougher on crime (figure 2.1), regardless of whether crime is trending up or down (figure 2.2.). A positive relationship clearly fits with the social order argument—more crime equals a greater need for the instrumental purpose of prisons. What might not be so clear is that a negative relationship also can support the social order perspective. Rising punishment (i.e., incarceration rates) and declining crime could simply mean that deterrence works. There is evidence to back up this claim. A 2014 report by the National Academy of Sciences investigated the causes of mass incarceration by sifting through decades of scholarly articles, government reports, policy studies from nonprofits and think tanks, and books by experts of all persuasions. They concluded that the weight of the evidence suggested the deterrent effect of prisons was real, though that same evidence also suggested that it was marginal.[25] There's a lot of disagreement on the exact extent to which increased incarceration decreases crime, but roughly speaking studies suggest a 10 percent increase in incarceration will buy you a 2 or 3 percent reduction in crime. There's a catch, of course. Those deterrent effects have diminishing marginal returns. In other words, the bigger the increase in incarcerated population, the smaller the deterrent effect.[26] As incarceration rates have increased by 400 or 500 percent in many states since the late 1970s, it is safe to say most of them shot past the sweet spot of deterrence gains a long time ago.

So, copious amounts of punishment, but the resulting deterrence gains seem, at a minimum, arguable on cost-benefit grounds. What about rehabilitation? If prisons are steering their charges into a greater embrace of law-abiding social norms, presumably a stretch in the big house will make a convict less likely to repeat the error of their ways. Does this happen? Recidivism rates seem to suggest prisons are not exactly hitting it out of the ballpark on the rehabilitation front. One review of recidivism studies found that in the United States recidivism rates ranged from 13 percent after six months to 70 percent after four years.[27] A study conducted by the Bureau of Justice Statistics looked at inmates released from states prisons in 2005 and found that more than 80 percent were arrested at least once in the following decade. Nearly half—4 in 9—were arrested within twelve months of being released.[28] There is, naturally, a lot of variation between states in recidivism rates, though systematic comparisons are difficult because not all fifty states report these rates in exactly the same way and there is no consensus on the most appropriate length-of-time window. Generally speaking, the longer the time window considered the higher the recidivism rate, and these can climb to two-thirds or higher in some states if windows longer than five years are used. World Population Review, a website that reports a wide variety of demographic data, ranked the forty-three states where data was available for three-year recidivism rates in 2020 and found they ranged from a low of 23.4 percent (Virginia) to a high of 64.5 percent (Delaware).[29] If we take those numbers as a rough ballpark, somewhere between a quarter and two-thirds of inmates will be arrested within seventy-two months of release. And keep in mind, that's just those who get caught. Push out beyond that three-year limit and the numbers go up, in some states dramatically.

Interpretation of these numbers can be subjective. If we stick to using state comparisons as the analytical yardstick, then having "only" a quarter of released inmates reoffend within three years arguably looks good (well-done, Virginia). Even in "low" recidivism states, though, that fraction clearly gets larger the longer the time window considered. Who knows what the actual proportion of reoffenders is, but a defensible low-ball rule of thumb is around 50 percent. And the prison experience almost certainly does not have much to do with the success stories, accounting for those who do not go on to reoffend. The single biggest factor contributing to a cessation of, or at least significant reduction in, repeated lawbreaking is not the deterrent or rehabilitative effects of prison but arguably nothing more than age.[30] Criminal behavior has a distinctive demography. It is, to a large extent, a young person's game. Assuming they survive (an admittedly shaky assumption for some violent offenders), the thing about young people is that they inevitably become older people. Older people are more likely to have families and to have accumulated some sort of stake in the social system like a job or property. With age also comes a degree of maturity and increased impulse control, or at least an acceptance that the young 'uns have an edge when it comes time to being quick on the draw and putting up your dukes. That maturity likely also brings a recalculation of whether the economic and social costs of criminal payoffs are worth the risks of incarceration. Sociologists and criminologists have long known of this "aging out" phenomenon. Indeed, there are good reasons to believe that crime took such a tumble in the 1990s not because states got tough on crime, but because their populations were getting older, and older convicts simply consume more prune juice and commit fewer crimes.[31]

The social order notion of what we use prisons for, then, stands on some pretty shaky ground. There clearly is an argument that incarceration was, at least initially, a response to increasing crime levels in the 1970s and early 1980s. Incarceration, though, kept its exponential upward trajectory going for *decades* even as crime was falling, or at least oscillating around a fairly stable plateau. Any way you slice the numbers, states are much tougher on crime (at least violent crime) than they used to be. What that orgy of punishment bought us from a social order perspective is arguable. Assuming prisons existed to deliver punishment, deterrence, and rehabilitation and further assuming that they perform these tasks with some minimum level of competence, the big expected payoff would be less crime and low recidivism. That may be happening to some extent. Increasing incarceration does indeed seem to bring a degree of deterrence, but it seems to be pretty small. Recidivism rates not only are high enough to cast doubt on the rehabilitation merit of prison, they contribute to the notion that the only way in which prison really addresses crime is by attempting to hold onto criminals until they are too old for the rough-and-tumble of felonious pursuits. That may be a net positive for society (who knows?), but it's hardly a score for the reformatory aspirations of a penal system justified by social order beliefs. States have been doggedly locking up people at ever-increasing rates regardless of crime rates and, apparently, regardless of the impact incarceration does or does not have on deterrence and rehabilitation. Maybe, prisons exist to do something else besides the goals suggested by the social order philosophy.

What might that be?

SOCIAL CONTROL

That brings us back to that second bucket of goals, which collectively represent the social control theory of prisons. Social control perspectives, which these days are accepted in one form or another by most social theorists, are anchored in a completely different set of assumptions about what prisons are for. They do not necessarily deny the instrumental purpose of prisons but argue it is naïve to think that is all prisons do. The social control perspective assumes that prisons also serve a variety of social, political, and economic goals that have little to do with addressing and correcting socially deviant behavior. De Beaumont and de Tocqueville provided an early eyewitness account of the most brutal and naked use of penal systems in this sense, that is, their use in Southern states to help prop up a racial slavery-based social and economic political order. Competition to control the economically valuable resource of prison labor also pushed reformers like Eddy away from their instrumental agendas and into more fraught political waters.

The social control function of prison has been embedded in the American penal system from the beginning but has become of intense interest to contemporary observers not just because of the modern phenomenon of mass incarceration, but also because the purpose of prisons has clearly become increasingly divorced from the social order perspective. If prisons do not exist solely—or even primarily—to punish, deter, and rehabilitate, then it raises some uncomfortable questions that the theory—more accurately theories—of social control seek to answer. Incarceration represents one of the single most blunt and brutal examples of the coercive power of government. When that power is exercised, an individual forfeits their liberty and a range of post-incarceration social and economic opportunities routinely withheld from all convicted felons. If the crime is serious enough, society may still exact the ultimate punishment and take an individual's very existence. The social order theory argues that sort of awesome power should be used in a limited way (to address the social problem of crime) for specific purposes (punishment, deterrence, and rehabilitation). Social control theories argue that power, in reality, is used to serve a much broader set of political, economic, and social objectives that may be only tangentially related to the larger problem of crime. As the name suggests, it is more about one social group exercising control over other groups to serve their own interests.

If prisons exist to help some groups achieve their political, economic, or social aims at the expense of other groups, what are those aims? Which social groups are wielding the coercive power of incarceration to achieve them? And at the expense of what other social groups? And what political, economic, and social interests might be served by all this? For answers, let's take a closer look at the main hypotheses of the social control theory of prisons.

Chapter 3

Discipline, Punishment, and Power

In which we find out what purposes prisons really serve. Sort of. Maybe. It's complicated.

Reading postmodern scholarly tomes is sort of like taking a balloon ride. Drop the gravity-hugging ballast of objective truth and delight in the ascent to view celestial panoramas. Just remember what makes those views possible: a big bag of gas drifting aimlessly in rhetorical ether and which is highly vulnerable to piercing by any number of sharp empirical objects. This is why many empiricists, and I count myself among their ranks, advise against such conveyances. Yet for good or ill they are unavoidable in any serious consideration of social control theories of incarceration.

This is largely due to yet another Frenchman, Michel Foucault. Foucault was a postmodern philosopher and author of *Discipline and Punish*, first published in 1975 and arguably the most influential social control takedown of the social order conception of prisons.[1] Like most works of postmodern historicism, reading this book requires wading though some pretty glutinous word porridge, but the payoff is worth it.[2] Foucault's central assumption is that the humanitarian and progressive motivations of the reformers who founded modern penal systems were in practice, if not intention, humbug. Foucault does not disagree that prisons were designed to punish and to habituate inmates into new norms and patterns of behavior, but he questions the ultimate objectives these institutions were designed to serve.

Foucault argues prisons exist not to lay claim on people's liberty in the name of social order, but to lay claim on their beliefs in the name of social control. In Foucault's accounting the arrival of the modern prison heralds a decisive shift in the social purposes of punishment, but not the change promised by reformers. Rather than inflicting physical pain for offenses against the commonweal, prisons re-orient punishment toward coercive re-education in the service of an amorphous state. Prisons impose on their charges an acceptance of social hierarchies, a belief that some have power, others do not, and that's just the way things are. This discipline-enforced socialization of the incarcerated seeps out into society at large, which like a sponge absorbs the coercive and inequitable social arrangements established in prisons. And broad adoption of such attitudes comes in very handy if you want to maintain a socially inequitable status quo. So, according to Foucault, prisons are less about dealing with crime and more about controlling people's will in order to model and maintain a set of social power relationships. Foucault doesn't make super clear who was pulling the strings behind the scenes to achieve these nefarious ends, is pretty opaque in defining those power relationships, and leaves readers to mostly guess about how they might be measured. Regardless, he claimed these dimly defined structural forces exercise a gravitational pull on how social relationships get oriented, serving to keep a mass of people relatively powerless and resigned to their lot. It wasn't just prisons doing this. Other social institutions like schools, the military, and even hospitals, Foucault maintained, perform similar functions.

Foucault's argument is lauded by some as a brilliant piece of historical analysis. It's harshly criticized by others. C. Fred Alford, a political philosopher who did extensive research in a maximum-security prison, reports that his observations of an actual prison didn't line up with Foucault's description at all. He describes the core of Foucault's argument thus: "Surveillance, categorization and classification, the time-table, non-idleness, and regimentation of the body: all are the mark of modern discipline according to Foucault. All . . . originate in the prison . . . subsequently migrating to the rest of society." Yet Alford didn't see much, if any, of this sort of thing going on: "Not only are these disciplinary practices absent, but what is in effect the opposite principle reigns: if you control the entrances and exits, you do not have to look."[3] Prisons aren't social control manufacturers, in other words They are warehouses. Society dumps people in there for lots of reasons, but social reprogramming doesn't seem high on the agenda. And if it is, recidivism rates suggest the attempt to condition soon to be ex-cons into social docility has been spectacularly unsuccessful.

Foucault's argument that prisons incubate a sort of Orwellian self-subjugation that metastasizes into society writ large has taken its empirically inflicted lumps. That in turn has prompted counter-arguments from non-empiricists of varying rhetorical viscosity. Postmodernists' incontinent production of gelatinous word goo, though, hasn't prevented empiricists from latching on to the key idea advanced by Foucault. The broader point that prisons are used to exercise social control is taken seriously by a wide range of social scientists whose analyses sprawl across multiple disciplines and draw on mountains of data. Foucault's ideas might have been a bridge (or two or three) too far, but his broader point about prisons functioning as political instruments of social control is an idea that demands to be taken seriously. Why? At least for some, it makes better sense of the available data than the alternatives.

These depart from Foucaultian analysis not just in rigorous empiricism, but in an assumption that prisons often serve more numerous and narrowly targeted political objectives than a universal "suppress the masses." Particular groups are targeted for incarceration for distinct purposes. Who are these targeted groups? In the United States, most prominently they are racial minorities, especially African Americans, and the poor. They can also include broader and less defined demographic groups, people who regardless of their income or race are perceived by influential constituencies as a threat to their safety and social standing. It matters little if those threats are real or imagined. The key idea is that democratic institutions will respond to any constituency with sufficient electoral clout. If influential constituencies want the criminal justice system to bully a particular group, democracy will oblige regardless of whether that group is some particular racial or economic category, or drug users, or the mentally ill, or illegal immigrants, or whoever.

Who are the groups doing the targeting? Again, it varies, though the most prominent cases are made for majority racial groups targeting minorities and the better-off targeting the socioeconomic underclass. How do white elites get away with this? Simple. State political systems are open and democratic, and that means sensitivity to majoritarian (or at least plurality) preferences is their warp and woof. If influential constituencies want the kibosh put on a group caught in their crosshairs, at least some parts of the political system will strain to oblige. The criminal justice system is a pretty effective way to achieve those ends. All you need are a set of laws whose burdens fall disproportionately onto the target group and a reasonably efficient enforcement mechanism. Incarceration, or at least its credible threat, thus becomes a coercive tool to keep certain groups of people in line. How does this play out in the American racial order? If a white racial majority sees a Black racial minority as a potential threat, it can elect legislators who pass laws that de facto if not de jure result in higher incarceration rates for the minority. Think three-strikes laws, the sort of thing that isn't necessarily explicitly aimed at racial groups but tends to result in people like Larry Dayries getting seventy years for stealing a sandwich.[4]

Social control arguments inevitably raise some uncomfortable questions about the democratic process, and there are a lot of social control arguments. Most of these, though, can be shoehorned into two basic categories. Neither reflects well on the political system. The first is the underclass hypothesis—the idea that incarceration is used as a means to exercise social control over particular socio-demographic groups. The second is the democracy-in-action hypothesis, which in its simplest form argues that we lock lots of people up because powerful and/or large constituencies want certain types of people locked up, and democratically elected officials have strong incentives to respond to those preferences.[5]

These are interlocking explanations and treating them as independent is something of an artificial exercise. They can both be true at the same time. Yet there are arguments for doing exactly that, assessing them independently. For one thing, presenting one argument is made easier by resisting the temptation to dive down every explanatory rabbit hole to see if it pops up in the other argument's meadow. For another, there's a long and productive record of taking this sort of singular approach. Huge research literatures in criminology, sociology, political science, and economics focus just on the underclass hypothesis. This largely represents an attempt to come to explanatory grips with the incontrovertible fact of the massive racial imbalance in incarceration. There's a lot to unpack right there without getting into a lot of arguments—everything from electoral cycles to institutional partisan control to state culture and ideology—making the rounds on the democracy-in-action side of the fence. It also makes sense to give the democracy-in-action hypothesis an independent and clear-eyed look because researchers, at least at the state level, have not fully followed through on the implications of its causal reasoning. Connect those dots to their logical conclusion and you end up with a diagnosis that is concerning as a theoretical possibility and gains a fast promotion to downright alarming if it withstands empirical scrutiny.

Independent of the underclass hypothesis, if the democracy-in-action hypothesis holds water it suggests Foucault might have been onto something. Not in the sense that discipline and punishment within prison serve as some sort of vanguard conditioning scheme to acclimate the proles to their social station. It would tell us something about what prisons are for, and that wouldn't be about dealing humanely with the larger social problem of crime. It would be about power.

THE UNDERCLASS HYPOTHESIS

The underclass hypothesis assumes society is hierarchically ordered on the basis of race and/or class and that those at the top want to stay there. Any hint of a reshuffle in the pecking order sends those higher up the social ladder hustling to ensure those on the lower rungs climb no further. In terms of race this was clearly a long-term historical reality in the United States. Most obviously—though far from exclusively—a race-based social hierarchy existed in Southern states where slavery was legal prior to the Civil War, and Jim Crow laws legally maintained a system of racial apartheid for a century after. We've already seen de Tocqueville and de Beaumont comment about prisons and punishment being put to such social control objectives in the antebellum South. More than a century later, scholars could still easily spot racially anchored social control political agendas.

These included V. O. Key, a political scientist, and H. M. Blalock, a mathematician turned sociologist. They are generally credited with formulating the racial threat hypothesis, essentially the underclass hypothesis in a specifically racial form. In his 1949 book, *Southern Politics*, Key noted that support for the segregationist Democratic Party was strongest in areas with larger African American populations.[6] Why? Key's analysis suggested a growing Black population made the white community increasingly worried about their social position. They responded by politically supporting the imposition of greater social controls on the racial minority. A couple of decades later (1967), Blalock published *Toward a Theory of Minority-Group Relations*, which argued that rising minority populations represent two distinct threats to the racial majority: economic threat (increased competition with the white population for good jobs) and political threat (the ability to use increasing electoral clout to wield political power).[7] Blalock's argument was later extended to a third type of threat: white fear of Black crime. Theoretically, the latter is pretty easy to directly translate into higher incarceration rates.

Regardless of the specific nature of the threat, though, these arguments have an obvious inference: if prisons are used as a means of social control over racial minorities, then incarceration rates should positively correlate with the proportion of racial minorities in the population (especially the Black population). There's no doubt that correlation exists.[8] Figure 3.1 plots the proportion of a state's residents that are Black and male against incarceration rates in 2010. The choice of year is arbitrary. This is a single example of a trend that has held for decades—a largely linear association between incarceration and the size of a state's minority population. While the precise estimates vary a bit from study to study, the positive association between a state's incarceration rate and the proportion of its population that is Black is arguably the most prominent and consistent finding of the relevant state-level academic research.[9] Racial threat theory also produced a range of related hypotheses for scholars to pursue. For example, if the criminal justice system is used to impose social controls on a racial minority, then if that racial minority managed to gain significant political clout—more representation in the state legislature, for example—there would be a lot less of this sort of thing going on. A number of scholarly studies suggest that's exactly what happens.[10]

The correlation between incarceration rates and the proportion of a state's population that is Black is, for the most part, clear and largely uncontested. What's less clear is the causal mechanism that produces that correlation. How, specifically, is the political system targeting Black Americans?

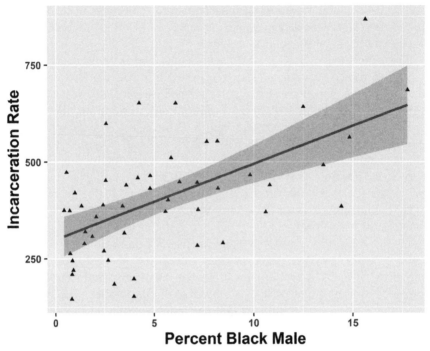

Figure 3.1. Relationship between Percent State Population Black Male and Incarceration Rate, 2010

Bald-faced racial bias has, for the most part, been mercifully stripped of legal standing and legitimacy. So, what's going on that results in disproportionate rates of Black incarceration? A popular and commonly accepted explanation is the war on drugs, which is argued to be a racially motivated effort to suppress the social advancement of Black Americans thinly disguised as a law-and-order initiative. Numerous historical precedents support this line of reasoning. Periodically, polite society gets the fantods over this or that mind-altering substance, then decides through their elected representatives that everyone would be better off if said substance was criminalized. No one seriously expects Gatsby-type one-percenters addling their neurons on no-no intoxicants to bear the costs of this legally enforced temperance. Those burdens inevitably fall more heavily on those at the lower end of the social scale. However, a range of social observers argue there was something different and more sinister about government-led anti-drug campaigns that began in the 1970s and accelerated in the 1980s. This wasn't just another cycle of respectable types getting the jim-jams over whatever psychoactive powders and potions the proles were using to get their jollies. This was a missile consciously aimed at the gains of the civil rights movement, one deliberately designed to employ the coercive power of government to snuff out hard-won social and economic opportunities before the Black community could fully take advantage of them.

Drugs and Violence

A powerful case for racial enmity as the war on drugs' raison d'être is laid out in Michelle Alexander's best-selling book *The New Jim Crow*.[11] This argues the war on drugs is rooted in white—especially rural, poor white—resentment of the Black social and economic gains in the wake of the civil rights era. Though systematically capitalizing on those fears for partisan advantage dates at least to the administration of Richard Nixon, Alexander says things really took off with the all-in anti-drug campaign launched by Ronald Reagan's administration in the 1980s. The latter made the war on drugs a high-profile policy priority, pouring massive amounts of money into enforcement efforts.

Not-so-coincidentally the repercussions of this putative law-and-order campaign dropped like a hammer on Black communities, with African Americans arrested and convicted for drug offenses at much higher rates than white Americans. This not only led to racially imbalanced levels of incarceration, all those felony convictions translated into permanent constraints on the social, economic, and political opportunities of disproportionately Black offenders. And that, Alexander suggests, was the whole point—the war on drugs led straight to the stealthy reestablishment of a socially acceptable form of Jim Crow. Open racial discrimination might be socially verboten, not to mention illegal, but it remains perfectly acceptable to discriminate against criminals. This is because they are criminal and not because—wink, wink—they are disproportionately Black. As Alexander put it: "Once you're labeled a felon, the old forms of discrimination—employment discrimination, housing discrimination, denial of the right to vote, and exclusion from service—are suddenly legal. As a criminal, you have scarcely more rights, and arguably less respect than a Black man living in Alabama at the height of Jim Crow."[12]

Academic research does much to support aspects of Alexander's arguments. Tough-on-crime policies (including tough drug laws) adopted by states do not seem to do much to reduce crime, but white attitudes toward Black inmates seem to influence support for get-tough policies that keep them behind bars.[13] Even though drug use is relatively proportional across racial categories, Black Americans are more likely to be arrested on drug-related charges, and they tend to get harsher sentences compared to white Americans.[14] And there's little doubt that social, economic, and political constraints that come with a felony conviction fall disproportionately on a particular racial demographic. Overall, about 3 percent of American adults

have a felony conviction, a number that jumps more than tenfold—33 percent—when applied to African American adult males.[15] Given the racial
imbalance and the big-time constraints of a felony record—it is harder to find
a job, get housing, and vote—this certainly looks like power-tinged social
control in action. Wink, wink, indeed.

While the war on drugs is arguably the best-known explanation of how
demographic imbalances in prison populations can be linked directly to racial
bias, the case for a backdoor Jim Crow system is not necessarily dependent
upon it. Heather Schoenfeld arrives at a similar conclusion to Alexander's via
a much more expansive route. She argues the politics surrounding the drive
for social equality led to a broader embrace of the coercive powers of government—read "locking people up"—that was aimed at African Americans. This
wasn't just about the war on drugs; it traces its origins to the social dislocations precipitated by the Civil War. Racial divides have cut through politics in
any number of ways since that time, frequently producing a range of policies
that disfavored African Americans. Most prominently, de jure segregation, a
legal system of racial apartheid implemented in many Southern states. One
outcome of that long, complicated historical process is a set of widely held
norms stigmatizing criminals as morally offensive and deserving of long sentences and more or less permanent social ostracism. And criminals (not just
drug offenders), wouldn't you know it, are disproportionately Black.[16] With
or without a war on drugs, in other words, the criminal justice system is
simply too tempting a tool not to be employed as a means to maintain social
control over racial minorities. The upshot is that racial minorities—especially
African Americans—are disproportionately arrested, prosecuted, convicted,
and incarcerated for a wide range of criminal offenses.

Although it is a powerful argument, the proposition that racial animus is
the not-so-hidden driving force behind the exponential leap in incarceration
rates is not uniformly supported by the available evidence. The war on drugs
argument starts wobbling with the realization that drug offenses actually
account for a small portion of prison populations. True, drug offenses account
for nearly half of those serving time in federal prison.[17] But remember, state
prison populations vastly outnumber those in the federal system. At the state
level, the best analyses available suggest only about 15 percent of state prisoners are behind bars for drug offenses, and that drug offenses are capable
of explaining, at most, only 20 percent of the growth in incarceration since
1980.[18] If state prisons were to let out all drug offenders tomorrow, incarceration rates would still be historically high, and racial minorities would still
constitute a disproportionate share of prison populations.

Even confining ourselves to the more-narrow slice of the explanatory pie
that the war on drugs can lay claim to—roughly a fifth of the growth in prison
populations—the racial targeting is far from uniform. Methamphetamine,

for example, is associated with poor, rural, and white America. The meth stereotype as a white, small-town version of the 1980s urban crack epidemic has been enthusiastically promoted by state and federal governments and is firmly entrenched in popular culture (think *Breaking Bad*—science teacher turned meth mogul Walter White is pretty darn white). Meth is seen as a "drug of White status decay," a psychoactive salve consumed by poor white trash to mitigate the pain of a nasty fall down the social and economic ladder.[19] The fact that this typecasting has about as much purchase in reality as the inner-city "crack babies" stories of the 1980s makes it no less powerful as a set of racial and social tropes. Certainly, it does nothing to dissuade rural and predominantly white states from putting meth dealers and makers into prison.[20] In short, the poor white population is also being locked up at alarmingly increasing rates too, and at least partially as a result of the war on drugs. This also goes for the poor Hispanic population. Are they just the collateral damage of a new Jim Crow project having difficulties keeping its racist aims on target? While prisoners under state jurisdiction are, by a considerable margin, disproportionately Black relative to the population as a whole, in terms of sheer numbers, white and Black inmate numbers are roughly equal, with Latino inmates not too far behind.[21] Those numbers seem to support the broader concept of the underclass hypothesis at least as much as the race-targeted version.

Racial targeting through the war on drugs is also not exclusively interracial, but also intra-racial. James Forman Jr. won a 2018 Pulitzer Prize for *Locking Up Our Own*, an account of how Black city leaders used their newfound political clout in the 1970s and 1980s to enthusiastically prosecute the war on drugs. These politicians saw drugs as a grave threat to their communities and tough criminal enforcement as a way to forcefully confront that threat. Those enforcement efforts were not only championed by Black political leaders, they were not infrequently implemented by Black police officers, Black prosecutors, and Black judges. Ironically, occasional opposition to these efforts by white city leaders were interpreted as counter to the interest of Black communities.[22] This seems somewhat inconsistent with the notion that the war on drugs is a covert social control project anchored in the fears and racial prejudices of white conservatives.

More broadly, the racial threat hypothesis also receives only limited support from a wide range of studies examining sentencing disparities. Clearly a key proximate cause of the racial imbalance in prison populations are racial differences in sentencing—African Americans are more likely than white Americans to be sentenced to prison and for longer terms. There is evidence of racial bias underlying those differences, but bias is not the whole or even the main explanatory variable. One review of more than forty studies concluded that legally irrelevant race and ethnicity concerns clearly do play some role in sentencing disparities. But the bottom line is that, "it is irrefutable that the primary determinants of sentencing decisions are the seriousness of the offence and the offender's prior criminal record."[23] Racial sentencing disparities are also at least partially the product of presumptive sentencing, that is, the use of strict sentencing guidelines up to and including the imposition of mandatory minimums for certain types of crimes.[24] This latter point is important because the demographics of prison populations are clearly tied to particular sorts of crime, and they are largely not drug offenses.

Most people incarcerated under state jurisdiction—roughly 55 to 60 percent—have been convicted of violent crimes like homicide, rape, robbery, and assault. All other categories of crime represent small fractions of the prison population. For example, property crimes like burglary and theft account for about 15 percent of inmates and drug offenses account for a similar proportion, though most—two-thirds or more—of the latter are for trafficking or similar crimes. The widespread belief that low-level drug offenders constitute a significant proportion of the prison population is mostly a myth: less than 5 percent of the state prison population is serving time because of simple drug possession.[25] All this is important because data suggests Black Americans are disproportionately more likely to commit and be arrested for violent crimes like murder, rape, robbery, and assault, exactly the sorts of crimes likely to result in longer sentences.

Scholars have two primary data sources to examine race and criminal offending. The first is the Uniform Crime Report (UCR), which collects data on a limited set of crimes reported to law enforcement agencies and arrest data for an expanded set of crimes. The UCR's findings are published annually by the Federal Bureau of Investigation, *Crime in the United States*. The second is the National Crime Victimization Survey (NCVS), which is a nationally representative poll of US households conducted by the US Census Bureau. That survey includes reports of rape, sexual assault, robbery, aggravated and simple assault, burglary, theft, and motor vehicle theft. It does not include measures of some crimes included in the UCR (most importantly it does not include a politically highly salient component of violent crime: homicide). The big advantage of the NCVS is that at least in theory it captures crimes not reported to law enforcement and thus should provide insight into what proportion of crime is reported and why some offenses go unreported, as well as who is or is not committing them. The rub is that because these two data collection operations have historically used different methods, different measures, and are conducted by different federal agencies, they are not always in agreement on sensitive issues such as rates of criminal offending by different racial and ethnic groups. Given that, there's inevitably a temptation to cherry-pick between these numbers to better support a given argument.[26]

I draw on both sources at various points in this book, but I lean more heavily on the UCR data because those numbers are readily available at the state level over long historical time periods—the NCVS is a national rather than a state-level survey. That said, it's important to note that these two data sets do not return identical estimates on rates of criminal offending across racial and ethnic groups. It is possible, as some have argued, that these reporting differences reflect systematic and widespread racial bias in policing and law enforcement actions, in other words, that what the authorities report (UCR) is a systematically (racially) biased subset of actual offenses in the larger population (NCVS). While acknowledging that possibility, there is evidence from studies drawing on both data sources that white and Black arrests occur in roughly proportionate numbers relative to their involvement in violent crimes. For example, in 2018 white offenders accounted for about 48 percent of the nonfatal violent crimes reported to police and about 46 percent of the arrests for the same sorts of crime. The comparable figures for Black offenders were 35 percent and 33 percent.[27] That general pattern has been observed for decades.[28] In short, there's a reasonable empirical case that Black Americans are disproportionately represented in the prison population because they disproportionately commit the crimes more likely to result in prison time, and those crimes are violent crimes rather than drug offenses. This relationship is exemplified in figure 3.2, which shows the relationship between violent crime and the proportion of state population that is Black and male in 2010.[29]

Just as there are clear racial disparities in who commits crimes, there are equally stark racial differences among victims. The vast majority of crime—especially violent crime—is intra-racial. This is particularly the case for African Americans, where roughly 70 percent of violent crime reported by Black victims is committed by Black offenders (the comparable figure for whites is 61 percent, and for Hispanics 43 percent). African Americans are also overrepresented as offenders in interracial crime—there are roughly five times as many violent crimes committed by Black offenders against white victims than violent crimes committed by white offenders against Black victims.[30] Yet it is unquestionably the case that Black communities overwhelmingly bear the costs of Black crime. Predominantly Black neighborhoods have rates of violence far higher than comparable white neighborhoods, as much as five times higher.[31] The cost of violent crime in those communities is not just exacted through higher rates of arrest, prosecution, conviction, and incarceration. Homicide is a top-five cause of death among Black males overall—astonishingly, it is *the* leading cause of death among young Black males—and medical journals have long called for it to be prioritized as one of the nation's most pressing public health problems.[32]

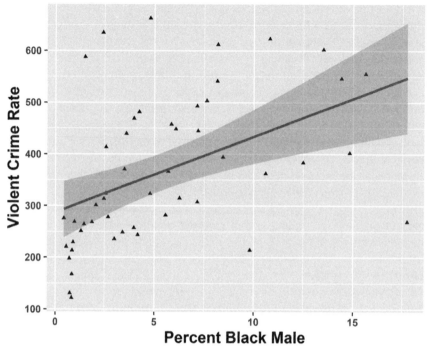

Figure 3.2   Violent Crime and Percent of State Population Black Males, 2010

Connecting the arrest-sentencing-incarceration dots suggests that the problem of socially stressed, highly segregated neighborhoods has at least as much to do with racial imbalances in prison populations as the war on drugs. A 2009 study seeking to explain the persistent racial imbalance in Minnesota's prisons—Minnesota has one of the highest Black-white incarceration ratios in the nation—went looking for an answer by working backwards from prison to see what forks in the path leading there might be prejudicial to minorities. The study, like many others, found that minorities tended to get substantially tougher sentences. Why did minorities get tougher sentences? Mostly because sentencing guidelines heavily weighted prior convictions and minorities were more likely to have prior convictions. Why were minorities more likely to have prior convictions? Because they tended to be arrested more. Why were they arrested more? Because of high Black crime rates relative to white crime rates, the greater willingness of victims to report crimes committed by Black offenders, and higher levels of police enforcement in Black communities. Why the over-enforcement in Black communities? Because in Minnesota (as in other states) the Black population is disproportionately concentrated in socially stressed, urban, and high-crime neighborhoods. The study concludes that, "Prison disproportionality largely reflects racial differences in presumptive sentences; presumptive sentences in turn, largely . . . reflect racial differences already present at arrest, which in turn reflect, in large part, racial differences in offending." Differences in offending were largely (but, it is important to note, not exclusively) tied to racial socioeconomic inequalities and high concentrations of Black residents in high-crime urban areas.[33]

This all seems to suggest that the social control iceberg starts to take on a lot more aspects of the social order argument the closer you look at it. There seems to be plenty of evidence that what drives incarceration rates boils down to crime, and what's driving racial imbalances in prison population are differences in criminal offending across different racial groups.[34] Is this exculpatory for the racial- or class-based Foucaultian social control argument? For several reasons, the answer is a reasonably hard no. First, even if racial bias is not *the* reason for rising incarceration rates, there's simply too much evidence for it not to be *a* reason. Second, the research trail seems to lead from racially imbalanced prison populations straight to severely disadvantaged communities serving as incubators of violent crime. As John Roman, a criminologist at the University of Chicago, succinctly puts it: "The recipe for violence in any city in the world is dense clusters of young men with nothing [to] do."[35] The reasons such communities tend to be disproportionately Black are way beyond the scope of this book, but any argument that neighborhood segregation patterns have nothing to do with deeply embedded, not-so-historical racism will get fact-slapped hard and fast (mortgage redlining, anyone?). Third, beginning in the 1990s crime went down in most states while incarceration rates went up. As we saw in the last chapter, social order explanations of that phenomenon fall short on several counts, so something else must be going on. Racial threat and the war on drugs might provide only a partial explanation here, but that doesn't make them non-explanations (drug offenses might constitute a small proportion of inmates, but they nonetheless also add up to a lot of people behind bars).

Finally, whatever questions this all raises about the racial threat hypothesis, the underclass hypothesis doesn't seem significantly dinged. There's simply no doubt that people on the lower end of the socioeconomic scale are much, much more likely to end up in prison. Pre-incarceration annual income is 41 percent less than comparable peer groups who are not incarcerated,[36] and roughly 40 percent of inmates in state prisons have not graduated from high school or received a GED. The comparable figure for the general population is 18 percent.[37] We shouldn't be super-surprised to discover prisons are disproportionately populated by the left-behinds in a society of growing economic inequality. Mass incarceration is a pretty good way to ensure the left-behinds stay out of the passing lane and in the rear-view mirror of those on the happy side of that growing economic gap. And it's hardly controversial to suggest that a close inspection of the faces in that rear-view mirror would reveal a painfully familiar racial imbalance.

So, it is not the case that the racial threat or the broader underclass hypothesis is definitively wrong. The argument that prisons are intentionally or unintentionally being used to keep a disadvantaged underclass in its place *can* find considerable support among the available evidence. What that body of evidence as a whole suggests, though, is that it is not that simple. The rise in incarcerations might be partially accounted for by a conscious or unconscious race- and/or class-based social control project, but there's clearly a lot more going on than that. What might that be?

THE DEMOCRACY-IN-ACTION HYPOTHESIS

The democracy-in-action hypothesis argues that prison populations could not leap to historically unprecedented highs unless we—the collective democratic, voting "we"—drove the political system to do exactly that. The means to do this are readily available. In all fifty states the criminal justice system is funded, regulated, and accountable to democratically elected officials. If those officials sense electoral advantage in advocating agendas that drive up incarceration rates, then basic democratic theory and more than a half-century of scholarly research on officeholder behavior says that is exactly what they will do.[38]

This, it should be emphasized, does not contradict the underclass or the racial threat hypothesis in the least. If fevered phantasms about redneck meth mafias or urban street gangs grip some politically influential constituency—say, the voting middle classes—then chances are more minorities and poor people are going to end up in jail. A classic example of this in action is the debate triggered by the "superpredator" theory. This was a popular 1990s argument that looming just over the horizon was a new generation of violent criminals, "radically impulsive, brutally remorseless youngsters, including ever more teenage boys, who murder, assault, rob, burglarize, deal deadly drugs, (and) join gun-toting gangs."[39] The fact it was complete codswallop—violent crime went down just as superpredator theory predicted the exact opposite—didn't prevent it from making catchy headlines, driving a popular narrative, and scaring the bejabbers out of the middle classes. Elected officials at all levels of government, well aware of how their ballot bread got buttered, responded to fear of superpredators with a whole raft of get-tough measures that fell hard on young, inner-city men. No prizes for guessing the economic and racial makeup of that group.

Like a Russian doll, the racial threat hypothesis fits inside the underclass hypothesis, which in turn fits into the democracy-in-action hypothesis.

What distinguishes the latter is that it recognizes that democratic systems respond not just to racial or economic group interests, but to *any* interest that accumulates enough political clout. This can include principled interests. Political conservatives have long championed law-and-order initiatives using a straight-up social order argument, that is, that crime is an important social problem best dealt with by swift and costly punishment to deter future social predation (rehabilitation, it must be said, tends to get short shrift in these arguments). Is it possible such reasoning provides cover for an agenda motivated by racial bias? Yes. It is also perfectly possible for such perspectives to be anchored in other value systems such as religious beliefs, or ideological first principles about individual responsibility, communal obligation, and the just desserts that should follow violations of those obligations. Indeed, exactly those sorts of values motivated the reformers that bequeathed us the modern prison. Figuring whether such arguments reflect principled beliefs, are camouflaging racial or class bias, or some mix of both, inevitably requires some subjective interpretation. It is impossible, at least on an individual level, to objectively disentangle a principled social order argument from not-so-principled social control dog whistling. Can political elites electorally cash in by feeding unfounded fears of "superpredators" and their ugly racial undertones? Sure. Can those same elites also be advocating for interests with legitimate concerns and principled notions of how to address them? Yep, that can happen too.

While underlying motivations can be difficult to objectively nail down, no one doubts that appeals to law and order are an excellent political mobilization tool. In any electoral contest where a victims-versus-offenders issue gets spotlighted, being on the side of the offender is a surefire ballot box loser. It is not just electoral hopefuls who know this, but a range of political interests with every incentive to create such campaign narratives. The latter are not limited to white constituents concerned about social competition from minorities, the better-off defending their privileged economic position, or support-your-neighborhood-G-man conservatives. Women's rights groups, for example, have called for crackdowns on domestic abusers and rapists. The LGBTQ community supported the establishment of the term hate crimes, that is, crimes punished more severely when seen as motivated by prejudice. Mothers in favor of gun control and/or against drunk driving have pushed for tougher penalties for gun violence or drunk driving. Adoption of these agendas by those in political power are also likely to put upward pressure on prison populations.

Among the best scholarly treatments of these sometimes-under-recognized components of the mass incarceration story is Marie Gottschalk's *The Prison and the Gallows*. This book lays out a highly persuasive case that feminist activists, victim rights groups—even public interest lawyers and anti–death penalty crusaders—have all contributed to creating what Gottschalk terms the "carceral state."[40] Gottschalk doesn't rule out other explanations like racial bias or the war on drugs. Rather, she expands the analytical lens and puts the politics of mass incarceration into a larger historical context. In doing so, she helps answer a question that has puzzled a number of political scientists: if mass incarceration is so terrible for the constituencies that progressive political elites often claim to advocate for, why did those progressive elites not fight harder against the predominantly conservative-led law-and-order push that filled prisons to overflowing? The answer seems to be that plenty of progressive interests were onside with that push because it served their political aims.[41] As Gottschalk succinctly puts it, being pro-victim and anti-offender helped knit together a hugely disparate set of political interests that collectively took to the political playing field asking voters whether they were for criminals or their casualties.[42] And in that competition, criminals always lose.

At the state level, political scientists have consistently identified exactly the pattern you would expect given those dynamics: conservative control of government consistently correlates with higher levels of incarceration.[43] It's not surprising that given a clear(ish) field, more conservative states will follow through on the opportunity to be tougher on crime. The bigger issue is whether such efforts are a product of an agenda anchored in principled social order values, a sneaky end run toward a new Jim Crow, or a payoff to the economic haves who want the have-nots to keep on not-having. Or maybe it's all of these things and more, simply the democratic system responding to a discordant scrum of political interests that includes, well, pretty much all of us. We might disagree on who the villains are, but we're united in demanding that government do something—preferably something appropriately punitive—about them. The government has obliged in no small part because no politician is eager to be painted in the colors of team offender. This is not news. Most political scientists and not a few criminologists argue that mass incarceration is above all a phenomenon more of politics than crime, a product of fifty democratic systems working in just the way that you would expect them to work.

While there is an enormous research literature that backs this argument by examining everything from electoral cycles to the adoption of specific policies, among the best exemplars of powerful, straightforward democracy-in-action arguments are those presented by John Pfaff and Peter Enns. Pfaff's book *Locked In* is skeptical of the "standard story" explanation of mass incarceration, in other words, the conventional wisdom that attributes mass incarceration to things like the war on drugs, increasingly tough sentencing guidelines, and the prison-industrial complex. He argues that while not necessarily wrong they misattribute the core problem and thus can at best explain a small portion of the growth in incarceration. So what is the core problem? Pfaff argues it is a combination of prosecutors and how violent crime is punished.

Pfaff calls prosecutors "the man behind the curtain," incredibly powerful but lightly regulated players within the criminal justice system. Legislatures might pass lots of tough-on-crime laws, but implementation—the translation of law into action—is undertaken by a set of mostly local (county) officials who operate with relatively little oversight. They have huge discretion on what to charge an offender with, and they often use that power as leverage in plea bargaining. If the options are pleading guilty and getting a defined prison term or risking a court trial on a harsher charge with a much longer sentence, we shouldn't be too shocked to find that many people opt for the former. This is especially the case for those lacking the means to hire white-shoe legal representation. For decades, swamped public defenders have grumbled that their numbers are too low and their caseloads too high.[44] In contrast, the number of prosecutors has been increasing fairly dramatically—by roughly 50 percent—over the past forty years. On a per prosecutor basis, you'd never guess that crime fell during this time. Between the mid-1970s and the first decade of the twenty-first century, the number of prison admissions per prosecutor went up.[45] Why would prosecutors be locking more people up? In simple terms, they have to justify their jobs.

An interesting fact about most chief prosecutors is that they are elected. There are several thousand chief prosecutors (commonly called district or state attorneys) with the responsibility for felony cases, and in forty-seven states they are elected.[46] Scholars have found elected district attorneys prosecute and convict more people.[47] Why would they do that? Well, it's not hard to predict the electoral fortunes of someone running for district attorney on a platform of sending fewer and fewer criminals to prison. Being tough on crime—and certainly avoiding any taint of being soft on crime—is an electoral prerequisite in such contests. And how do you prove you are tough on crime? As Pfaff documents, you lock people up. More prosecutors equals more people with strong incentives to pack people off to jail, and that includes non-elected prosecutors who work for elected bosses.

Pfaff devotes less analytical attention to judges, the officials who actually wield the ultimate decision-making power to impose prison sentences. The core of his argument, though, seems equally applicable to these actors. Indeed, if there is a single office in the political system where decisions to incarcerate are concentrated it is arguably not prosecutors, but the presiding officers of the courts of original jurisdiction handling felony cases. A fairly extensive body of research suggests that elected state judges are sensitive to the democratic process; for example, they tend to hand down tougher sentences as reelections get closer.[48] States being states, the actual form of the democratic selection process for judges comes in a bewildering variety.

Elections can be partisan or non-partisan, involve competing candidates or only a single judge running in a retention election at the expiration of an appointive term. States mix and match these systems not only between themselves, but within their court systems, using different methods for general jurisdiction and appellate court.

The electoral mechanics are less important than the recognition that, unlike their federal counterparts, most state court judges are periodically exposed to the ballot box. So getting and/or keeping the job ultimately depends on getting votes. And how do you get votes? Hint: not by being soft on crime. This raises an important issue with the other key problem underlying mass incarceration that Pfaff identifies—the punishment of violent crime. If most people are in prison for being convicted of violent crimes, then significantly reducing incarceration levels inevitably means figuring out how to have fewer of those people behind bars. Reducing the incidence of violent crimes would seem the obvious optimal solution, but that doesn't seem to work: when crimes actually went down, incarceration went up. That suggests something is out of whack on the sentencing end, which is partly why Pfaff's "man behind the curtain" argument is so persuasive. But it's not just prosecutors who would have to change to reduce prison population. Perhaps even more importantly, so would judges. Could a state judge campaign successfully on a platform of reducing sentence lengths for violent criminals as a way to reduce incarceration levels? Could the same judge successfully seek reelection on a record of doing exactly that? Maybe, but democratic theory and a truckload of scholarly analysis suggest it is unlikely.

The reason for that boils down to the ultimate power in a democratic system—voters. If the electorate is in favor of a less punitive criminal justice system and willing to express those preferences at the ballot box, then democratic officials will respond. Or at least, they will if they want to keep their jobs. There seems little risk of this happening. Public opinion has become increasingly punitive over the past four or five decades, and reversing that trend—especially in the sense of figuring out alternatives to lengthy sentences for those convicted of violent crimes—will not be easy. We know a good deal about these trends in public opinion and their relationship to incarceration rates at the state level through the work of Peter Enns. He helped address one of the central challenges of doing comparative state-level public opinion analysis related to incarceration: the lack of reliable comparative polling data. Historically, we've never really known how public opinion on any issue consistently differs across states. This is because as a rule polling organizations do not administer identical, independent surveys to representative samples in each of the fifty states (an expensive proposition), or if they do it tends to be a rare one-off event. In the past, state scholars seeking to get some sense of state-level public mood had to work with a mishmash of polls that had huge gaps—some states were not surveyed at all, and even those that were could not be directly compared because different polls used different questions. Lacking good polling data, researchers tended to rely on indirect measures of public opinion such as interest group ratings of legislators.[49]

The severity of that problem was lessened by some smart statistical types who figured out that national polls could be reweighted on the basis of state demographic data. This is a statistically intensive procedure, but the result can get you a pretty darn good estimate of state-level public opinion.[50] Enns used this approach to create measures of state-level ideology (the proportion of a state's population identifying as conservative/liberal and Republican/ Democrat), and more specifically of punitiveness (the latter uses such questions as support for the death penalty).[51] Using these sorts of measures Enns found public opinion to be a robust predictor of incarceration at the state and national level. In *Incarceration Nation* he reports that politicians followed public attitudes rather than vice versa, that public attitudes got more punitive in response to news coverage of crime, and that news coverage of crime fluctuated with actual crime rates.[52] These findings gored oxes in a number of academic meadows where causality is claimed to run in opposite directions. Still, the idea that the news media responds to crime levels, the public responds to news coverage with harsher attitudes toward lawbreakers, and politicians respond to public opinion by cracking down all has a very familiar ring to it. That, in a nutshell, is democracy in action.

Enns's work has helped convince criminologists that political scientists might be onto something with this whole public-opinion-as-a-driver-of-crime-policy thing, and they have called for more research in this area.[53] However, there still remain a number of gaps in the democracy-in-action hypothesis that even political scientists seem blind to. Gottschalk, Pfaff, Enns, along with many others, have by now identified most of the dots in the democracy-in-action argument yet haven't connected all of them. *Locked In* and *Incarceration Nation* are terrific books, each making important advances in our understanding of mass incarceration. Yet Enns focuses on public opinion and pays little attention to the mechanisms used to translate these majoritarian preferences into action.[54] Pfaff does the opposite, highlighting the role of the "man behind the curtain" with big incentives to get tough in order to satisfy particular political constituencies, while paying relatively little attention to the attitudinal dynamics bubbling out of varied interest blocs. If the democracy-in-action hypothesis holds any explanatory water, it requires the interaction of these two core themes, not the independent effects of one or both.

Even if not fully fastened together, the "dots" laid out by such scholars as Pfaff, Enns, and Gottschalk paint a pretty clear picture of the democracy-in-action hypothesis. Public attitudes became harsher, a trend likely kicked off by rising public awareness of increasing crime levels (especially violent crime) in the 1960s and 1970s. Being tough on offenders became an important political mobilization tool employed by a range of political interests across the political spectrum. Politicians responded to all this and supported policies—three strikes, mandatory minimums, and so on—that set the stage for locking more people up.[55] Those who actually determine who goes to prison, prosecutors and judges, had the same incentives to respond to harsher public opinion, so they used those tools and their own independent decision-making leeway to drive up incarceration rates. The end result: supporting criminal justice stopped being a mostly symbolic commitment to social order and legislators responded to the will of the people by forging a range of legal tools capable of radically increasing incarceration. Those tools were then put in the hands of officials with strong incentives to enthusiastically put them to use.

If there is any veracity to this story then we should be able to build a statistical model capable of predicting variation in incarceration at the state level. States where public attitudes are tougher on crime, states with elected judges, states where conservatives exercise more legislative and executive control should, all else equal, have higher incarceration rates. There still remain some missing pieces. For example, near as I can tell, nobody has ever bothered to take a systematic look at how political culture might predict state-level incarceration rates, which seems decidedly odd from the perspective of the democracy-in-action hypothesis. If you remember the discussion from a couple of chapters ago, culture captures a stable set of attitudes over what government should do and, to a certain extent, who it should be doing it to. I won't repeat the theoretical details again, but different political sub-cultures clearly can be expected to have different notions about how many people should be locked up and why, and following the logic of democracy in action we would expect governments to reflect those broader attitudes.

SOCIAL ORDER OR SOCIAL CONTROL?

There are, no doubt, other pieces worth examining that go unconsidered here. Still, by now we have a reasonably comprehensive set of responses to the first critical question addressed in this book. Why did we become the world's biggest jailer? The social order answer is that prisons exist to deal with the problem of crime through a reasonably humane process of punishment and deterrence. So, if prison populations are high, it is either because we have a lot of crime, or if crime is low then it's because those high levels of punishment are doing a bang-up job of deterrence. As we saw in the last chapter, evidence for this argument is, at best, mixed. The social control argument is that prisons are less about dealing with crime than serving an interest or interests to shape society in a desired direction through punishment and coercion. This can take the form of a racial majority deliberately seeking to constrain the social and economic opportunities of a racial minority. It might be the economic haves trying to ensure the have-nots don't get ideas above their station. It might also simply be a diverse set of political interests pressuring government to go after a whole range of target groups, everything from domestic abusers to homophobes to drunk drivers to people hanging out on street corners and transmitting a frisson of fear up the spines of people who don't hang out on street corners. Again, there is mixed evidence and also a recognition that the democracy-in-action story still has a number of unread chapters.

So, which of these stories has the best evidentiary claim as the correct answer to our question? Social order? Social control? A bit of both? Are any social control effects mostly accounted for by the racial threat hypothesis? Let's bring some data to bear on these questions and see if we can figure that out.

Chapter 4

What's in the Box?

In which an Englishman who learned to blow up bridges
helps us find out why we lock up so many people.

George Box left school at age sixteen and apprenticed himself to a sewage plant manager, an oddly fitting start to a long and storied career scraping crap out of the machinery of scientific analysis. These contributions were mostly made as a statistician, a trade he came to wholly by accident. Trained as a military engineer during World War II—an experience that left him incapable of seeing a bridge without mentally working out how to blow it up—he ended up working on a top-secret project using mice to study the effects of poison gas. Disentangling the signal from the noise in some of these experiments was a task that fell to Box. His sole qualification for the job was a confession that he'd once read an important book on modern frequentist statistics, a thin qualification at best.[1]

Box emerged from these rather random vocational beginnings to become one of the most significant statistical and scientific thinkers of the twentieth century. According to an obituary published by the Fellows of the Royal Society, he "made seminal contributions to theory and practice in the areas of quality control, time-series analysis, the design of experiments, and Bayesian inference."[2] All very impressive, but why is he sneaking in a prominent guest role in a book about mass incarceration? Mostly because this chapter is going to directly tackle one of the book's key questions—why do we lock so many people up?—and do so by following an analytical approach championed by Box. While Box is still revered among academics, outside the academy, if he's remembered at all it's for some version of this aphorism: "All statistical models are wrong, but some are useful." That's what this chapter is about. I'm going to build statistical models to predict incarceration rates. They are, inevitably, going to be wrong, as all models by definition are. They are also, I sincerely hope, going to be useful.

THE SCIENTIFIC BOX STEP

If statistical models are always wrong, then statistical models of any aspect of human endeavor or experience are more incorrect than most. The social world is very complicated and trying to capture all that complexity with equations applied to data is like catching whales with basketball nets. So why bother? Because done with care statistical models can still tell us much about how the real world works. For example, they can help us determine which theoretical explanations of mass incarceration—the underclass hypothesis, democracy in action, and so forth—actually have real-world predictive power. If we observe relationships in the real world that, a) are consistent with the causal associations suggested by these hypotheses, and b) refuse to go away after a good statistical kicking, we can assign them probabilistic credence. In other words, even if we cannot definitively prove anything (remember, the model is wrong), we can say it's a reasonable bet that the world works the way the model says it does.

Landing on that point with confidence, though, is not easy. Box described science as an iterative process of deduction and induction. Connect dots on some facts and assemble them into a theory. Test the theory against facts. Use discrepant facts to reject, modify, or create a new theory. Rinse and repeat until what's left comprehensively accounts for what's observed in the real world. There are pros and cons to applying this process to mass incarceration. The past couple of chapters make clear that scholars have been putting together facts and building theories for a while, so we're already some way down this road. That's good. The problem (typical in social science) is that there is not one theory to test, but lots of them pointing in different explanatory directions. The social order and social control arguments are families of theories rather than two specific and well-defined causal explanations. Each clan within those pedigrees claims a causal right to include its favored predictor in any statistical model seeking to explain state-level incarceration. There are so many of these that there's no practical way to include all of them. So how do you decide what makes the cut?

One approach is to stuff as many predictors into a model as you can. Box cautions against this, saying the better approach is to produce a pared-down model that is not "importantly wrong." As he put it, don't worry about mice when there are tigers around.[3] Okay, so how do you tell a mouse from a tiger? Statistical models of incarceration are notoriously incontinent in their inclusion of predictors and there is little consensus on which of these, in Boxian terms, has stripes and big teeth and which has a twitchy nose and a weakness for cheese. Something on the order of 40 to 50 variables (typically 10 to 20 of them in a given model) are at least semi-routinely used in academic studies to predict state-level incarceration rates.[4] Including all of them means committing to something immensely complicated and hard to interpret.[5] Yet taking the opposite tack, ditching the confusing complexity for a super stripped-down model using as few variables as possible, can leave you with a model that is systematically biased. For example, it creates the temptation to cherry-pick predictors based on whatever particular mix of them returns the most subjectively pleasing result to the analyst.[6]

Picking predictors is hard enough. But even if there were some sort of universal consensus on the key drivers of mass incarceration (and there most emphatically is not), that does not mean data on those variables is available, or that if the data exists that it's available for all states for every time point targeted in an analysis. Comparative state scholars typically scrape materials from a patchwork of sources: multiple federal and state agencies, organizations like big polling outfits, and often each other (they're a pretty generous bunch who readily share the fruits of their data collection efforts). Even so, one of the not-so-secret tricks of the trade is that we often end up analyzing the data we have rather than the data our theories argue we need. There's more. Even supposing we get nothing "importantly wrong" in the mix of predictors, and by some good fortune have access to data on those measures, we are still some way from producing a useful model. We still need to figure out dimensionality—measure once across space or repeatedly across time? If across time, how far across time? To do any useful data analysis we also need to pick the right analytical, that is, statistical, tool. Box cautions against "cookbookery," or the practice of whacking data with whatever handy algorithm is fashionable or familiar. He also recommends avoiding "mathematistry," or doing fancy-schmancy algebraic somersaults that might impress quant nerds but do more to obscure rather than reveal the story lying in the data.

Given this lengthy list of challenges it's obvious why all statistical models are wrong. Nonetheless, being aware of those challenges is important because it provides a path to consciously address and mitigate them. Being wrong, remember, does not mean you cannot still be useful.

OF MICE AND TIGERS

Let's begin with the easy stuff. The analytical target is state-level incarceration rates, defined here as an annual count of non-federal prisoners per 100,000 population serving one-year terms or longer. The goal is to build a statistical model assessing the explanatory powers of the social order and social control arguments by testing their ability to predict that measure of incarceration. Here's the plan to achieve that aim: round up a set of variables representing the key causal arguments, sort out which ones consistently associate with incarceration rates, and use those variables with stable predictive capacities to provide answers to why we lock so many people up. To do this I assembled a data set that includes a bunch of candidate variables for all fifty states for all years between 1980 and 2010. Choosing this three-decade time span represents the first trade-off between the desire to get nothing "importantly wrong" and analytical feasibility. This window captures the big rise in incarceration rates in the 1980s and early 1990s and extends through the plateau and, in some cases, declines in those same rates during the early part of the twenty-first century. Whatever the answers to why we lock so many people up, the meat of it seems likely to be available in that time span. It also gives us plenty of variance to work with—fifty states at thirty different time points, or a total of fifteen hundred "state-years"—so if there are any systematic patterns across states, or within states across time, the predictor variables have plenty of opportunity to lock onto them.

That time period, though, is also a compromise. The further back in time, the sketchier data availability becomes for the variables clamoring for inclusion in the model. This is simply the longest time period where I could reasonably reassure myself that the input variables representing the hypotheses bubbling out of the last two chapters could be comprehensively accounted for. I am making a guess—educated, informed, and obsessively ruminated over, but still a guess—that this time window reduces the likelihood I get something importantly wrong because I just ain't got the data.

The analytical approach chosen is consciously designed to steer away from cookbookery and mathematistry. There will be a few math-ey fireworks rumbling in the background, but I've chased most of those off to a methodological appendix that interested readers can find on the book's website. All you really need in order to follow the arguments in this chapter is a vague grasp of basic regression, which is relatively straightforward if you remember your eighth-grade algebra. I know. Me neither. So, here's the general idea—think of an equation that looks like this: $Y = a + X$. Y represents incarceration rates and X a set of predictor variables—"a" represents a constant, which we won't worry too much about (its job is to tell us the estimated value of Y if all the X's are zero). Regression models apply this basic idea to data by estimating coefficients for X that do the best job of predicting Y. All that's really happening under the mathematical hood is the application of a set of algorithms that seek to isolate what happens to Y when a particular X moves away from its mean.[7] Technically, what I'm ultimately aiming at is a series of panel analyses, or models where the X's and Y's account for variation between states in space and within states across time.[8] Typically, that'd be pretty much it. To build useful statistical models, analysts generally find data for the desired X's and Y, feed them into a statistical program that applies a desired estimation approach, and use the output to make inferences on the relationship between

X and Y.[9] I'm going to go two steps further: (1) I'm going on a tiger hunt, (2) when I get to those panel analyses, I'm going to use a whole bunch of different estimation techniques to see what predictors keep roaring and what starts to squeak.

To bag the big cats, I gathered a bushel of variables to represent the social order and social control arguments, randomly pulled out a handful, fed them into a statistical model, looked at the results of that model, tossed the variables back into the basket, and then repeated the exact same process thousands and thousands of times.[10] Technically this is what is known as an extreme bounds analysis, and as used here it is an attempt to differentiate consistent from inconsistent predictors of incarceration. Rather than argue that this or that variable must be included because it tickles my theoretical or ideological fancy, I've let the variables duke it out on their own. This is important because for various technical reasons how a variable performs in a statistical model can be highly dependent on what mix of other variables are included. Change that mix and you might get very different results—tigers in one model can be mice in another. It is not unheard of for variables to change direction entirely depending on how a model gets tweaked. What I'm attempting to do here is make a predictor earn its stripes before being included in anything used to make inferences about what's driving incarceration rates.

The entire list of variables included in this exercise are listed in table 4.1. Predictors representing the social order argument are violent crime and property crime. If the social order argument has any weight, then incarceration rates should respond to crime, especially violent crime. The other variables are divided into the two buckets of the social control argument. For the underclass hypothesis I'm using percent Black male and percent of a state legislature that is Black. The reasoning here is simple: if racial threat is driving incarceration rates it makes sense that increasing minority—especially Black and male—populations should trigger an increased use of prisons in response. If the minority population has some measure of political power—represented here by the proportion of Black legislators—that influence can be used to dampen that response. The Gini Index is a measure of income distribution, where higher values mean greater income inequality, and the poverty rate is self-explanatory. If prisons are used to subdue the economically disadvantaged, in theory these variables should systematically co-vary with incarceration rates. I've also included the percent of a state's population between the ages of fifteen and thirty-five, which, as noted in the previous chapter, is a span covering the prime ages for engaging in criminal behavior. The other two variables in the underclass hypothesis category are policy related. The first is whether a state has decriminalized marijuana (an attempt to assess the effects of the war on drugs) and whether a state has a three-strikes law. These

Table 4.1. Predictors of State-Level Incarceration Rates

Theoretical Argument/Hypothesis	*Variables to Test Theory/Hypothesis*
Social Order	Violent Crime
	Property Crime
Social Control—Underclass Hypothesis	**Percent Black Male**
	Percent Black Legislators
	Gini Index
	Poverty Rate
	Percent Young
	Three Strikes
	Marijuana (De)criminalization
Social Control—Democracy in Action	Partisan Control of State Government
	Percent Conservative
	Punitive Attitudes
	Racial Diversity
	State Culture
	Judicial Selection

Note: Bolded variables displayed ≥ 90 percent directional consistency within 105,839 separate regression models that included all permutations of variables in cross-sectional (ordinary least squares) models predicting incarceration rates at five-year intervals between 1980 and 2010. For details see methodological appendix.

are the sorts of laws directly implicated in the "new Jim Crow" arguments as important drivers of incarceration.

The variables in the democracy-in-action bucket are all institutional, attitudinal, or designed to capture the broader sociopolitical environment. Partisan control of state government is straightforward enough (higher values represent Democratic Party control), as is the percent of a state's electorate that identifies as conservative or holds punitive criminal justice attitudes (for example, favors the death penalty). Judicial selection captures whether a state uses elections to select judges in courts of original jurisdiction, an appointment method, or some hybrid system. The idea is to capture a democratic process with a direct connection to incarceration. State culture, though rarely included in studies of state-level incarceration, has an obvious place here (see chapter 1).

I'm also including a measure of racial diversity, specifically what is known as the Blau Index. This is simply the probability of two people chosen at random from a state population being the same race or ethnicity. It is important to note that the Blau Index says *nothing* about any specific racial group—a state that is 70 percent white and 30 percent Black, a state that is 70 percent

Hispanic and 30 percent white, and a state that is 70 percent Black and 30 percent Asian would all have identical scores on the Blau Index.[11] What the index does is give a sense of racial and ethnic diversity. Scholars are divided over the impact of such diversity on social harmony and the potential knock-on effects for prison populations. Some—with justification—champion the "contact hypothesis"—the idea that as people become more likely to encounter people different from themselves they become more tolerant of differences.[12] Others back the "conflict hypothesis," the idea that more heterogeneity leads to more groupish behavior, which in turn leads to more group conflict and less social harmony.[13] The conflict hypothesis is supported by such journalists as David Goodhart and such academics as Eric Kaufmann, who argue that rapid demographic shifts over the past several decades have led to significant social and economic dislocations in the United Kingdom and the United States.[14] This in turn has fomented a form of politics that undoubtedly has racial and ethnic overtones, or at a minimum politics with increasingly intense skepticism toward liberal immigration policies. At its core, though, these changes are argued to be rooted not simply in racial or ethnic differences but in a growing unease about the erosion of social norms, a growing sense that, as Arlie Russel Hochschild put it, people increasingly feel like "strangers in their own land."[15] The end result are communities that are increasingly less tolerant of shifts from traditional norms and much more likely to support politicians and policies that defend them. One way for that political dynamic to manifest itself is in higher support for a more punitive approach to rule breakers, regardless of who they are. Hence higher incarceration rates.[16]

I cannot emphasize enough that these fifteen variables do not exhaust the list of plausible theoretical predictors of state-level incarceration rates. Far from it. I also freely acknowledge there are reasonable arguments that might challenge how I've classified them (for example, Black legislators arguably should be in the democracy-in-action bucket, racial diversity in the social control bucket). That said, I believe I'm on safe ground in declaring this list is fairly representative of the predictors scholars employ in statistical models of state-level incarceration rates (state culture is the big exception). I'm also confident in saying that this is a list that gives the social order and social control arguments a fair crack at making their case. Could other variables be included? Absolutely. Could the variables I use be employed to test hypotheses differently than how I've set them up in table 4.1? Yes. As I've tried to make perfectly clear from the get-go, my model—any model—is going to be imperfect.

I used the list of candidate tigers and mice in table 4.1 as the basis for the extreme bounds analysis mentioned earlier. This consisted of predicting incarceration rates in all fifty states between 1980 and 2010 at half-decade intervals. In each year I used every mix and match of the fifteen variables possible—a total of more than 100,000 separate statistical models. The bolded and italicized variables in table 4.1 are those that emerged from this gauntlet as stable predictors, which I defined using the rough rule of thumb of a variable pointing in a consistent direction at least 90 percent of the time.[17] This wasn't a hard and fast cutoff—as I'll explain in a minute there were a handful of cases where it seemed reasonable to accept variables that didn't quite meet that threshold. The bottom line, though, is that I started by trying to identify the variables that regardless of the year and regardless of what other grab bag of variables get tossed in the model, kept punching through all the noise and signaling the same story. Both the list of variables that did this (the tigers) and those that did not (the mice) provide some useful—and sometimes surprising—information about the arguments laid out in the last two chapters.

The first surprise is crime—neither property nor violent crime consistently predicted incarceration rates by the standards of my 90 percent threshold. At first blush, this seems a substantive blow to the social order argument though there are two big mitigating factors. First, crime, particularly violent crime, *was* a consistent predictor until around the turn of the century. In 1980, 1985, 1990, and 1995, violent crime positively predicted state-level prison populations in close to 100 percent of the roughly 65,000 models run in those four years (97.4 percent, 97.8 percent, 97.9 percent, and 94.5 percent, respectively). That positive relationship cratered in 2000, dropping to 61 percent before moving up somewhat in 2005 and 2010 (81 percent and 75 percent, respectively). So violent crime was a positive predictor of incarceration rates until the mid- to late-1990s, but after that the correlation became much more likely to turn negative. This leads to the second big mitigating factor: crime is the only variable tested here where that pattern could emerge from a tiger rather than a mouse. This is because there are defensible theoretical explanations for crime rates to have positive and negative relationships with incarceration.[18] If crime goes up and incarceration rates go up, then score for the social order argument, that's exactly what you'd expect. Yet if crime goes down and incarceration rates go up, that too can be interpreted in support of the social order argument. This is because a negative correlation suggests that higher incarceration rates may be having a deterrent effect and depressing crime. In other words, maybe it's not crime that's driving incarceration rates, but incarceration rates that are driving crime (down). That reasoning does seem like the social order argument is getting its cake and eating it too, but as discussed in the last chapter the fact is both relationships can make sense. The results are consistent with both of these possibilities: incarceration rates responded to high levels of crime, and this (partially) helped depress crime rates, so the once-tight positive correlation started to become much looser.

Admittedly, this is a bit of a shaky start, but I'm declaring violent crime a tiger. I could make the same defensible argument for property crime, but declaring one tiger over the muffled squeaking coming out of the social order bucket seems plenty.

The second big surprise is that the democracy-in-action bucket contains mostly tigers, while the underclass hypothesis holds mostly mice. That pattern holds even if we switch the assignments of Black legislators and racial diversity. That said, arguably the biggest tiger to emerge from this exercise was percent Black male. Regardless of year or what other variables it competed against to explain incarceration rates, percent Black male positively predicted incarceration rates with virtually no directional variation. The *lowest* performance of this variable came in 1995 where it was a positive predictor in 93.2 percent of the 8,100 statistical models it was included in. Twice—in 1980 and 2010—it was a positive predictor in more than 99 percent of the models. This suggests the racial threat hypothesis has real predictive chops. Other variables in the underclass hypothesis bucket, though, didn't meet hypothetical expectations. They mostly just squeaked. Marijuana decriminalization and three-strikes laws bounced between positive and negative with some regularity between 1980 and 1995, and though they did stabilize somewhat after that they never broke the 90 percent consistency threshold. Percent young was highly unstable across the entire range of years and models—there's simply not much evidence prisons are being used to keep emerging "superpredators," or at least some groups of stroppy youngsters, under society's thumb.

The possible exceptions were the Gini Index and the poverty rate, which were unstable predictors from roughly 1980 to 1995 and stable, positive predictors after that. This is particularly true of the Gini Index. Income inequality hit the 90 percent threshold in four of the seven years examined (1990, 1995, 2005, and 2010) and just missed it in a fifth (88.2 percent in 2000). This is close enough that I'm willing to grant the Gini Index provisional tiger status. This is fudging the *a priori* qualifications I set for such qualification with no theoretical fig leaf to whip over the decision as I did for violent crime. There's simply no causal path in the theoretical landscape I've examined where greater economic inequality leads to lower incarceration rates. That said, I am sensitive to what seem like systematic shifts in across-time patterns in these results.[19] Violent crime was a rock-solid predictor of incarceration in the first half to two-thirds of the years analyzed. Income inequality was a rock-solid predictor in the second two-thirds. Given the arguments examined in the last chapter, that incarceration rates became less responsive to the violent crime rates and more responsive to high income inequality during these three decades seems entirely plausible.

Unlike the variables in the social order and underclass buckets, predictors in the democracy-in-action category do not need much in the way of a squint-hard-with-thumb-on-scale treatment to see stripes. With two exceptions all of them perform exactly as theoretically expected. Regardless of year or what other variables are included, these four factors—conservative electorates, high rates of racial diversity, state culture, and electing judges of courts of original jurisdiction—are consistent, positive predictors of incarceration rates. The failure of punitive attitudes to consistently predict incarceration rates was a surprise, especially as there are a number of other studies out there reporting a strong relationship with this same, or a very similar, variable.[20] Part of what might be going on here is that punitive attitudes may already be getting captured by other variables (for example, conservative identification, partisan control, or state culture). Regardless of the explanation, the bottom line is that punitive attitudes were a positive predictor roughly half the time and a negative predictor the other half, and that 50–50 split held reasonably consistently across different years. That's a definite squeak. Partisan control is a different story. It met the 90 percent threshold in 1980, 2005, and 2010, and what really kept it from winning its stripes was a single year—1985 when it was positive roughly 52 percent of the time and negative 48 percent. Who knows what happened here—maybe the last gasp of the conservative wing of the Democratic Party? Regardless, partisan control averaged 81 percent across all years and models, that is, 81 percent of the time, higher levels of Democratic control of state government were associated with lower incarceration rates. That puts it well outside my 90 percent cutoff, but it's hanging around in that same gray area as the Gini Index, so I'm going to include it in the final models.

Bottom line, then, the tigers pulled from this analysis are the variables bolded in table 4.1. and I'm adding to their ranks violent crime, the Gini Index, and partisan control of state government. Do these eight variables incontrovertibly account for all that was driving incarceration rates between 1980 and 2010? Probably not, and I'm not claiming they do. What I am claiming is that they represent a set of variables that demonstrate substantive predictive consistency through a pretty grueling weeding-out process. The results provide an initial hint that the mass incarceration phenomenon was originally rooted in rising violent crime rates, but by the late 1980s it had been overtaken and accelerated by broader sociopolitical currents predicted by the democracy-in-action hypothesis. The socio-demographic targeting forecast by the underclass hypothesis was considerably less prescient, though far from absent. The correlation between Black males and incarceration was not only consistent but consistently large, and there certainly seemed to be some evidence that in the second half of the time series, economic inequality had started to squeeze out the predictive role previously held by violent crime.

These conclusions, though, are all highly preliminary. The exercise thus far was about trying to get to some irreducible set of variables that provide some minimum assurance that nothing important would be left out of a final statistical model. It is the latter that is going to be used for inference, that is, for making any broad claims about why we lock so many people up.

WHAT FULL STATISTICAL MODELS SAY ABOUT INCARCERATION

The preceding analyses, whatever their merits for classifying tigers and mice, have significant limitations as platforms for answering the question of why we lock so many people up. While totting up an impressive number of iterations, each individual model included a maximum of only fifty observations (i.e., the fifty states) in a single year. That's pretty small potatoes given the fifteen hundred observations (fifty states, thirty years) available in the entire data set. An awful lot of explanatory variance has been left on the table. A better way to get comprehensive answers is to use the eight short-listed variables on all fifteen hundred observations at the same time, simultaneously accounting for differences between and within the states. That's a much richer data environment for identifying systematic patterns.

That means conducting a panel analysis, a form of statistical modelling conducted on data that includes observations across time (years) on distinct units (states). While it has mighty tempting advantages, panel analysis can also be what's known in technical terms as a royal pain. This is because all forms of statistical modelling rest on a set of underlying assumptions and almost by definition panel analysis violates some big ones.[21] Try to solve one of these problems and it inevitably creates another. I'll skip the technical detail, but bottom line: panel analysis estimation choice often boils down to a judgment call on which statistical work-around represents the lowest threat to the fitness of inference. Make the wrong choice and the model can end up lying its ass off, presenting as if it's in the pink of statistical health while in reality being spurious to its duplicitous core.

In an attempt to avoid such outcomes, I am not lashing my inferences to a single estimation approach. I'm going to use different flavors of panel analysis—each designed to deal with a particular set of assumptions—and see what variables tell similar tales across different analytical choices. If a variable makes it out of the extreme bounds ordeal and then sticks to its story under differing varieties of panel analysis estimation, I am going to believe what it is telling me. I will not automatically assume that variables lacking such firmness are committing statistical perjury, but I am going to be a heck of a lot more cautious in using them to crawl out on any inferential limb.

Table 4.2 summarizes the results of all the modelling approaches I tried. The top half of this table (the half labeled *Individual Models*) represents a half-dozen traditional approaches to doing panel analysis. The bottom half of table 4.2 (labeled *Grouped Panel Model*) reports the results of a more recently developed alternative approach that basically allows the mixing and matching of the traditional approaches within a single model. Interested readers can find full results and technical details in the methodological appendix.[22] The columns—models A through G—report summary results from six different defensible ways to set up the panel analysis. A "+" symbol in the table indicates a positive predictor of incarceration rates and "-" represents a negative predictor. For example, in the first row, violent crime shows itself to be a positive predictor in all modelling approaches where it was used as

Table 4.2: Panel Analyses of State Incarceration Rates, 1980–2010

	Model A	Model B	Model C	Model D	Model E	Model F	Model G
Individual Models							
Violent Crime	+	+	+	+	+	+	*
Percent Black Male	+	+	-	+	+	-	*
Gini	+	+	+	+	+	+	*
Partisan Control	-	-	-	-	-	-	*
Conservative Identifiers	+	+	-	-	-	-	*
Judicial Democracy	+	+	*	+	*	*	*
State Culture	+	+	*	+	*	*	*
Racial Diversity	+	+	+	+	-	+	*
Grouped Panel Model							
Violent Crime	*	+	+	*	*	*	+
Percent Black Male	*	+	+	*	*	*	+
Gini	*	+	+	*	*	*	+
Partisan Control	*	-	-	*	*	*	-
Conservative Identifiers	*	+	+	*	*	*	-
Judicial Democracy	*	+		*	*	*	
State Culture	*	+		*	*	*	
Racial Diversity	*	+	+	*	*	*	+

Notes: + = positive predictor of incarceration rates, – = negative predictor, * = not included in model. Bolded symbols indicate significant predictor at p < .05, except for cross-section averages, which are all bolded as baseline. The models represent different estimation approaches to predicting incarceration rates: Model A = mean from individual cross-sectional models in 1980, 1985, 1990, 1995, 2000, 2005, 2010; Model B = between estimator, Model C = fixed effects estimator, Model D = random effects estimator, Model E = OLS model with all variables first differenced, Model F = OLS model with all independent variables lagged at t-3, Model G = time (year) based common effect on all states. For full details see methodological appendix.

a predictor. This suggests that it doesn't matter much what assumptions you make or what estimation approach you use, holding all else equal, states with more violent crime tend to have more people in prison.

Attacking from multiple angles like this reduces the risk of drawing conclusions from a single potentially flawed estimation approach, but it has its downsides. Even as a very bare-bones report of all the statistical labor undertaken there's a lot going on in table 4.2.[23] The big advantage that table 4.2 gives us is the 10,000-foot view—we can see how the predictors perform in different statistical environments. And that perspective is pretty interesting. Five predictors tell wholly consistent stories: violent crime, the Gini Index, partisan control, judicial democracy, and state culture. In short, it doesn't matter what you do to the data or how you generate the statistical estimates, in all the models where they are eligible for inclusion, those variables keep roaring out the same story. What is that story? States locked more people up in response to violent crime and increasing economic inequality and because of the institutional and cultural dimensions of their political environments. It bears repeating: This conclusion comes not from reading the tea leaves from a single statistical analysis, but from hopping on multiple statistical conveyances and recording their common end points.

The variables with inconsistent stories also tell us something useful. The proportion of a state's population that is Black and male was mostly positive, turning negative only in two models (Models C and F). Given the assumptions underpinning those models (see appendix) those results indicate that if you isolate a state and track increases in the Black male population over time, those changes probably won't do a great job of predicting shifts in its incarceration rate. If you zoom out and look at states with higher proportions of Black males relative to other states, and if you look at the growth of the Black male population nationally (shown in the *Grouped Panel Models* section), they do have something to do with higher incarceration rates. This suggests demographic history and national trends are where the racial threat hypothesis finds empirical traction. In other words, the predictive power lies in where a state starts out relative to other states and how all states are reacting to changing demographic trends at the national level, not the growth of a minority population within a state.

The racial diversity measure is consistent and positive in all models except one (Model E), and in that particular case it's really not saying anything meaningful (the predicted impact in that model is indistinguishable from zero, which given the assumptions embedded in that particular model is not surprising).[24] The real takeaway here is that incarceration rates do seem to respond to shifts in racial diversity, though the analyses also suggest that response might take a while. What we see here is what we'd expect if the conflict hypothesis realistically described the world at least as far as incarceration goes: as state populations become more diverse, states tend to be more willing to lock people up.

The only out-and-out mouse here was conservative attitudes, which were all over the place. Some models suggested more conservatives meant more incarceration, others suggested more conservatives meant less incarceration, and there's no obvious pattern (at least to me) in all this directional somersaulting to suggest any sort of a systematic relationship. I strongly suspect that attitudes are important but that in these models that effect is being channeled through the institutional and cultural variables. In other words, the institutional and cultural elements of a state's political environment are sponging up the attitudinal orientations of its electorate and translating them into more or less exactly what you'd expect if the democracy-in-action hypothesis held water.

While we're getting a clearer picture of what does—and just as importantly, what does not—predict incarceration, we have yet to touch on the relative strength of these relationships. Being a consistent predictor of incarceration rates, after all, holds no guarantee of substantive impact. If massive changes in, say, violent crime rates predict but a piffling change in prison populations it's probably not a good candidate to explain the mass incarceration phenomenon. Figure 4.1 shows the relative impact of these variables by showing how much change in an explanatory variable would be required to increase incarcerations rates by an estimated 100 inmates per 100,000 population. Lower numbers indicate relatively little movement in a variable can translate into more people behind bars—in other words a lower number means a bigger impact. For example, the graph suggests that to result in another 100 people behind bars, violent crime would have to double (increase to 200 percent of its average) and racial/ethnic diversity would have to increase sixfold (move to 600 percent of its average).[25]

What figure 4.1 suggests is that economic inequality and a state's political culture have outsized impact on incarceration rates. Interestingly, the former is a dynamic measure, that is, it changes across time, while the latter only changes across space (from state to state). Some interpretive caution is warranted here as both these variables have hard left and right walls, they are strictly bounded in the minimum (0 for the Gini, 1 for culture) and maximum (1 for Gini, 9 for culture) values possible. These limited ranges makes them different animals from, say, violent crime, which at least in theory has no maximum limit. Nonetheless, this seems to be saying something useful. Specifically, that growing economic inequality destabilizes society, which in turn moves pretty sharply to control that instability by becoming much more punitive toward those on the lower end of the socioeconomic scale. The culture variable is saying that states might look very similar in terms of inequality, violent crime, or any of the other variables in the model, but pretty

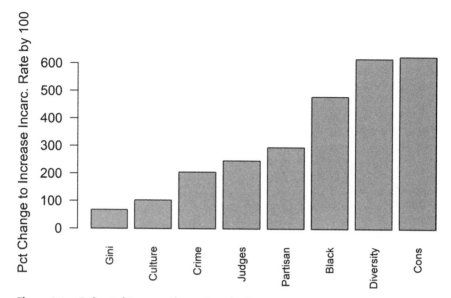

Figure 4.1. Estimated Percent Change Required to Increase Incarceration Rates by 100

Note: Bars represent the estimated change required in a variable to increase incarceration rates by 100 per 100,000 population, expressed as a percent of a variable's overall mean between 1980 and 2010 (absolute values used to aid comparison). These estimates are calculated using the results of Model G (the random effects panel model). Full model reported in methodological appendix.

small differences in political culture can have outsized effects on prison population numbers. Violent crime is particularly interesting because not only is it directionally consistent, but different models spat out a remarkably uniform point estimate: give or take, they suggested roughly ten more violent crimes translate into incarceration rates going up by one. That's a pretty unambiguous result supporting an equally clear inference: the social order argument retains a good deal of real-world substantive bite.

The percent Black male variable represents perhaps the most challenging set of results to interpret in terms of relative impact. This variable chugs through the statistical storms to report that the racial threat hypothesis is (yet again) confirmed. To be sure, there are exceptions, but the main finding is that the higher the percentage of Black males in the population, the higher the rate of incarceration. The difficulty comes in figuring out the impact this variable has. If we ignore the one negative estimate from table 4.2, overall the statistical models suggest that an increase of 1 percentage point in this demographic is associated with around a 4 to 12 percent increase in the incarceration rate. Interpreting those numbers is an exercise that unavoidably tacks onto subjective shoals. On the one hand, *any* consistent evidence backing the racial threat argument is not just noteworthy but disturbing: it suggests incarceration is to some extent racially driven. On the other hand, the estimates consistently suggest the impact is not particularly large. On average, the proportion of a state's population that was Black and male in this period was 4.8 percent.[26] Between 1980 and 1995, when most of the increase in incarceration occurred, the average state Black male population shifted from 4.4 to 4.8 percent (it was 5.2 percent in 2010). At the upper bound of the estimates a half-percentage point increase in this demographic—in this data, a pretty hefty increase across a decade—would translate into roughly another 6 people incarcerated per 100,000 population. For comparison, this is an era when the average state incarceration rate was never below 119 and often topped 400. Adding 6 to either of those numbers can be argued to be 6 too many with complete justification, especially when you consider that translating it into total numbers means something like 15,000 more people behind bars. As percentage of the total, though, it's not large. All else equal, the models are suggesting that the proportion of a state's population that is Black and male would have to jump by an extraordinary and unobserved amount to have played a major role in the incarceration explosion. Other variables that I assessed had a larger impact.

Two factors from the analyses argue against consigning the racial threat hypothesis to a real but somewhat limited phenomenon. One comes from the group panel model summarized in the bottom half of table 4.2. Remember, this is kind of a mix-and-match approach where a single statistical model contemporaneously generates some of the same estimates generated independently by the models represented in the top half of the table. Two of these group panel estimates—those analogous to Model B and Model C—echo the small effects described in the previous paragraph. The methodological appendix has the details, but the bottom line is that these point to roughly a similar half-dozen (maybe even less) more people in prison per 100,000 population with each half-to-one percentage point increase in Black male population. The big finding is in the *common trend*—basically the trend in Black population nationally across the entire time period studied—which is an estimate that only the group panel model generates. That estimate predicts a 1 percentage point increase in the common trend will result in an increase of 96.3 in the incarceration rate. That, by any yardstick, is a whopping effect.[27] It is important to understand what this estimator is capturing: variation in a time-based average, that is, the average for all states in a given year. This suggests a general rule of thumb that any national, across-time trend in this demographic is accompanied by a pretty sharp uptick in incarceration across all states. Conceivably that effect may be dampened by the fact, already alluded to, that across time the national average for state-level percent Black population simply didn't change a whole lot, slowly rising from 4.4 percent in 1980 to 5.4 percent in 2010. Still, even if it was across a thirty-year span, that 1 percentage point difference has a hard-to-ignore substantive impact on prison populations if the group panel model is to be believed.

The second factor is the performance of other variables that cover some pretty broad sociopolitical ground—state culture, for example. Traditionalistic states are heavily concentrated in the old Confederacy, in other words, Deep South states with long and troubled histories of race relations. While Sharkansky's measure of culture was not designed as a measure of racial attitudes, it would take a braver academic than I am to argue culture was not accounting for some portion of those orientations.[28] In short, just as systematic differences between the states in their sociopolitical environments might be statistically blotting up punitive or ideological attitudes, so too might they be absorbing and reflecting racial attitudes.

WHY DID WE LOCK SO MANY PEOPLE UP?

So what does all this modelling wonkery and data analysis tell us? Running tens of thousands of statistical models, employing multiple estimation approaches, and generally trying to let the data drive the narrative is no guarantee of getting everything, or anything, right. This is a good place to bring back a final word from George Box: these models are wrong. And that's okay. Definitive proof was never in the cards, I was chasing a more modest and achievable goal: to avoid being importantly wrong and to provide useful information. Assuming my rather catholic approach to appeasing various methodological gods has accomplished these more humble aims, what is that useful information? What's the story? Why *did* we lock so many people up?

At least according to the empirical investigation laid out here, the answer goes something like this. By 1980 state governments were facing a serious crime problem. In 1960 the average state-level violent crime rate was around 115 (i.e., 115 violent crimes per 100,000 population). That had more than doubled by 1970, and it doubled again by 1980. That year, when our data set picks up the story, the average state's violent crime rate had increased something like fourfold over a two-decade span. That average crime rate went right on climbing through roughly the first half of the time window analyzed, peaking in 1993. In 2010, the analysis's stopping point, the average crime rate was 366—way down from the peak but still roughly on par with the late 1970s, a period when those sorts of crime levels were considered extremely alarming. This is particularly so because we're talking about *violent* crime. Compared to itself fifty years in the past or to other wealthy liberal democracies at similar time points, America is a fairly violent place—some states are way more violent than others—and the data set covers a period when violent crime rose to a recent historical peak.[29] The heart of the social order argument is that prisons exist to provide an instrumental response to crime, so more crime, especially violent crime, should equal more people in prison. And that, pretty consistently, is exactly what we see in the data, especially in the 1980s through early 1990s, which account for the bulk of the historical increase in prison populations.

That, of course, is far from the whole story. The rise in violent crime overlapped with some huge shifts in state sociopolitical environments. These included the ideological realignment and subsequent polarization of political parties and electorates, growing economic inequality, and increasing racial/ethnic diversity. Combined, that's a recipe for social instability, which according to the social control argument will trigger increased use of incarceration to mitigate threats to those with power and a stake in the political, economic, and social status quo. That's exactly the story told by the analyses reported here. Whether those changes pushed a state's incarceration elevator up a floor or two or blew it through the roof was heavily dependent on broader context, things like state culture, partisan control of state government, and the proximity of those with sentencing authority to the ballot box. It's interesting to note that four of the five states with the lowest incarceration rates in 1980 were still in the bottom five in 2010: Maine, Massachusetts, Minnesota, and New Hampshire. Comparatively speaking, what those states consistently have in common is lower levels of violent crime, a moralistic-leaning political culture, a Democratic Party with a realistic shot at capturing power, judges a step or two removed from the ballot box,[30] and less racially and ethnically diverse populations.[31] There was quite a bit more churn in the top five incarcerators in 1980 and 2010, but even though the names changed, the sociopolitical profile of states with high prison populations did not. Regardless of which end of the era you pick, high incarceration states tend to have high violent crime rates, traditionalistic (or at least individualistic) leaning political cultures, a streak of Republican Party dominance, judges who are exposed to the ballot box, and a racially diverse population. De Tocqueville could have made a pretty good guess at the states on this list—they are heavily concentrated in the South.[32]

This story is likely not particularly satisfying to partisans of specific hypotheses, whose arguments sometimes suggest *an* explanation for mass incarceration is *the* explanation. The analyses here point squarely toward an inference that arguments like Marie Gottschalk's are likely closer to the mark than those of Michelle Alexander. That is, we locked so many people up for lots of reasons, not all of them obvious and many of them deeply rooted in regional sociopolitical context. Change the latter and you might change what story explains prison populations—each state is at least a little bit different. Just to be clear, this most definitively is not a claim that Alexander is necessarily wrong; there's plenty in my analyses to corroborate suspicions of an ugly racial undertone to the rise in prison populations. The point is more that the rise in mass incarceration has multiple factors (it's a multivariate phenomenon) and, across the states, is highly uneven. The social order argument cannot account for the entire phenomenon, but it sure seems to be the consistent contributor. What jump-started the era of mass incarceration and sustained its upward trajectory for at least a decade to a decade and a half was violent crime. Its explanatory power, though, was never fully comprehensive and seems to have faded badly in the mid-1990s. Part of that fade might be hiding a real deterrent effect, but even if that's true it doesn't fill in a fairly large explanatory hole about what else drove up prison populations. That gap is better covered by social control explanations.

I've already fessed up that pulling apart the independent effects suggested by the underclass and democracy-in-action hypotheses is a somewhat artificial and perhaps forlorn exercise. That said, even allowing for a good deal of real-world overlap, mass incarceration seems to be at least as much about the latter as the former. The mass incarceration phenomenon was not a product of crime or race or politics or inequality or institutions or culture or the war on drugs. It was all of that and more, a set of mutually interdependent forces crossing streams at a particular historical moment to create an irresistible shove toward depriving vast swaths of the population of their liberty. Though not always agreeing with their empirical findings, if forced to provide a succinct summary, my own analyses push me toward the larger conclusion drawn by scholars such as Peter Enns and Jonathan Pfaff. Why did we lock so many people up?

For lots of reasons, but mostly because: (a) we were worried about high rates of violent crime, and (b) because we wanted to.

Chapter 5

Throwing the Bomb

*In which we investigate mass incarceration's explosive
implications for social cohesion and trust.*

The most famous bombing mission in history was successfully completed
on August 6, 1945, by the B-29 Superfortress *Enola Gay*. At 8:15 a.m.
local time, 31,000 feet above the Japanese city of Hiroshima, the bomber's
belly disgorged "Little Boy" into freefall. Little Boy was a ten-foot-long
finned cylinder encasing an atomic Pandora's box, a compact fifteen-kiloton
exploratory experiment in nuclear species extinction. He whistled earthward
for a minute or so before having a very big-boy detonation roughly two
thousand feet above his unsuspecting victims. In an instant he flattened five
square miles of the city and left seventy thousand of its residents lifeless.
Captain Robert A. Lewis, *Enola Gay*'s co-pilot, stunned and troubled by the
apocalyptic power he had helped unleash, made the following note in his
logbook: "My god, what have we done?"[1]

Mass incarceration and nuclear holocaust are not really analogous, but
Lewis's question can be applied to the former with a similar sense of awed
disquiet. Thanks largely to state governments' enthusiastic forty-year commitment to putting their own citizens in the clink, Americans are now more
likely to have served a prison term (3 percent) than have green eyes or red
hair (2 percent). Black men are more likely to have a prison record (15 percent) than to be a plumber or to be left-handed (less than 10 percent).[2] One
in four Americans have siblings (mostly brothers) who have been incarcerated, and a third of eighteen- to twenty-nine-year-olds have a parent (mostly
fathers) who has spent time behind bars. Overall, nearly half of all Americans
(45 percent) have a family member with a prison record, a number that climbs
to 63 percent for the Black community.[3] Vast swaths of the population—possibly a majority of all Americans by the time you read this—have direct or
indirect experience with incarceration. Somewhere along the line incarceration leapfrogged its role as an instrumental response to a social problem or

even as an institutional tool for social control. It somehow burrowed itself into a normed part of the social environment.

Given all that, swiping Lewis's line doesn't seem such a stretch: My god, what *have* we done? The only honest answer to that is we're not really sure. The one thing we definitely do know about putting huge numbers of people in prisons is that they tend not to stay there. Even with a long trend toward tougher sentencing, the median time served in state prisons is less than a year and a half, and even most violent offenders are sooner or later paroled or complete their sentence.[4] So not only have we been stuffing huge numbers of people into prisons for four decades, we've also been sluicing roughly equally huge numbers of people out of prisons in what amounts to a massive revolving door. The end result is a society where mind-boggling numbers of the population have prison records. As of 2010 (the most recent estimates I could find), the best estimate was roughly 7.3 million who were currently or formerly in prison or on parole. Roughly 20 million had a felony record (not all convicted felons serve prison time).[5] States being states, there is of course wild variation. Fewer than 1 in 100 adults living in Massachusetts were or had ever served a prison term. In Louisiana it was roughly 1 in 20.[6] Pick a person at random in some states and they are more likely to have a prison record than to have shopped at Whole Foods or used a dating app.[7] We have more veterans of prison sentences than veterans of tours served in Iraq or Afghanistan.[8]

Shuffling such vast numbers through penal institutions is bound to have implications for society and—spoiler alert—they are not likely to be good. At the individual level we hardly need another academic study to drive home the point that a prison record can limit individual social, economic, and political opportunities by corroding relationships, limiting job opportunities, and precipitating the loss of voting rights.[9] We can quibble about the reasons individuals end up in prison, but there's no arguing the consequences faced on getting out. While the ramifications of incarceration and reentry for individuals—loss of liberty, ruptured family relations, loss of reputation, diminished earning potential, disenfranchisement—are well established, what about the larger social impact? Is there a collective price, a reckoning that mass incarceration exacts from all of us? The rest of the book is aimed at trying to get some answers to these questions, at assessing the impact of mass incarceration on the social, economic, and political health of the society we all live in. The social impact is the focus of this chapter.

It is hard to extract clear insight into the spillover effects of mass incarceration simply by gaining some sense of why we lock so many people up in the first place. Assuming the analyses in the last chapter clear the Boxian hurdle of not being importantly wrong, then at least in a rough sense we possess that knowledge: mass incarceration is a phenomenon rooted in a social order reaction to rising violent crime rates colliding with a historical period marked by roiling social changes—rising inequality, increasing racial/ethnic heterogeneity, sharpening ideological and partisan differences—that acted as a powerful accelerant to the use of prisons as means of social control. This happened pretty much across the board though differences in degree if not kind varied enormously from state to state. That state-level variation is linked to historical and institutional context, the contemporary distribution of partisan power, and the extent to which all those socio-demographic changes were reflected within state borders. Yet getting that tentative grasp on causes tells us nothing about consequences. Did states that tightened down hard on punishment actually get rewarded with more social stability? Or was there blowback, a negative feedback loop where states that incarcerated more people ended up creating more of the social destabilization they presumably were seeking to control? Most importantly, how could we possibly test any of this? Before pulling anything out of the Boxian tool kit to try to answer these questions, let's first figure out what attributes are, (a) collectively valued at the state level as important contributors to social success and harmony, and (b) could possibly be threatened by mass incarceration.

THE IN-AND-OUT PROBLEM

The impact that entering and leaving prisons has on offenders and their families, friends, and community has been the subject of a good deal of academic scrutiny. An important lesson from this research is that incarceration involves a lot of collateral damage, exacting costs that fall particularly heavily on children and their caretakers. These include not just separation trauma, the economic constraints accompanying the loss of a provider, or the economic and psychological strains suffered by a left-behind child, parent, or loved one. It can have long-term developmental implications, shaping both emotional well-being and social behavior. Children with an incarcerated parent—especially if that parent is the mother—are more likely to experience problematic behavioral and psychological responses, both external (e.g., anger, fighting, substance abuse) and internal (e.g., withdrawal, depression). Not infrequently children witness the criminal behavior that triggers incarceration, worrisome not just for what it says about the antisocial environments this all takes place in—some children are more likely to interact with a convicted criminal than a doctor—but for piling on an added ration of psychological trauma and stress.[10] Children may have to move, and parents or custodians may struggle to provide adequate childcare or even to put food on the table.

This can have a depressing and all too predictable cyclical effect. Behavioral problems crop up at school, academic performance suffers, antisocial behavior tips into lawbreaking, and soon enough another person gets swept up by the criminal justice system. Incarceration's negative influence on family stability can lead to cycles of trauma and abuse that repeat through generations. As one study concludes, "in families touched by incarceration . . . criminal behavior (especially substance use and violence) may be recurrent, observable features of children's lives. Over the long haul . . . the realities linked to such family context channel the child's own developing social ties (peers, romantic partners) that serve as proximal influences on behavior and reduced life chances."[11] As people headed to prison are much more likely to come from already precarious social and economic positions (less educated, lower income), even relatively intact and functioning family and social networks struggle to remain resilient to these sorts of shocks.

Given those distressing difficulties, it's not surprising that getting people out of prison does little to mitigate the broader social problems associated with sending them to prison in the first place. Indeed, communities where significant numbers are regularly going to, serving in, and returning from prison suffer not only higher crime rates, but higher levels of social dislocation that extend well beyond the erosion of family and friendship networks. Ex-offenders often return to their communities with limited financial resources and job opportunities; they may also feel the stigma of being a convicted criminal and have difficulty re-entering family or social relationships, especially if those friends and family are dealing with economic and social hardships of their own. This can create spillover effects that blanket entire neighborhoods, triggering not just higher rates of reoffending and family dysfunction, but lower levels of social cohesion and trust that get communally institutionalized.[12] Two concepts are commonly evoked to describe the negative macro-level social outcomes associated with incarceration-reentry cycles: collective efficacy and social capital.

Though the term and the concept predate his work, social capital is most famously associated with political scientist Robert Putnam and the two best-selling books he wrote on the subject. In *Making Democracy Work*, Putnam argued that civic engagement and social relations marked by reciprocated trust were foundational to a well-functioning civil society.[13] More controversially, Putnam argued in *Bowling Alone* that social capital—again, broadly conceived as the interwoven relationships of trust and participation foundational to civil society—was in a precipitous decline in the United States.[14] Though less associated with Putnam's work, in crude terms the concept of collective efficacy is basically social capital plus, the idea that in order for social capital to have any effect it must be harnessed to a collective sense of agency. Collective efficacy is succinctly described as the "social cohesion among neighbors combined with their willingness to intervene on behalf of the common good."[15] Regardless of the specific concept employed, the basic idea is that civic communities—places where people are involved and, crucially, willing to take action rather than turn a blind eye to anything undermining the commonweal—are better governed, safer, and generally more successful and pleasant places to live. Those sorts of places are much harder to sustain where a non-trivial proportion of the community is headed to prison, in prison, or has spent time in prison.

This hypothesis, unsurprisingly, has attracted considerable attention from criminologists and sociologists who have devoted considerable effort to probing the link between social capital/collective efficacy and levels of crime. They have found that plonking what amounts to a giant conveyor belt going to and from prison into the middle of a spatially concentrated, economically and social stressed community is immensely destabilizing. The incarceration-reentry processes create a "coercive mobility" problem that serves to increase single parent households, joblessness, poverty, and ultimately the higher crime rates that continue the cycle. In a nutshell, there is general agreement among academics that mass incarceration has helped corrode the social cohesion of communities—especially, but not exclusively, urban neighborhoods with high minority populations. Bottom line: mass incarceration or at least a much-accelerated incarceration-reentry cycle seems to have stripped communities of vast reserves of social capital.[16] As the latter decreases in a community so does its social cohesion, its economic opportunities, and even its political influence.

All this is already reasonably well established at the neighborhood or even municipal level, but do those negative effects scale to the level of states? If so, it matters little whether a state employed incarceration with an eye toward achieving social order or social control. The end result of an over-profligate use of prisons would result in less of either.

SOCIAL CAPITAL AND THE STATES

Francis Fukuyama once described social capital as the "sine qua non of stable liberal democracy," in other words as *the* absolutely necessary ingredient to create and sustain a well-functioning and prosperous polity such as a state.[17] Given that, figuring out whether mass incarceration is shorting states of such a crucial social additive is obviously a big and important question. Criminologists and sociologists have supplied considerable evidence that accelerating incarceration-reentry cycles depress stocks of social capital (and social efficacy) at the neighborhood and community level, and that this is generally bad for the people who live in those places. Moving up a level to assess whether the same is true at the state level would seem a fairly straightforward exercise. Unfortunately, as is often the case in social science, it is anything but straightforward. The problem with looking at the correlation between the current or formerly incarcerated population and social capital is that while good, reliable estimates of the former are readily available, arguably no equivalent exists for the latter.

Part of the problem is that we (social scientists) can't agree on what social capital is. Broadly speaking, it's agreed that it underpins a range of beneficial communal outcomes—social harmony, economic success, better governance—but it has proven a maddeningly difficult concept to define, let alone measure.[18] The basic idea makes intuitive sense. Obviously, there are some places where people rub along better with each other, are more engaged in and contribute more to communal life, and are generally willing to do the things that make for a safer and more vibrant social environment. Equally obvious is that there are places with a less salutary civic vibe, where neighbors are strangers and people feel unsafe venturing out at night. It stands to reason that the former sorts of communities are going to be more successful and harmonious than the latter. As a metaphor to explain these sorts of differences—as the critical ingredient to a civic soup—social capital is readily communicable and easily comprehensible.

The problems start when you try translating this intuitive and commonsense idea into something that can be precisely qualified or quantified. There's been a huge interdisciplinary effort to study the effects of social capital and its various analogs and extensions like collective efficacy. It is not at all clear, though, that these efforts are looking at the same thing. There are at least twenty or so definitions of social capital floating around. All clearly circle notions like levels of trust and behavioral norms deeply embedded in social networks, but none are exactly the same. Definitions include the "norms and networks that enable collective action," "all factors that foster social relations and social cohesion," "obligations and expectations, information, channels, and social norms," and the "features of social organization, such as trust, norms and networks that can improve the efficiency of society."[19] These particular definitions all suggest something that is characteristic of a social aggregate—a community, neighborhood, city, state—but social capital has also been argued to be something that is rooted in individual-level traits such as willingness to trust others.

Given the definitional incontinence it's no surprise that there's no such thing as a standard way to measure social capital, including and especially at the state level. Roughly speaking, there are three approaches to quantifying a state's stock of social capital: (1) use survey data, that is, simply ask people if they trust other people and like to do stuff with them and aggregate that up to the state level; (2) skip the individual reports and go right to aggregate characteristics, in other words, use state-level measures that presumably reflect more or less social cohesion or associational activity (e.g., divorce rates, or membership in social organizations); (3) use a bit of both and statistically combine them.[20] All of these measures correlate with each other which can, and has, been argued as evidence that lurking under the surface of the statistical Loch Ness is the actual social capital monster. Yet what combination of specific variables best bait that Nessie out of the depths has never been settled.

To start with, all the challenges of getting reliable state-level survey data discussed in some depth in the last chapter apply here too. There's also the added problem that, assuming the survey data does exist, it's not exactly clear what to take from it. Putnam, for example, relied heavily on data from DDB Needham (a marketing and communications company), who asked people questions like whether they attended church, had family breakfasts, sent greeting cards, and, most famously, went bowling. A follow-up study on social capital measurement took a close look at Putnam's source material and concluded you simply couldn't drag a coherent state-level social capital concept out of it.[21] If anything, using state-level indicators (as opposed to aggregating from individual-level indicators) adds to the problem. Recipes for state-level social capital indexes cover an extravagant list of potential ingredients, everything from voter turnout to the number of public golf courses to the proportion of births to unwed mothers. Alarmingly for present purposes, these ingredients sometimes encompass crime and incarceration rates, which presents an obvious problem for any attempt to figure out if mass incarceration is eroding social capital. Going down that measurement path—using crime and/or incarceration to index social capital—effectively means we're headed toward correlating something with itself. That's an exercise guaranteed to produce robust statistical relationships with the unfortunate downside of being utterly meaningless.[22]

This points to another big problem: the indiscriminate use of such variables in studying social capital. Because we don't really know what it is or how to measure it, it's really hard to figure out where it comes from and what might influence it. Take the number of public golf courses, a variable used as a component in one well-known social capital index.[23] Say a state's citizens collectively decide they don't want their tax dollars supporting duffers who, as Winston Churchill once described it, spend their time trying to put exceedingly small balls in exceedingly small holes with implements ill-suited for that purpose. What does that mean? Will course closures cause the decline of social capital? Or are the closures evidence of already declining social capital? Both? Neither? Regardless of the causal path, is it even possible for aggregate levels of social capital to substantively change across relatively short time windows? This last question is far from trivial. Most scholars treat social capital as a product of historical context and a set of long-standing, norm-supporting institutions that sustain it. It's no accident that state-level social capital indexes like Putnam's are cross-sectional, that is, they vary across states but not across time. These measures treat social capital as if it were a fixed state characteristic, sort of like a personality trait. Put like that, social capital starts to sound a lot like political culture.[24] It looks like it too: the correlation between Elazar's measure of state culture and Putnam's state-level social capital index is large enough to raise legitimate questions about whether they are measuring the same thing.[25]

If state-level social capital is a permanent feature of a state's "personality," it undercuts the reason for examining how it will respond to growth in prison populations. This is for the simple reason that if social capital doesn't change across time, it *can't* respond to temporal fluctuations in other variables like incarceration rates. We can look at whether states with higher prison populations have lower levels of social capital, but we can't really figure out what happens to social capital within a state if its prison numbers change across time. Ideally that's what we'd like to do here, and that can't be done with a cross-sectional measure of social capital.

GETTING BACK TO BOXING

The last section tells a pretty glum story given the central goal of this chapter. To sum up: the goal is to figure out whether and how mass incarceration has affected the social health of states. Down at the neighborhood level, scholars have pretty well established that super-sizing incarceration-reentry cycles leads to dysfunction across a number of social dimensions and that the latter can be more or less collectively captured by the concept of social capital or closely affiliated analogs like collective efficacy. A large research literature independently argues that social capital makes a big contribution to generating things we'd like more of (e.g., social tolerance, economic prosperity, good governance, better schools) and tamping down things we'd like less of (e.g., social conflict, crime, community dysfunction).[26] This points to a straightforward blueprint for the chapter goal: just see whether state-level stocks of social capital respond to variation in the size of prison populations. The big obstacle to pulling this off is that, while intuitively appealing, social capital is hard to precisely define and quantify, especially at the state level. We're not completely sure what it is, or how to measure it, or where it comes from. We're not even sure if we can think of it as something that is temporally agile, shifting in response to things like changes in incarceration rates, or whether it is a historical and institutional bequest of long-ago forebears, forged and frozen in the primordial mists of time and soldiering on mostly unchanged from year to year. This sounds pretty bad. Does this mean we can't do the tests we want?

Nah.

Social scientists rarely let things like conceptual opacity, imprecise measurement, and extended causal head-scratching slow down the investigative enterprise (if we did entire disciplines would be struck mute). Dealing with poor-quality input materials is simply an unfortunate reality of the job. This, however, does not mean our investigations are doomed to uselessness. Properly done they can reveal much. The key to getting those efforts to illuminate rather than just make the shadows flicker faster is to recognize and accept the limited wattage of the lamp we're carrying. As long as we stick to what we can see with that restricted beam—as opposed to imagining we know what's going on in the dark—we can, however dimly, make out a path to answers. In Boxian terms, staying on that path requires knowing and being upfront about all the conceptual and measurement limitations, as well as the pretty crude causal understanding we're using for a compass. In other words, because we know setting out that we're running an above-average risk of getting something importantly wrong, we want to consciously mitigate those risks at each step, and, where they can't be tamped down, we take particular care to look out for things we might stumble over.

The immediate need for such a risk-reduction exercise is a state-level measure of social capital that is a valid index of the core concept and also varies across time and space. While there are a range of state social capital measures out there, as far as I'm aware only one measure really fills that latter requirement.[27] Luckily, this is also a measure that has a good claim to the former. It was developed by a trio of political scientists—Daniel Hawes, Rene Rocha, and Kenneth Meier—and was designed from the outset to be a dynamic measure of state social capital, in other words, to capture shifts in social capital from year to year as well as state to state. It uses a wide range of mostly survey-based measures to tap into three core dimensions: community organizational life (e.g., belonging to a civic club or a fraternal order), engagement in public affairs (e.g., voting, contacting a government official), and volunteerism (e.g., volunteering for a non-political cause or organization, donating to public television). These were statistically combined into a single index that has been validated by showing that it works as well as cross-sectional alternatives and that it predicts the things social capital is expected to predict, including incarceration rates.[28] It is available for forty-eight states (Alaska and Hawaii are excluded) for all years between 1984 and 2010.

The extent to which this measure accurately operationalizes a core concept of social capital is, admittedly, open to the same arguments that dog all other state-level measures. Yet it is at least as good in that respect as any other available measure (it correlates highly with all other measures I am aware of), and it has the unique advantage of actually being an annual measure available for a healthy chunk of the era that saw incarceration rates exponentially rise. At a minimum, we can say with a reasonable degree of confidence that it tracks the relative levels of things like civic engagement and communal cohesion, the building blocks of collective efficacy and social capital. So if we take this as the best available dynamic index of state-level social capital during the mass incarceration era, what does it tell us about the distribution and temporal change in social capital stocks?

Figure 5.1 provides an initial answer. This shows the distribution of state social capital scores by year. The score is standardized so the overall average is zero and a shift up or down of 1 indicates a change of roughly a standard deviation.[29] Two things are immediately made apparent by this graph. First, the dispersion of state-level social capital stocks tightened between 1984 and 2010. In other words, social capital–wise states became more similar. The distribution in 1984 is pretty flat—it looks kind of like a stomped-on hat. In the years that follow the hat seems to be slowly springing back to shape, its crown expanding upward and pulling in its rims. What this suggests is that over time states gravitated toward a more similar social capital profile. Second, social capital across the states trended in exactly the way predicted by Putnam: it declined. The yearly distributions not only become more compact, they also steadily shift to the left, in other words, they become less positive. The key takeaway from figure 5.1, then, is that across time, state-level social capital stocks declined and became less variable.

Of course, states being states there is a lot of variation hiding within this general pattern. The vast majority of the total variation in the social capital is concentrated *between* states (roughly 67 percent) rather than within states or across time. That said, that still leaves a lot of idiosyncratic differences within states, and a good chunk of those idiosyncratic differences (between a fifth and a quarter) occur across time. Inspection of a couple individual states can tell the general tale: South Dakota shows a pretty steady decline in social capital across time, while South Carolina shows a pretty steady increase. Still, most states showed a fairly nonlinear shift in social capital in this time period—a pattern of decline through the 1980s hitting a plateau, or even a bounce back, during the 1990s. That sounds suspiciously like what we already know happened to incarceration rates, though the latter went up and plateaued rather than down. Regardless of what wending path social capital took across time to get to 2010, for the vast majority of states that journey ended with a lower number compared to the 1984 starting point.

If social capital has half the positive impacts a large research literature attributes to it, this is all worrying enough; it suggests the collective civic soup is getting watered down, including ever smaller measures of its key ingredient. The larger question here, though, is whether the distributions we see in figure 5.1, or in the across-time patterns in individual states, were in any way moving in response to a gravitational pull from incarceration. In effect, was it locking up more and more people that kicked social capital to

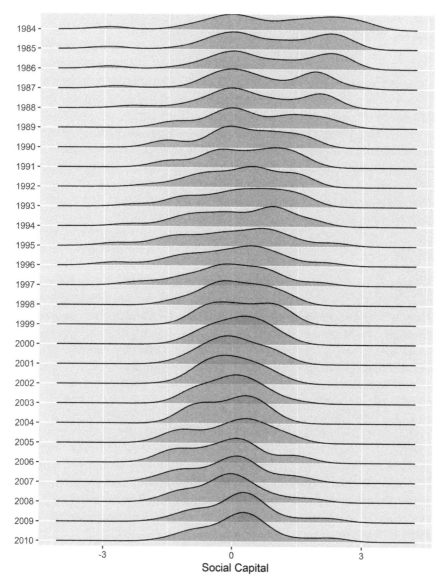

Figure 5.1. State-Level Social Capital Distribution 1984–2010

Note: The mean is standardized to zero and the vertical line serves as a reference point for how state-level capital has shifted relative to its mean over time.

lower levels? Given all the ambiguity surrounding what social capital is and where it comes from, in answering that question we also need to keep in mind that maybe it was social capital doing the kicking. In other words, maybe it was a decline in social capital—an erosion of social cohesion and trust—that actually was driving the rise in incarceration rates.

One way to get a handle on what's driving what is to use a statistical technique called a Granger causality test. The reasoning underlying a Granger causality test is pretty straightforward: If X causes Y, then X and Y will correlate, a change in X will be followed by a change in Y, and any changes observed in Y really are being driven by X and not some other variable Z. The goal of a Granger test, then, is to see if the patterns observed in data line up with that causal logic. If they do, then X is said to "Granger cause" Y. As Granger tests go both ways, it can be used to determine whether incarceration rates (Granger) cause social capital, or vice versa.[30]

While this all sounds pretty simple, it can get way more complicated in practice, and choices have to be made that inevitably invite objections. Perhaps most importantly, to establish the temporal precedence criterion— changes in Y follow previous changes in X—you have to choose what past values of X to use. What do we do here? To predict social capital this year do we use last year's incarceration rates? The year before that? Five years ago? Ten? There are good reasons to argue for a three-year lag, at least on the side of incarceration influencing social capital. If the median time served is roughly eighteen months, then double that—three years—is a defensible window that is wide enough for the incarceration-reentry churn to occur. If incarceration and release is actually detrimental to social capital it should start to be measurable at the end of that three-year cycle.

Still, rather than pin inference to a single choice, I ran the analysis with lags ranging from one to seven years. The results consistently showed clear evidence of reciprocal causation. The hypothesis that changes in social capital caused changes in incarceration rates was supported in five out of those seven tests. Using a minimal bar for statistical significance, the hypothesis that changes in incarceration rates caused changes in social capital was supported seven out of seven times.[31] This could be interpreted as slightly more evidence for incarceration driving social capital rather than vice versa, but that's a debatable take. The more cautious interpretation is that, at least at the state level, incarceration and social capital are tied together in a feedback loop. Movement in one leads to movement in the other, which leads right back to another cycle.

None of this necessarily means much. The effects, even if they are causal, could be trivial. The big issue here is not just whether social capital responds to incarceration rates, but if it does so in a *meaningful* way. To get at an answer to this question, I ran a separate analysis using the same basic approach but with the specific aim of getting a point estimate of how well lagged incarceration rates predicted social capital while controlling for all past values of social capital. The results of that analysis are presented in figure 5.2. This shows estimates from that analysis expressed as movement from overall averages. For example, if incarceration rates increase by 25 percent from their overall 1984–2010 average, the model estimates social capital will respond by dropping about 25 percent from its overall mean value. If the average incarceration rate doubles—it increases by 100 percent—the model estimates that social capital will respond by dropping roughly 40 percent from its average.[32]

Needless to say, if those effects are anywhere close to reality's ballpark—let alone actually in it—they suggest a very large and substantive effect. If social capital is the critical ingredient in the civic soup, this series of analyses suggest it is being consumed at an increasing clip by the states' long-standing commitment to locking up huge numbers of their own citizens. And if those lower social capital stocks actually lead back to more incarceration, the bad news in figure 5.2 is literally only half the story.

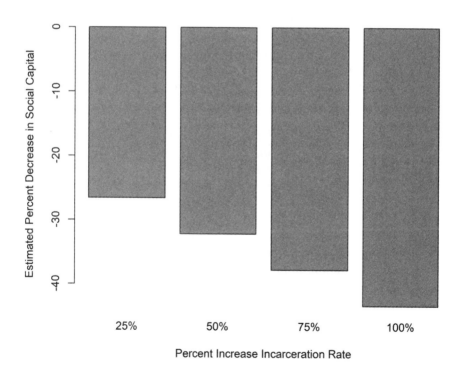

Figure 5.2. Impact of Incarceration Rate Increase on Social Capital

Note: Effects are expressed as percentage change from overall averages based on statistical model described in methodological appendix.

WHAT WE'VE DONE

We need to be careful about overinterpreting these results, especially in the sense of granting specific point estimates high degrees of confidence (in other words take figure 5.2 with a pinch of salt). I freely confess that by the standards of cutting-edge causal methods, this is all pretty rudimentary. The comparatively simple and straightforward approach employed here, though, is perfectly capable of ferreting out patterns in the data without piling on an extra ration of technical assumptions to accompany the social capital conceptual and measurement leaps of faith.

Even a cautious interpretation of the findings raises some pretty big concerns. Bottom line, these analyses support reasonably confident claims that:

a. State-level stocks of social capital have steadily declined across time (see figure 5.1).
b. Social capital is negatively correlated with incarceration rates, both between states and within states across time. The overall correlation is pretty substantive (95 percent confidence intervals suggest the actual correlation is between -.61 to -.53), and the correlation within states and across time is also persistently negative.[33]
c. The hypothesis that decreases in social capital scores are preceded by increases in incarceration fits with observed patterns in the data.
d. Whatever the precise effect of incarceration rates on social capital, they seem to be substantive and far from trivial.

What does this mean? Well, if social capital is as vital an ingredient to a cohesive, stable, prosperous, and harmonious polity as numerous scholars have repeatedly argued, and if the state-level social capital measure used here more or less accurately reflects that concept, then alarm bells should be going off. The vital ingredient of civic society, the sine qua non of stable liberal democracy to use Fukuyama's words, is in increasingly short supply. Why? Well, if you believe what the data used here seem to suggest, it's in no small part because states have coercively deprived their own citizens of liberty in historically huge numbers. This may well be a symptom of deteriorating social cohesion, but there's a justifiable case that it is also its cause. Mass incarceration has contributed—likely in large and substantive ways—to a fraying of the norms, networks, and trust that underpin the commonweal.

So, what have we done? Socially speaking, it appears we've dropped a bomb onto the central political units of the republic. The resulting detonation has sent shrapnel tearing through the civic fabric, including all of us in its collateral damage.

Chapter 6

Cheap Labor Is Damn Expensive

*In which we investigate how low-priced prison
labor costs a lot more than you'd think.*

Sometime in the early morning hours of February 25, 2016, a wildfire broke out near the Mulholland Highway, inland and north of the Southern California city of Malibu. Wildfires are common there—Malibu has been scorched dozens of times in the past century—and these blazes can move fast, fueled by the combustible scrub that blankets the hills and ravines.[1] Uncontained, these can quickly pose serious threats to lives and property. The job of Crew 13–3, based in Malibu Conservation Camp #13, was to make sure that did not happen. They received an alarm at 3:00 a.m. and responded to the Mulholland fire. Among those tumbling out of bed and heading toward the blaze was Shawna Jones. Like everyone else on 13–3, she was not a career firefighter. She was a convicted criminal, a ward of the California Department of Corrections and Rehabilitation (CDCR).

Fighting fire is not a typical inmate job responsibility, though there's nothing unusual about inmates having jobs. Indeed, prison labor can be and is legally mandated, and not just in the sense of inmates being assigned to clean the bathrooms or run the library. Correctional industries—divisions of state corrections departments that make and sell stuff and/or contract out labor—are big operations. Cornhusker State Industries in Nebraska, for example, employs hundreds of inmates to make everything from bookcases to lounge furniture. Corcraft Products operates fourteen manufacturing shops in New York prisons.[2] Inmates in Idaho do agricultural work, and their counterparts in Kentucky run a million-dollar cattle operation. All told, more than sixty thousand captive laborers work in correctional industries, and collectively they are a billion-dollar-a-year business.[3] And none of this includes the sort of work Shawna Jones was doing. The CDCR estimates California inmates alone contribute an annual average of three million work hours to state and local emergency services work like fighting fires.[4]

Prisoners, in short, represent a valuable economic resource—they represent a huge labor pool that can be tapped extraordinarily cheaply. As an inmate firefighter, Jones was earning a prison salary of $2.56 a day, plus an additional $1.00 an hour for time she spent actually on a fire line.[5] As far as prison wages go, that's actually not that bad. California inmates can be paid as little as 8 cents an hour for regular prison jobs like cleaning and laundry. And that's generous compared to other states where doing basic institutional maintenance chores pays bupkis. Astonishingly, given the barely-there wages we're talking about, over the past couple of decades, inmate labor has been getting steadily cheaper. Between 2001 and 2017 the average maximum daily wage for doing prison jobs dropped from $4.73 to $3.45.[6]

Though much-criticized, exploiting inmate labor has a very long history and is perfectly legal. As we saw in chapter 2, mandatory labor was woven into the reforming agendas of the penal pioneers who created the modern prison. Work was considered a triple good; good for the soul, good for balancing the books, and a good kick in the pants to remind offenders of what society did to scofflaws. So much good was seen here that compulsory inmate labor got itself some pretty high-level legal protection. The Thirteenth Amendment is best known for abolishing slavery and involuntary servitude. What's less known is that it also grants explicit constitutional blessing to convict peonage: "Neither slavery nor involuntary servitude, *except as punishment for crime* . . . shall exist in the United States" (italics mine). It's totally kosher, in other words, to coerce prisoners to labor against their will. The economic incentive for state governments to milk that loophole is obvious. Locking people up is expensive, but the very act of doing so also creates a pool of workers that can be coerced into working at far below market-rate wages.[7] It just makes economic sense to take advantage of the free labor to offset the costs of incarcerating them.

This is the combo correctional logic that justifies putting the likes of Shawna Jones, a twenty-two-year-old from an underprivileged and hardscrabble background, on a fire crew. It goes something like this: the hard work serves a punitive function, pays something back to the taxpayers—at a fraction of minimum wage—and hopefully teaches some valuable life and vocational skills that reduce the probability of recidivism. That's the sort of winner, winner, chicken dinner argument that drew Dickens and de Tocqueville into checking out places like Auburn and Cherry Hill. Unfortunately, this logic has repeatedly been shown to be less than airtight. If recidivism rates are anything to judge by, forced labor doesn't have much of a deterrent effect, so at best its punitive benefits boil down to believing that reciprocal trades of peepers and dentures, punishment for punishment's sake, serves its own worthy retributive purpose. As for transferring useful skill sets, even when that does happen it doesn't seem to do much for ex-inmates or society. It can be really tough to translate prison jobs into gainful employment after release. The payoffs of, say, having extensive prison cafeteria experience on your resume are debatable. And it can be tough to take economic advantage of even highly prized skill sets if they were acquired in prison. Some of Shawna Jones's Camp 13 colleagues struggled to get jobs as firefighters or emergency medical technicians after their release, even though they were qualified, experienced, and had often developed a passion and commitment to the work.[8] Jones didn't even get the chance to try. She was struck in the head by a falling rock that February morning, then evacuated by helicopter to Ronald Reagan UCLA Medical Center, where she died without regaining consciousness. While there are certainly rehabilitation success stories, it's fair to say that the involuntary servitude clause hasn't actually done much to support social order hopes of using prisons to inculcate good habits and industry.

On the other hand, it inarguably offered a pretty darn effective tool of social control. The ink was still smudgeable on the Thirteenth Amendment when some (especially Southern) states used the loophole to create what amounted to backdoor slavery. They hustled up "Black Codes," laws with tough sentences that targeted African Americans, forcing them back into bondage for the same planter class the Thirteenth Amendment supposedly just emancipated them from.[9] The brutal system of convict leasing—renting out inmates to labor in often appalling chain-gang conditions—was openly justified as a means to make prisons turn a profit.[10] The worst of these practices have been outlawed, though their contemporary antecedents continue to raise disturbing questions of social justice. Peek under this rock and you'll find the social control condemnations of the criminal justice system toured in chapter 3 staring back with discomfiting moral force.

That force is generated by stories like those of Shawna Jones, who died doing a dangerous job for peanuts to help lower the financial burden of incarceration. Yet while tragic and raising all sorts of ethical and social justice issues, the economic math of exploiting her labor—and the labor of thousands upon thousands of other inmates—still seems to make sense. Regardless of the whiff of bondage and the ethical issues that follow, cheap labor is an always in-demand economic resource. Maybe that labor serves no real deterrent purpose, and maybe it does little to set inmates up to become better economically and civically contributing citizens on their release. No matter. Someone or something—governments, for example—will always have a use for labor selling at far below market rates. Using that resource to reduce the financial burden placed on society to support the costs of incarceration just seems to make irrefutable economic logic. After all, by some estimates it costs California $81,000 a year to incarcerate a single inmate.[11] Inmate labor on emergency and community services alone—the sort of work Jones was doing—is worth an estimated $100 million annually to

California taxpayers.[12] In the state's macroeconomic ledger that's equivalent to the costs of 1,250 inmates. So, even if it doesn't provide any universal benefits to inmates, it still serves the larger economic interests of the state that locks them up. Right?

The main goal of this chapter is to try to answer that question. The focus here, though, is not going to be on the extent to which inmate labor does or does not offset the costs of incarceration. Instead, we're going to focus on the broader economic implications of cycling huge numbers of people through prisons. The economics of a cheap labor pool of inmates might look attractive in terms of balancing out the cost of corrections. But what if this process also creates an even larger pool of people whose economic skills, opportunity, and productivity are limited simply by the fact they have served prison terms? Putting the likes of Shawna Jones into a dangerous job for chicken feed might make bean-counting sense while a sentence is served. But what of the millions upon millions like her who get tossed back into society with little in the way of economically valuable skills or, perhaps even worse, socially valuable skills that are harder to sell because of the stigma attached to being an ex-con? If prisons are serving as a sort of de facto labor regulator—scooping in massive numbers of people and returning them to society with limited abilities or opportunities to compete economically—that raises some serious questions. Having inmates do custodial chores or fight fires might indeed fractionally offset prison costs. But if prison records are limiting the economic potential of millions who find themselves back in the workforce, there's a good possibility that cheap labor might turn out to be damn expensive. For all of us. The macroeconomics of mass incarceration might not make any sense at all.

PENAL KEYNESIANISM: THE MACROECONOMICS OF MASS INCARCERATION

Scholars have known for some time that prison populations are large enough to exert measurable macroeconomic effects. Prison populations, for example, are big enough to artificially lower the national unemployment rate. How do they do that? It's a matter of calculating percentages. The US government defines the labor force as people who have a job (the employed) and those who don't but would like one (the unemployed).[13] The latter's proportion of the labor force—expressed as a percentage—is the unemployment rate. The keeper of these labor force sums, the Bureau of Labor Statistics, does not count inmates as employed or unemployed. They are, quite literally, off the books. There is simply "no trace of an inmates' existence in the labor force while they are behind bars."[14] Crew 13–3 might have done a lot of hard, dirty, and dangerous work, but it was all invisible as far as official employment and unemployment estimates were concerned. The net effect of defining away the prison population from the labor force—more than two million people with less salutary job prospects than most—is to artificially reduce the official national unemployment estimate. And not by just a little bit. Some studies suggest prison populations reduce male unemployment estimates by 30 to 40 percent.[15] That deflationary impact is almost certainly much higher for certain demographic groups, particularly African American males.

Mass incarceration's economic impact is not limited to supporting statistical jiggery-pokery on unemployment rates. Prisons are massive public works and employment projects. More than 430,000 state employees draw more than $2.3 billion in annual paychecks while working in corrections. In total numbers, there are more people working for state corrections in the United States than for Google, Facebook, and Apple combined.[16] These numbers are so big that prisons are seen in some quarters more as public program ATMs than as houses of correction. Prisons are prized as local economic development engines, especially in rural areas where they are seen as a source of scarce well-paying and stable jobs.[17] Abilene, Texas, once offered the state government an incentive package valued at $4 million to lure a prison project. This included not just land for the actual prison, plus new roads and infrastructure to provide access and services, but also an adjacent 1,100-acre farm (a potential profit maker with inmate labor), and even use of a private plane.[18] Prisons can be—and are—thought of as ever-so-slightly-shady New Deal or Great Society operations, public programs where the government spending is big enough to exert a Keynesian supply-side economic effect.

The concept of "penal Keynesianism" is taken seriously by academics who study the economic spillover effects of mass incarceration. That research, though, raises serious doubts about prisons priming any economic pumps, that is, performing as a supply-side stimulus in classical Keynesian fashion. Prisons might provide a steady source of paychecks to be spent on local goods and services, but they have less beneficial knock-on effects for the labor market. L. Randall Wray, an economist, illustrated this by comparing the Keynesian differences between prisons and the military, the two big programs that sweep vast numbers into government institutions and legally limit their individual liberty and rights (albeit in very different ways and for very different purposes). The military, Wray argued, has clear supply-side benefits. Large standing armies tend to take a lot of less educated and lower-skilled people (especially males), give them a job that is valued by society and a source of individual pride, and in the process inculcates values and transfers skill sets that make people more employable outside of military service. At a minimum, being a veteran can provide a significant leg up in the civilian labor market where veteran's employment preferences are not uncommon. So, the military takes a lot of people with a higher probability of being unemployed, trains them in useful skill sets, and puts them to work in a way that does not compete with existing low-wage labor. Long story short on the net effect of all this: veterans return to the civilian world better able to compete in the labor market. For the taxpayer, the investment in a soldier thus pays off twice—a short-term return in national security and a long-term return in the form of a more economically productive citizen.

Wray argues that prisons do not throw off similarly beneficial economic effects. Like the military, prisons take in a lot of less educated and low-skilled people. What most of them are put to work doing as inmates, though, is low-skill labor for little to no pay, often in ways—agricultural work, custodial and food services, and so on—that put them in direct competition with low-skilled workers outside the prison walls. Even at minimum wage, the latter are way more expensive so they have no shot in a direct competition for those positions. Upon release inmates are often returned to a world where they are less competitive in the labor market. There is a pretty low probability of going into prison with no skills and coming out, say, a qualified plumber. There's certainly not much of an ex-con's hiring preference policy.[19] It must be said that having a prison record is far from an insurmountable barrier in terms of getting a job, and there are programs (and companies) that work really hard and often successfully to get ex-inmates jobs. That said, there's also little doubt that a prison record is not exactly an ideal means of expanding your job opportunities. At a minimum, serving a prison sentence clearly seems to exact a considerable earnings penalty. All else equal, a prison record is estimated to reduce an individual's earnings from 10 to 30 percent.[20]

If there is any truth to this it suggests the cost-benefit ratio of prisons might be seriously out of whack when considered in the context of the broader economy. The economic justification of inmate labor rests, and has always rested, on the argument that it can offset the costs of incarceration. Doing everything from basic institutional operation and maintenance to fighting fires on the cheap with inmate labor saves taxpayers money. And, fair enough, that *does* make sense. The open labor market is certainly not going to supply many workers willing to go through an intense training program so they can land a brutally physical job humping up and down hills to fight fires for $2.56 a day. There are not many people willing to do anything at all for 8 cents an hour. Labor that cheap has to save the government money somewhere, even if the people doing the labor aren't exactly enthusiastic about jobs they are forced to do. The problem comes when inmates are released back into society and expected to compete for jobs that put a few more zeroes on a paycheck. What are the employment consequences of spending a year or two behind bars doing menial work for pauper's wages? Bruce Western, a sociologist, has published some of the best known and cited studies relevant to this question. His research consistently suggests that serving a prison term reduces access to (and perhaps the ability to hold) a steady job and lowers earning potential, and that the US penal system generally provides the economy less in the way of Keynesian supply-side honey and much more in the way of labor market regulatory vinegar. Specifically, by locking so many people up the government makes a huge, coercive intervention in the US labor market. It removes millions from the labor market and in doing so saddles them with, at a minimum, more limited earnings potential for life.[21]

It almost goes without saying that those effects are unevenly distributed and almost certainly exacerbate class- and race-based economic inequality. Still, the basic lesson that many may draw from all this is: tough—if you don't want to hobble your economic opportunities then don't do anything that will get you sent to prison. Rather than take up the invitation this presents to wander out into the social justice minefields, I want to raise the sights a little. What if mass incarceration exacts an economic price from *all* of us? Government statistics might hide prisoners from the labor force while they are inside, but what happens when millions upon millions of convicted felons are released and return to the labor market? This is a population that is already comparatively under-educated and under-skilled, and by definition they have huge gaps in their employment histories, which translates into smaller employment-relevant social networks. They are also frequently dealing with a range of challenges—not the least of which is the stigma attached to a prison record—that hamper their ability to successfully compete in the job market. As one review of the labor market issues of a prison record put it, "The negative 'labor supply' effects of incarceration are not limited to the impact on job skills and job networks. For many inmates, incarceration can have serious, long-term consequences for physical and mental health."[22]

These characteristics do not describe the sort of labor force you'd choose if the goal was to maintain a vibrant and dynamic economy. Indeed, it's reasonable to speculate that sort of labor force, if anything, could act as a drag on economic growth. Inmates might get swept under the rug in labor force calculations while they are inside prison. There's no statistical sleight of hand that can hide them once they are outside the prison walls. Is it really possible that mass incarceration has had a big enough negative effect on the labor force to actually hamper economic growth? This is a supportable hypothesis. In some states, after all, the proportion of the population with a prison record is starting to catch up to the proportion with an advanced degree.[23] There is also a reasonable argument, though, that the labor pool impact of mass incarceration—whatever its costs to individuals—might be an overall economic boon. The depressed earnings power of ex-prisoners might be signaling states have been unintentionally using prisons to create a big pool of low-cost labor outside the prison walls. Having lots of people willing to work cheap (or, perhaps more accurately, having little choice about earning less) might be a good thing for the economy. There's some evidence for this.

Figure 6.1 shows a scatter plot of the relationship between the percent of a state's population that has served time in prison with per capita Gross State Product (GSP) in 2000. As you can see it's a positive relationship.[24] What this tells us is that, at least in 2000, states with higher per capita GSP also tended to be states with more ex-prisoners. This is purely a cross-sectional picture, however; it shows the relationship between states at a given time point. It doesn't tell us anything about how the growth of the ex-prison population within a state over time might predict economic growth.

We can get some sense of this by looking at growth within a state over time. Figure 6.2 plots the relationship between annual growth in per capita GSP and ex-prisoners in the state of California from 1980 to 2010, where each data point is a single year. This serves to make the point that within a state, across time, higher numbers of people with a prison record could indeed act as an economic drag.[25] The relationship here, though messier that the one portrayed in figure 6.1, is clearly negative. California wasn't chosen arbitrarily for this example. It is the largest economy within the United States and by some counts is the fifth largest economy in the world. If anything is shaving even a fraction of a percent off the annual growth of the California economy it translates into very big numbers. Currently the GSP of California is in the neighborhood of $3 trillion. One percent of that—30 billion dollars— is roughly the equivalent of the entire GSP of Wyoming.

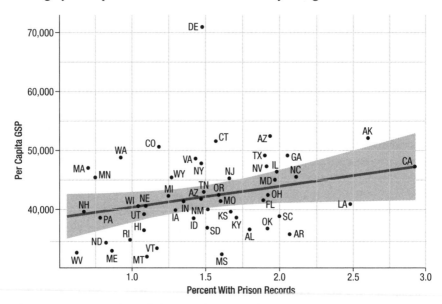

Figure 6.1   Percent of Population Ex-Prisoners and Per Capita GSP 2000

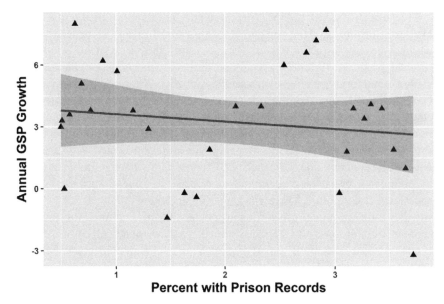

Figure 6.2 Percent of Population Ex-Prisoners and Annual Growth in GSP in California, 1980–2010

To anticipate some perfectly reasonable objections, I am sort of mixing levels and differences in figures 6.1 and 6.2 (GSP in the former and changes in GSP in the latter). The point I'm trying to make, though, is expository rather than to plant a flag for any grand analytical inference. The point being that *any* economic impact of mass incarceration's de facto regulation of the labor market—positive or negative—is likely to be a big deal. How big? Let's see if we can find out.

MODELLING STATE ECONOMIES

The basic analytic goal here is simple and straightforward: see whether the proportion of ex-inmates in a state's labor force can predict its economic performance. There are, as far as I know, no readily available estimates of ex-prisoners as a percent of the labor force by state and by year. There are, however, good estimates of the number of ex-inmates in state populations.[26] Some of these former prisoners will be retired and some won't be looking for work, be unable to work, or be otherwise ineligible to be employed and thus won't technically belong to the labor force. States with higher ex-prisoner populations, though, almost certainly have more ex-prisoners in their labor forces, so this is a measure that can serve for our purposes even if it doesn't meet the Bureau of Labor Statistics technical definition.

Measuring state economic performance is also no problem. Gross Domestic Product (GDP) per capita is a standard means of benchmarking national economic performance. This is simply the value of all goods and services produced for each person, and nations with higher per capita GDP are reckoned to be more prosperous and productive. This is handy because the US Bureau of Economic Analysis (BEA) calculates and reports a state-level equivalent: Gross State Product (GSP), the economic measure already used in figures 6.1 and 6.2. Though GDP and GSP have their critics (e.g., they don't say much about economic equity), they are largely accepted as a standard measure of economic performance. GSP has certainly been widely employed by political scientists and economists interested in things like the effects of state-level fiscal policy. There is a lingering argument among scholars about whether state economies are sufficiently independent of national (or regional) economic conditions to make these sorts of analyses practically useful. State economies are undeniably highly permeable: they have no trade barriers, labor is highly mobile across state lines, and ditto for capital. Furthermore, states have unique constitutional constraints (e.g., balanced budget requirements) that can make for disorderly responses to economic downturns and increase dependence on federal stimulus spending. This all adds up to a reasonable concern that state economies are so thoroughly folded into the national economy that it doesn't make sense to treat them as independent economic units.[27]

There are two big answers to that concern. First, state policymakers certainly act as if they are independent economic actors. Indeed, economic development has been called the, "Esperanto of state politics . . . virtually every policy is now weighted by its anticipated impact on economic development."[28] Second, and more convincingly, the by now large research literature on state political economy provides extensive evidence that states are fully capable of being, "independent and influential economic policymakers."[29] If states can exercise policy influence over their economic fates, it seems safe to say that comparative studies of those same economies are capable of telling us what might or might not predict economic growth. The number of ex-prisoners in the labor force, for example.

So, we're in a much better position in terms of analytical clarity than we were in the last chapter. In contrast to social capital, we don't have to take any great leaps of faith about what we're even measuring and how we're measuring it. We have a globally meaningful measure of economic performance and simply want to know whether this systematically co-varies with the size of a state's ex-prisoner population. The challenge, as is typical in comparative state studies, is figuring out the right statistical approach. We're really only interested in the ex-prisoner/economy relationship so I'm not going to agonize too much about what other variables are fed into the model. All I want is a set of statistical controls strong enough to make any claims about that relation-ship—or lack thereof—defensible. Accordingly, I'm just going to pinch what has worked just fine in other studies and call it good. As long as the models in those other studies are within shouting distance of wrong-but-useful territory, they provide a turnkey set of statistical controls that, at least in theory, should boost confidence in any finding about the relationship of interest. So, what exactly am I poaching from previous research?

Like pretty much every other concept that has attracted the interest of comparative state research, there is no standard, universally accepted statisti-cal model of state—or even national—economies. That said, there's a good deal of commonality to the models that are out there. Broadly speaking, cross-national studies find that access to capital, certain labor pool traits (e.g., education levels), initial levels of development, and government fiscal poli-cies consistently predict economic performance. Much the same is true at the state level: capital, labor, public investment in things like infrastructure and education, and relative tax burden have all been found to predict economic performance at the state level. At least among political scientists there has also been a lively debate over whether partisan control of state government has economic implications, with at least some counterintuitive evidence back-ing the claim that Democrats are better for business than Republicans.[30] So, if we control for all of this stuff, does the percent of a state's population with a prison record tell us anything about economic performance?

The short answer is yes. Full details are in the methodological appendix, but I ran a set of statistical models controlling for a wide range of commonly used predictors of per capita GSP for all states between 1980 and 1997 (the time span was dictated by a shift in how GSP was measured in 1998).[31] These tended to kick out a pretty consistent estimate about the relationship between economic performance and the size of the ex-prison population: a percentage point increase in the latter predicted a decrease in per capita GSP of roughly $3,000. To put this into perspective, I used one of these models to provide a baseline estimate of a theoretical average state. In other words, I asked the model to give me an estimate of per capita GSP of a state that had not just the average proportion of ex-prisoners in its population, but also had average per capita education expenditures, average levels of taxation, average levels of everything all predictors in the model. This across-the-board average state had a per capita GSP of right around $35,000.[32] I then took a look at what hap-pened if that ex-prisoner number jumps a percentage point while all the other variables in the model were held at their means. The answer is that it pulls down per capita GSP to roughly $32,000. If the ex-prisoner number goes up 2 percentage points it drops to about $29,500 (this impact is presented graphi-cally in figure 6.3). The average state population during this time window was, give or take, around 5 million. In other words, the per capita GSP loss

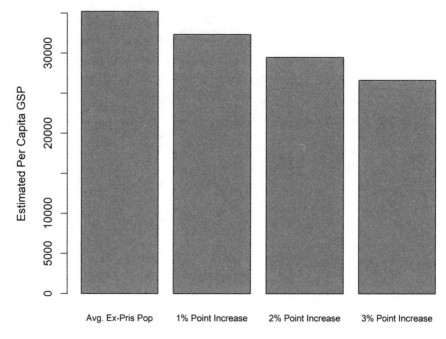

Change in Percent Population with Prison Record

Figure 6.3 Impact of Ex-Prison Population on GSP

associated with a 2 percentage point increase in ex-prisoners comes to a total of $6,000 multiplied by 5 million, or $30 billion in inflation-adjusted dollars. To an average state that's a real economic hit. To smaller states like Wyoming, that's pretty much the entire economy.

I also ran an identical set of statistical models predicting annual percentage growth in GSP. The results here were not quite as consistent, but the general takeaway was very similar. A percentage point increase in the ex-prisoner population predicted a reduction of somewhere between a third and a full percentage point of GSP growth. The average annual growth in GSP between 1980 and 1997 was about 3 percent. Something that shaves somewhere between a tenth and a third off that number is a big economic drag. Which is exactly what these statistical models suggest large ex-prison populations represent.

Before we get too carried away, it needs to be emphasized that these estimates should be taken with a healthy sprinkle of salt. They are all attached to a statistical creation, a perfectly average state. And even if we do accept the results as pretty faithful reports of general patterns in the data, we shouldn't get too attached to the precision of these estimates. Depending on the specific model, there's some walloping levels of potential variation accompanying the point estimate. In other words, the lower border of potential values suggests the impact on our theoretical state might be significantly smaller (though, by the same token, the opposite border of possible values suggests they could also be much higher). The analyses also consistently supported a version of the story told in figure 6.1—that is, statistical models focusing on *between*-state variation found economic performance is positively associated with the size of the ex-prison population. This sounds like a contradiction of the results reported so far, but it really isn't. What this suggests is that states with higher than average ex-prison populations also have higher than average per capita GSP. The story told by the analyses reported above simply suggests that the negative relationship is not between states, but *within* states—in other words, it is how a given state's ex-prison population increases across time that produces the economic drag, not where that state stands relative to other states. The between effect is about $500, a fraction of the $3,000 hit estimated by the within effect. If this is all sending you a little cross-eyed, just subtract $3,000 from $500, which gives us negative $2,500—this is the additive between/within effect of a 1 percentage point increase in the ex-prisoner variable. In other words, if we account for the between effects we still end up with a pretty hefty economic hit.

Again, though, all of these estimates should be treated as ballparks rather than the precise coordinates for the pitcher's mound. Even treating these numbers in a close-enough-for-hand grenades-or-horseshoes sort of way, though, there's a pretty clear inference emerging from the data: across the two-decade span when states were most enthusiastically stuffing as many of their citizens into prisons as they could, that same effort was systematically co-varying with a pretty serious brake on their economies. Precisely how much force that brake was applying on economic growth is open to healthy debate. But if our conceptual Average State is anywhere close to representing actual effects, one of the unintended consequences of mass incarceration is, economically speaking, a huge "own goal."

THE HIGH COST OF CHEAP LABOR

It's more or less universally agreed that going to prison is not good for anyone's economic prospects. And that a prison record acts as a significant disadvantage in the labor market. Had she lived, Shawna Jones—the inmate who died fighting the Mulholland fire—was likely facing dodgy job prospects on her release. Jaime Lowe lays out in heartbreaking detail the struggles of the post-prison struggles of Jones's colleagues, those who fought fires as inmates, in her book *Breathing Fire*. They struggled to get jobs, and remember in some cases that meant difficulty landing emergency service jobs—highly in-demand work they had done and been trained to do at taxpayer expense while incarcerated. Some might argue that this is tough, but individual choices have individual consequences. Yep, you worked hard in prison, and yep, a prison record is a kick in the pants to your employment opportunities. Bottom line, though: you broke the law, your labor was legitimately forfeit as a consequence, and if after release it's harder to get the same opportunities as someone who didn't break the law, well, tough. The obvious lesson to all here is social order flashing in neon: don't break the law . . . or else.

That doesn't quite wash, though, at least not if the analyses described above are in shouting distance of reality. Cheap prison labor turns out to be damn expensive, not just for the people dragging a prison record into the employment sweepstakes, but for all of us. Though the ethics involved in coercing convicted criminals to work are debatable, I suspect most people have no serious objections to those arrangements, at least as long as there are no egregious abuses going on, work conditions are safe, and assuming convicts did indeed commit the crimes that sent them to prison. There's an undeniable appeal to the social order insistence that lawbreakers put in some honest labor to atone for their sins, even if many of the supposed benefits of that toil turn out to be suspect. But that's not really what we're talking about here. The issue isn't whether inmates should be put to work while serving a sentence, the issue is whether mass incarceration is hobbling the labor pool on the outside. The analyses reported here suggest that is indeed the case. We have gone so hog wild locking people up that an inevitable result is a massive number of people—at least five million and likely considerably more—face challenges in the labor market because of their prison record.[33] Mass incarceration has not just created millions facing those challenges individually, the resulting drag on labor force productivity exacts an economic hit that affects all of us. That cheap labor does indeed turn out to be damn expensive.

Chapter 7

For Whom the Cell Polls

In which we learn how those with prison records help determine who holds an obscure local office. And maybe the most powerful office of all.

In June 2021, Joel Caston emerged from a crowded field to win a seat on Washington, D.C.'s Ward 7F Advisory Neighborhood Commission. It wasn't exactly a landslide. He captured a third of the vote in what might charitably be described as a low-turnout race. Only 142 people cast a ballot.

Nothing too out of the ordinary in that. Local elections include offices that, rightly or wrongly, many judge to be humdrum, obscure, and lacking in influence. Voter interest in such affairs is frequently modest and stimulate turnout rates that routinely amount to a fraction of state and federal contests. Indeed, they can be such sleepy affairs that even political scientists don't pay that much attention to them. Advisory neighborhood commissions make a weak case for an exception to this general rule of yawning disregard. They exercise little real power, operating mainly as forums for public grumbling about municipal ineptitude. Competitions for the power to preside over provincial complaint conclaves are, unsurprisingly, rarely characterized by epic ideological donnybrooks and sharp-elbowed mobilization campaigns.

While advisory commissions might be as prosaic as it gets down in the democratic salt mines, there was absolutely nothing typical about Caston or his election. Indeed, both he and the constituency supplying his margin of victory were conspicuously unusual. When elected Caston was in prison, serving the tail end of a lengthy sentence for a murder conviction.[1] That's not exactly the resume you'd expect for a seeker of elective office, and certainly not a successful one. It helped that the four other candidates on the ballot were also inmates in the D.C. jail. So were 141 of the 142 voters.

Inmates electing inmates to public office is, needless to say, astonishingly rare. In some states a prison record—or at least a felony conviction—is a disqualification for running for office, let alone holding one. Inmates are legally prevented from voting in all but two states, and in a dozen or so a felony

101

conviction may mean a permanent loss of the franchise.[2] States, in other words, built tough barriers to wall off the democratic process from those with a criminal record. So, however minor the office or diminutive the electorate, Caston's win is something of a democratic unicorn: a genuine example of people with a prison record exercising actual political power.

Though rare in practice, demonstrations of political power by inmates and, especially, ex-prisoners, are a hypothetical taken seriously by academics and partisan activists. There's a simple reason for this: the population of ex-prisoners has grown so large that, at least in theory, it represents a slumbering electoral kingmaker. If permitted and willing to vote, a motivated constituency of ex-prisoners could certainly have made a radical difference to the political history of the first quarter of the twenty-first century. In 2000 George Bush's presidential ambitions rested on a nail-biting win in Florida. His margin of victory, after extensive recounts, was a piffling 537 votes out of roughly 6,000,000 cast. There were roughly a quarter-million ex-prisoners in Florida in 2000, and it's a good bet Al Gore could have lapped Bush in the voting sweepstakes among that group. He didn't, of course, because a huge proportion of them were ineligible to vote thanks to felony convictions. In 2016 Donald Trump took the White House thanks to the thinnest of cracks in the Democratic "Blue Wall." His presidency was decided in Michigan, Pennsylvania, and Wisconsin, where roughly 100,000 voters decided who took all of their state's electoral votes and with them the key to 1600 Pennsylvania Avenue. At the time, there were between 300,000 and 400,000 ex-prisoners in those states.[3] If they had all cast a ballot and, as academics would predict, voted heavily Democratic, then Hillary Clinton would have been the forty-fifth president. In short, as potential voting blocs, ex-prisoners represent meaningful election muscle, a latent democratic force powerful enough to determine much more than the electoral fortunes of arcane local offices.

That possibility is well known to the poo-bahs of both major political parties. It causes higher-ups in the Republican Party no small amount of heartburn, and it helps explain why restoring voting rights to inmates or ex-prisoners is politically controversial. Democrats see removing felony disenfranchisement—especially after a sentence has been served—as a way to unlock an untapped resource with huge potential to boost their electoral prospects. Republicans fear that Democratic assessment is correct. Former Alabama GOP chair Mart Connors explained his party's reluctance to return voting rights to felons thus: "As frank as I can be, we're opposed to it because felons don't vote Republican."[4]

Generally speaking, academics see Republican fears and Democratic hopes on this front as wildly overblown. While the math works out under generous assumptions about ex-prisoners turning out in high numbers and voting a mostly straight ticket, the simple fact is that for most election scenarios those assumptions do not rub shoulders with reality. Academics have repeatedly found people with prison records simply aren't that interested in electoral participation. Even if all current and former inmates got the franchise tomorrow, their D.C. advisory-commission-race levels of enthusiasm for the ballot box means it's unlikely they'd have a decisive impact on any high-profile electoral outcome. It's hard to swing an election if you don't vote.[5]

How ex-prisoners might or might not reshuffle the odds on the horse race aspects of electoral politics, though, is not the whole story. Rather than determining who does or doesn't win at the ballot box, the growing population of ex-prisoners may be doing something more worrisome. A range of scholarly studies suggest that contact with the criminal justice system is a powerful form of political socialization. Even a short time behind bars makes people less trusting of the political system and more likely to avoid it, an attitude that may diffuse to friends and family.[6] Rather than latent electoral power waiting to be animated to life, perhaps prisons are snuffing out that very possibility? In other words, are prisons socializing current and former inmates—and perhaps those in their social networks—to effectively drop out of democracy? And if that is actually happening, what does it mean for the political system? Given the millions of people we're talking about, those are perhaps more interesting questions than just figuring out in what partisan column they'd line up in some theoretical election. Let's see if we can find some answers.

THE POLITICS OF PRISONERS

Folk wisdom about the partisan leanings of ex-prisoners mostly rests on their demographics. Like the inmates they once were, ex-prisoners tend to be socioeconomically disadvantaged and disproportionately racial minorities—especially African American males. That sounds like a Democratic Party constituency. Democrats thus tend to favor opening the felony disenfranchisement gate, while Republicans want it kept firmly locked. For example, Democrats mostly cheered a 2018 Florida ballot initiative that restored voting rights to felons who had completed their sentence. This was a big deal: in one swoop it created a pool of roughly a million-and-a-half newly eligible voters. That's a pretty significant chunk of the electorate given Florida is a place where statewide contests can be decided by a fraction of that number. The Republican-controlled state government responded to the re-enfranchisement initiative by passing a law to keep ex-felons disenfranchised until they paid off all their accrued court costs and fines. That had the practical effect of continuing to keep most of those newly enfranchised voters legally at arm's length from any ballot box.[7]

While political parties are convinced of the latent partisan intentions of the millions of current and former inmates, hard data to support these assumptions is in relatively short supply. There is not a ton of good scientific surveys of ex-prisoners, and even fewer for prison inmates. In terms of reliable, comprehensive, and comparable state-level surveys, at least as far as I'm aware, we're talking about a totally bare cupboard. While we can make some informed guesses, we don't really know if, say, inmates or ex-prisoners in Texas and Georgia identify more as Republicans than ex-prisoners in Wisconsin and Illinois.

One of the very few serious attempts to broadly poll the political beliefs of prison inmates was undertaken in 2019 and 2020 by the Marshall Project, a nonprofit news organization that covers the criminal justice system, and the online magazine *Slate*. They included a survey in a widely circulated prison newspaper (*News Inside*—distributed to roughly five hundred prisons) and received 8,266 responses. Though a large sample, this is not a representative poll by any stretch of the imagination. There's no way to ensure that responses are limited to inmates serving sentences of one year or more in state institutions, the incarcerated population as I defined it way back in chapter 1.[8] It does not allow for meaningful state comparisons (the analytic method the entire argument of this book rests upon).[9] But it is the only large sample survey of its kind that I am aware of. Still, even with all its limitations, the results put the sagacity of folk wisdom up for some serious questioning.

Survey respondents indicated a pretty even split between Republican and Democratic Party identification: 23 percent identified as Republican, 24 percent as Democratic, 28 percent as independent, and the rest as something else. Voting intentions are also something of an eyebrow-raiser. Asked who they would vote for if the presidential election was held tomorrow (keep in mind the 2019/2020 time frame) the candidate who came out on top by a healthy margin was . . . Donald Trump. Trump was favored by 28 percent, and the only other response in hailing distance of that total was "don't know/ would not vote" (25 percent). The ten Democrats then in contention for their party's presidential nomination mustered between them a total of just under 40 percent.[10] In other words, combined Democratic support was well short of the combined preference for Trump and what amounts to "none of the above." Results were equally surprising on the political engagement front. Nearly half, 47 percent, said being incarcerated increased their motivation to vote, while only about 12 percent said it decreased their zeal to cast a ballot. Perhaps academic warnings of prison acting as an agent of political demobilization are overblown? Maybe. A solid majority of those polled, 55 percent, also admitted they'd never voted. Whether the enthusiasm for getting off the voting schneid survives an outward-bound trip past the prison gates is debatable.

The most generous scholarly estimate of the potential electoral impact of ex-prisoners, and almost certainly the best known, comes from a series of studies done by sociologists Jeff Manza and Christopher Uggen.[11] Their statistical models suggest roughly 35 percent of those disenfranchised because of felony convictions would vote if given a chance and that about 73 percent of those would cast a ballot supporting a Democratic candidate. Those numbers imply a potentially massive impact on the nation's political fortunes, an underground electoral force that could change outcomes for powerful offices like governor, the US Senate, and even the presidency if it ever fully surfaced. Think of those 1.5 million newly (sort of) enfranchised voters in Florida. If 35 percent of that number voted and 73 percent of them ticked a ballot for the Democrats, it would represent a net gain of roughly a quarter-million for a theoretical statewide Democratic candidate.[12] That's bigger than the margin of victory in the state's 2000, 2012, and 2016 presidential contests, as well as its 2010, 2014, and 2018 gubernatorial races.

Those sorts of numbers set Democratic strategists' hearts to beating faster and give their Republican counterparts arrhythmia. Whether triggered by hope or dread, though, academic research indicates the extra cardiac activity may be for naught. Manza and Uggen's estimates are considered to be unrealistically high by other studies, which report the dormant Democratic constituency's actual size doesn't justify all the partisan tingles. For example, one of the few studies of ex-prisoner voting based on big nationally representative samples concluded that Manza and Uggen overestimated the number of disenfranchised felons who would vote by roughly ten to twenty percentage points.[13] A study analyzing the voting behavior of inmates in Vermont and Maine—the two states where incarcerated people remain eligible to vote—found that less than one in ten actually bothered to do so. The same study looked at statewide election outcomes assuming their *entire* incarcerated populations voted as a block. It concluded that even in this wildly unrealistic counterfactual world, few, if any, election outcomes would change.[14] Returning to the observed rather than assumed world, scholars have found that ex-inmates who legally have the franchise rarely bother to register, let alone actually vote.[15] In New York, less than 20 percent of ex-felons are registered (around half as Democrats, a fifth as Republicans) and less than 10 percent regularly vote. In North Carolina roughly a third are registered (slightly more than half as Democrats, 10 percent as Republicans) and about 10 percent regularly vote.[16]

While the lack of good comparative state data means any estimates are speculative, a reasonable guess pulled from the academic research is that in the typical state somewhere between 10 and 20 percent of ex-inmates will cast a ballot, or would do so if legally eligible. Any estimate of their partisan split amounts to what's known in the prediction trade as a WAG (a "wild-ass guess"). A not-too-awful-WAG-ey range would be something like 50 to 60 percent voting Democratic and 10 to 20 percent Republican. Obviously, that still leaves a chunk of this constituency up for grabs, and even these highly hypothetical partisan divisions are almost certainly going to differ considerably from state to state. Still, let's take the middle of those ranges and re-apply them to those 1.5 million potential voters in Florida to get a comparison with estimates taken from the Manza and Uggen estimates. If you run this math, what you end up with is a statewide Democratic advantage of roughly 90,000 votes.[17] That's a long way from nothing—give Charlie Crist that many extra votes in 2014 or roll them into Andrew Gillum's column in 2018 and Rick Scott and Ron DeSantis's narrow gubernatorial wins become narrow losses. That sounds like a big deal—and it is—but zoom out and 90,000 votes just doesn't look like a fundamental game changer for the overall electoral landscape. Why? Well, something like eight to ten million voters participate in Florida's presidential and gubernatorial contests so, while 90,000 seems like a big number it represents only about 1 percent of total votes cast. In other words, it has to be a very tight race indeed for ex-prisoners to determine who ends up popping champagne corks and planning a move to Tallahassee.

The bottom line is that most academics who have taken a serious look at this issue conclude that the potential impact of ex-inmate voting on statewide election outcomes is minimal. In races where razor-thin margins separate the major party candidates, everyone agrees the numbers could, at least in theory, be decisive. Most races, in most states, though, just aren't close enough for the ex-prisoner constituency to provide the critical difference for Democratic candidates. For example, the closest of the eleven governor's races run in 2020 took place in North Carolina, where incumbent Democrat Roy Cooper won by nearly 5 percentage points. Winners in the other races coasted home with double that margin. In 2020 the average margin of victory for the thirty-five US Senate races was 18 percentage points.[18] Those are pretty typical numbers for twenty-first-century elections. You have to make some mighty heroic assumptions about anticipated ex-prisoner voting patterns to conclude they could change contests routinely being decided by averages of 10 to 20 percentage points.

In sum, rather than a lurking powerhouse capable of putting a decisive finger on the partisan scales, ex-prisoners are more realistically a potential source of an extra percentage point or two for the Democratic candidate in a statewide race. Yep, that's enough to shove a Democratic candidate into office in a hotly contested campaign. That won't happen often, though, because there simply are not that many races decided on such wafer-thin margins. There is one potential major exception to this general rule, and it's the big kahuna of American electoral prizes: the presidency of the United States.

PRISONERS AND PRESIDENTS

The presidency is a race for states, not votes. This is because presidents are elected using a Rube Goldberg parliamentary doo-dad dreamed up by Founding Fathers who didn't trust kings, didn't trust voters, and, truth be told, weren't too thrilled with the perceptible whiff of power lust fumigating their own wigs. I'll skip the civic lesson details, but in practice the Electoral College means states elect the president. And these days, that puts a lot of power in the hands of very few states because in most states, in most presidential elections, there is no real Electoral College competition to speak of. The majority of electoral votes are sewn up before we even know who the candidates are. This is because all states except Maine and Nebraska award all their Electoral College votes to the state's popular vote winner.[19] As many states, including those particularly rich in electoral votes, are one-party dominant, you don't exactly have to be a professional crystal ball jockey to accurately call their presidential election outcomes. California hasn't voted for a Republican presidential candidate since 1988, and Texas hasn't voted for a Democrat since 1976. It is a small number of so-called battleground or swing states—states with meaningful electoral vote swag that feasibly could go either way—that routinely play the kingmaker. And races in those states frequently get very tight indeed.

Indeed, half of the six presidential elections between 2000 and 2020 were decided by a crucial percentage point or two in no more than four or five states. The hanging chads fell for Bush in Florida in 2000. In 2016 Trump edged Clinton by roughly a point in Wisconsin, Michigan, and Pennsylvania. In 2020 Trump was pipped at the post by similar tissue-thin margins in Georgia, Arizona, Wisconsin, and Pennsylvania. In other words, a percentage point or two in a few states not only *could* determine who holds the most powerful elective office on the planet, they *have* been doing exactly that on a pretty regular basis. The big question is whether ex-prisoners, in theory or in fact, supply those margins.

To get at that answer, I'm most interested in what happens to a state's voting patterns as its population of ex-prisoners grows.[20] In other words, do increases in the ex-prisoner population reliably predict an uptick in share of the popular vote won by the Democratic presidential candidate? Such Democratic gains could not rely directly on voting by people with prison records. Felony disenfranchisement, after all, means that in some states many ex-inmates cannot legally cast a ballot. Friends and family without felony records, though, certainly can. If, as some scholars have suggested, the political socialization effect of prison spills through social networks, this could be a general relationship rather than one tied to the turnout and voting proclivities of an ex-prisoner constituency.[21]

Preliminary evidence for that hypothesis can be found in figure 7.1. This provides a visual representation of the presidential election outcome/ex-prisoner relationship in four swing states between 1980 and 2008 (the maximum time span given data availability). That relationship is clearly positive and linear. I picked these four states specifically for their role as realistic determinants of who ends up picking out new curtains for the White House, but they are pretty representative of a general relationship. The correlation between ex-prisoners and Democratic vote share is positive for forty-one states. At least it is using data from the eight presidential contests between 1980 and 2000. The nine states where the correlation is negative are also instructive. They are all traditionalistic states and heavily concentrated in the Deep South, where partisan loyalties started shifting away from conservative Democrats to conservative Republicans in the 1980s.[22] Those exceptions, in short, do not really undermine the rule inferred from figure 7.1, that there's a tight, positive relationship between Democratic vote share and the size of a state's ex-prisoner population.

This is a pretty simplistic analysis to hang this inference on, though, especially given its implications. The analysis represented in figure 7.1 suggests an unintended effect of mass incarceration is a long-term boost to the electoral odds of Democratic presidential candidates. Yet there are a lot of other things that could potentially account for state-level election outcomes, especially given the nearly three-decade span we're talking about. Could this

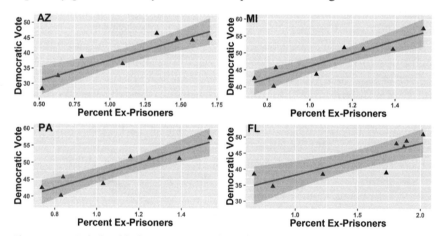

Figure 7.1.   Relationship between Proportion of Population with a Prison Record and Democratic Presidential Candidate Vote Share in Arizona, Michigan, Pennsylvania, and Florida, 1980–2008

Note: X-axis is the estimated proportion of a state's population with a prison record, Y-axis is the percent of the popular vote received by the Democratic presidential candidate.

relationship survive a good Boxing, in other words a good statistical kicking that accounts for the tigers of presidential election predictions?

To help answer that question I turned to presidential election prediction models. This is a well-established cottage industry in political science. Every four years different scholars or teams of scholars vie to produce the most accurate forecast, which are published in the journal *PS: Political Science & Politics* before the election. The competitors use different predictive strategies, constructing statistical crystal balls out of economic conditions, primary performances, opinion polling, and so forth. Regardless of the modelling minutia, the bottom line is that these forecasts repeatedly demonstrate that political scientists have become *really* good at predicting presidential election outcomes. A majority of the ten models included in *PS* symposia were within a percentage point of predicting Hillary Clinton's share of the popular vote in 2016; the most inaccurate was off by only three points or so (keep in mind that these predictions were published the summer before the election). In 2020, the models forecast Trump's share of the popular vote would be 47.8 percent, pretty darn close to his actual total of 46.9 percent.[23]

Political scientists are not quite so hot at predicting the Electoral College tally, but they are still pretty good—the average 2020 modelling forecast predicted Trump with 237 electoral votes, while he actually received 232. The drop-off in accuracy between popular and electoral vote predictions is due in no small part to that same handful of states where a tight race or two can dramatically alter the results. The big problem in making electoral vote forecast more precise is that there are lots of variables—some state and/or election specific—that could potentially tip a neck-and-neck contest, and it's simply not practical to account for all these possibilities. Still, while no model is perfect, political scientists have constructed plenty that are quite good. One of the most parsimonious and accurate models of state-level presidential outcomes was developed by Jay DeSart. His model uses only four predictors: a state's presidential voting history (how it voted in the last election), national poll numbers, home states of the candidates, and how many consecutive terms the incumbent's party has held the White House. By political science standards that's as stripped down as a model gets. Yet it's also good enough to correctly call 276 of the 300 state-level presidential outcomes that occurred between 1996 and 2016—an accuracy rate of 92 percent.[24]

Rather than reinvent statistical wheels to conduct a more sophisticated look at the relationship portrayed in figure 7.1, I simply pinched DeSart's model and added two variables: state culture and the percent of the state's population with a prison record. The latter is obviously what I'm most interested in, and I included the former as state culture in the bivariate analysis discussed above suggested traditionalistic states as potential exceptions to a general relationship rule. DeSart used his model to predict the Democratic share of the two-party popular vote between 1996 and 2016. I'm trying to predict the same thing but in a different time window: 1980 to 2008, the longest time span where estimates of the ex-prisoner population are available. In simple terms, what I'm doing is adding an ex-inmates predictor to a validated model to see whether it "pops." In other words, within the constraints of a model proven to be a fairly accurate predictor of state-level presidential outcomes, can the size of the ex-prisoner population elbow its way through the queue and grab a piece of explanatory variance for itself?

Well, does it? Sort of. One of the models I ran showed a huge effect; on average, a 1 percent increase in the size of the ex-prisoner population predicted an increase of roughly 2 percentage points in the Democratic vote share. That's eyebrow-raising. If we interpret this causally (and this should be done with caution), it suggests that a jump in ex-prison populations in those swing states could absolutely tip presidential races. Before getting too excited, though, the overall picture emerging from the statistical analyses is not nearly so definitive (see methodological appendix for full details). For one thing, a 1 percentage point increase in the portion of a state's population with a prison record is, relatively speaking, huge. For the average state, that sort of growth takes about twenty years, which gives a lot of time for the political environment to adjust to modest shifts in demographic voting patterns.[25]

For another, alternative statistical models estimate much more modest effects. Roughly speaking, they suggested that a 1 percentage point increase in ex-prisoners between presidential electoral cycles increased Democratic vote share by about a 0.2 percentage point. That suggests more of a non-effect than anything else, at least in the short term. A realistic increase in ex-inmate population share over a four-year span is not 1 percent but something more like a tenth of a percent. Plug that smaller number into the model and it estimates a Democratic bump that comes out to a fraction of a fraction of a percentage point. Outside of Florida-in-2000 situations, that is just not big enough to make a difference. Over the long-term, though, the cumulative three-decade effect looks more substantive. Roughly speaking, the long-term effect of a 1 percentage point increase in ex-prisoners—a level of growth easily achieved in most states between 1980 and 2000—translates into something between a 1.5 and 2 percentage point increase in Democratic vote share. That's enough to make a difference in key states, even if absorbed into the political environment over a long time in small increments.

As the statistical analyses failed to consistently rule out the possibility of no effect, that the impact of growth in ex-prisoner population on Democratic vote share was zero, inference inevitably depends on the subjective spectacles the numbers are viewed through. A reasonably safe conclusion would be that there is no evidence that increasing ex-prisoner populations harms the electoral prospects of Democratic presidential candidates, and none that it benefits their Republican counterparts. Somewhat more contentiously, the evidence suggests more ex-prisoners translates into Democratic candidates taking a bigger slice of the popular vote pie. Whether that slice is enough to appreciably fatten their (electoral) vote share is debatable, but the positive case is, I think, defensible.

BIG HOUSE TO THE BALLOT BOX: A
ROAD LESS TRAVELED

To recap the story thus far: repeated readings of the statistical tea leaves suggest that increasing numbers of ex-prisoners predicts Democratic electoral chances will increase by a smidgen. For most races, in most states, that appears to be too small a smidge to have any determinative impact on election outcomes. On the other hand, that same smidge expands to a more robust jot, tinge, or trifle in presidential races, thanks in no small part to the odd electoral mechanism we employ to catapult people over the White House fence. A small effect does not persuasively argue against the very real possibility that, though a modest proportion of the overall electorate, ex-prisoners could regularly influence presidential outcomes. After all, in the Gore-Bush, Clinton-Trump, and Trump-Biden contests, the political impact of a voting share smidge has shown itself to be politically seismic.

Still, given that we're talking about very modest effects emerging from inconsistent statistical results, the effect—or lack thereof—of ex-prisoners as a voting constituency can be debated until the cows come home. There's no gray area when it comes to the impact of ex-prisoners on political participation: mass incarceration has led to a huge increase in the numbers of people who simply do not vote. What makes that statement hard to argue against is felony disenfranchisement, state laws that bar convicted felons from the ballot box. In some states, those numbers affected by these laws are jaw dropping, especially when broken down by race. In 2020 an estimated 7.7 percent of the voting-age population in Florida was legally denied the franchise because of a felony conviction. If we exclude those incarcerated or on parole and only include people who have completed their sentences, you still end up with the vast majority of those people—about 6 percent of the state's voting-age population—disenfranchised. Even if you take the conservative estimate that only 10 percent of that population would vote if allowed, that means there were more than 88,000 Floridians who wanted to participate in the 2020 election but could not because of their criminal record. That same year, nationwide there were more than 5 million people with no right to vote because of a felony conviction, and 2.25 million of them were not incarcerated or on parole. These are people who had served their sentence but were consigned to continuing and perhaps permanent second-class citizenship because of state law.[26]

Break these numbers down by racial categories and the picture quickly goes from concerning directly into *The New Jim Crow* territory. In 2020, an estimated 15 percent of Florida's African American population was disenfranchised. Even that shocking number hides the real impact. Given the huge gender disproportion in felony convictions (approximately 90 percent are male), what you're likely looking at is something in the neighborhood of 30 percent of African American males being disenfranchised in the Sunshine State. Debates about the underlying causes of that conviction rate should not, in any way, detract from the small-d democratic implications here. If a third of a sizable racial group are being legally deprived of the most basic democratic right, it suggests something down in the engine room of participatory democracy is seriously out of whack.

It is possible to smear some lipstick on this participatory pig by staying focused on the national numbers. And, fair enough, the 2.25 million disenfranchised who are not incarcerated or on parole represent only about 1 percent of the nation's voting-age population. That's a statistical dodge, though. These people are not evenly spread geographically. The percent of the voting-age population disenfranchised because of a felony conviction is zero in Maine and Vermont, and it's less than 1 percent in Illinois, California, and Ohio. On the other end of the scale, it's 10 percent in Mississippi, and 9 percent in Tennessee and Alabama.[27] Felony disenfranchisement is obviously a state issue, not a national one. None of this accounts for any of the potential spillover effects that scholars have long suspected, the potential for prison experience to filter through social networks and depress political engagement more generally.

The key question here, then, is not whether mass incarceration reduces political participation, especially for a specific demographic group. It does, period, full stop, and end of story. The extent of de jure exclusion varies wildly state to state, but even granting low turnout rates among ex-inmates it is inarguable that felony disenfranchisement prevents, at a minimum, hundreds of thousands from voting who would otherwise willingly participate.[28] Indeed, this fact—the huge growth in the numbers of prisoners and ex-prisoners—has already helped solve one of the big puzzles of voter turnout studies: the mystery of the vanishing voter. Political scientists who study participation started noticing a steady decline in turnout that first became apparent in the early 1970s. That trend continued through the last few decades of the twentieth century. This did not seem to make a whole lot of sense. Barriers to the ballot box (poll taxes, age limits, etc.) were falling left and right in the 1960s and 1970s, while rates of educational attainment—about the best predictor of turnout ever identified—were on the rise. So where the heck did all the voters go?

As a discipline, political science threw a ton of horsepower at that question for a decade or two without really solving the puzzle. The answer finally arrived in 2001 in an *American Political Science Review* article by Michael McDonald and Samuel Popkin. The title says it all: "The Myth of the Vanishing Voter."[29] In a nutshell McDonald and Popkin argued that the turnout decline we were all wringing our hands about didn't actually exist—it was almost entirely an artifact of how turnout was being measured. Traditionally, turnout studies used the percent of the voting-age population (VAP, to those in the know) as the yardstick of participation. McDonald and Popkin pointed out that across time this measure scooped up an ever-increasing proportion of groups that could not legally vote. One consisted of non-naturalized immigrants. The other big, rapidly expanding ineligible demographic group in the VAP was, you guessed it, convicted felons. Statistically adjust for these groups—that is, throw them out—and what you are left with is the voting eligible population (VEP). Use VEP rather than VAP and the great turnout decline disappears. As McDonald and Popkin succinctly put it: "The apparently decline in voter participation in national elections since 1972 is an illusion."[30]

McDonald and Popkin's analysis focused mainly on national and regional trends, but scholars who took the analysis down to the state level found similar, if perhaps more modest, results.[31] Unsurprisingly then, scholars of turnout have heavily favored VEP since McDonald and Popkin's article. VEP, though, is in no way a perfect measure, especially for present purposes. For one thing, it is conceptually set up to explicitly remove the impact of mass incarceration from participation—it deals with the problem of rising felony disenfranchisement due to a criminal record by just getting rid of it. For accounting purposes, VEP tosses out convicted felons and sweeps them under the rug. For another, despite its name it doesn't actually measure those eligible to *vote*, it measures those eligible to *register* to vote. In other words, VEP almost certainly includes lots of ex-prisoners who have never, and are unlikely to ever, bothered to register. Overall, only about two-thirds of eligible citizens register to vote.[32] The data is less reliable for ex-prisoners, but as we've already seen their registration rates are likely less than half of that for the general population. In some states, it's likely way less than half. One way to deal with this is simply to measure turnout as the proportion of registered voters who actually cast a ballot. This measure has its own problems—some states are notorious for being less than vigilant about keeping voter rolls updated and accurate. Still, it is perhaps the best estimate available of what proportion of a state's population in a given year can, if they so choose, actually show up to the polls and exercise their right to vote.

So, what happens to that proportion as the number of ex-prisoners increases? As far as I am aware there's no statistical model for state-level turnout that has the sort of 90 percent–plus accuracy guarantee found in electoral vote models. Still, there's a fairly universal agreement that turnout in the states is driven to a large extent by a handful of key variables, such as competitiveness, ease of voter registration, state culture, and relative education levels.[33] I put together a set of statistical models based on those predictors, but that also included the proportion of a state's population with a prison record. Though more stable than the Democratic vote share models, the point estimates did some wobbling depending on what set of assumptions drove the model. That said, the most defensible model on statistical grounds suggested a pretty whopping effect.[34] The estimate was that a 1 percentage point increase in ex-prisoners predicts a 3 percent decline in turnout. It is worth emphasizing that this is a 3 percent decline among *registered* voters. In other words, it not only accounts for ex-prisoners ineligible to register, it accounts for ex-prisoners who are eligible and have registered. This effect size suggests a pretty substantial spillover, that the rise of mass incarceration has a political socialization effect that acts as a participatory drag even for those signed up and qualified to vote. At a minimum, it seems pretty unlikely that a turnout decline of that size can be chalked up to ex-prisoners alone.

As already noted, a 1 percentage point increase in the number of ex-prisoners across the time ranges considered here is not untypical; indeed, ten states had double that between 1980 and 2010.[35] This suggests that once you pull those with felony records back into turnout consideration, that vanishing voter might not be as mythical as it seems. If we take the 3 percentage point decline as a reasonable average associated with that 1 point increase in ex-prisoners, that's adds up to a lot of missing voters. Their partisan leanings are unknown, and unrecoverable from the available data. But they wouldn't have to show Manza and Uggen sorts of Democratic preferences to represent a potentially big effect on statewide election outcomes, especially close races. Three percent of registered voters with a strong partisan tilt could make a real difference, especially in swing states.

This, of course, is statistical speculation. Especially given the unclear signal sent from the statistical models I ran, it would be foolish to make any bold and definitive claims. Still, maybe those racing Democratic hearts and incipient Republican coronaries tied to ex-prisoner electorates are not quite as unjustified as we social scientists have made them out to be.

CONCLUSION

There's little doubt that the era of mass incarceration has produced a large enough population of inmates and ex-inmates that, collectively, represent a potent electoral force. To what extent that force is being applied to the democratic system remains, to put it mildly, not fully understood. Still, it's not an outrageous speculation to think of Joel Caston's election to a little-known local office as a visible signal of a trend that's been rumbling underground for four decades. Scholarly and statistical ears to the ground have strained mightily to make coherent sense of what those subterranean grumblings portend for the political system. Some argue, with evidentiary support, that it amounts to not much more than a minor settling of the political landscape. Maybe this constituency helps produce a Democratic win here and there in the odd tightly contested race, but the general rule boils down to "not much to see here." Others run the numbers and conclude a tectonic shift registering in the mid- to high-reaches of the political Richter scale is possible.

The reality lies between those two extremes. There is no doubt that mass incarceration has measurable impacts on political participation. If nothing else, it's a stone-cold certainty that it removes millions from the pool of eligible voters. Inmates are, with very few exceptions, legally disenfranchised, and there are a lot more of them than there used to be. And in many states, release from prison does not guarantee reinstatement of voting rights. Indeed, some states—looking at you, Florida—have gone to pretty extreme lengths to keep ex-prisoners legally barred from the ballot box. It's equally certain that a single demographic group—African American males—disproportionately suffer this legal exile from democratic participation, the imbalance in some states being disturbingly spectacular (I'll again serve up Florida as the exemplar). Beyond this, what's less certain is the extent of the mass incarceration era's broader demobilizing effect. Some argue contact with the criminal justice system acts as an agent of political socialization, leaving not just those with prison records but also members of their family and social networks less trusting of the system and eroding their willingness to participate. That view is certainly consistent with the analyses I ran, which point to rising populations of ex-prisoners being associated with some pretty eye-popping reductions in turnout among registered voters.

It's hard to vest full confidence in the latter conclusion, mainly because the available data doesn't allow a direct test of the core underlying question. Ideally, what I'd need in order to address that question is high-quality survey data of eligible voters who did not cast a ballot, a survey that specifically asks these non-voters about their prison records, as well as the prison records of friends and family. Of course, I'd also want that data collected in, and individually representative of, all fifty states. As far as I'm aware, no such survey exists (this is not surprising—what I'm describing is a pretty expensive proposition). Lacking that, the spillover effect of turnout depression remains more than a little murky—the available data provides suggestive patterns though. Even accepting these limitations, the weight of the evidence clearly supports the conclusion that large numbers of people who want to vote are either discouraged or legally prevented from participating. In the average presidential electoral cycle, the only real debate on this point is whether that population is in the hundreds of thousands or stretches into the millions. Accepting even a modest spillover effect clearly pushes the probabilities toward the latter end of the scale.

The real question, then, is not whether the era of mass incarceration has reduced political participation. It has. The question is by how much, and what sort of partisan advantage is gained or lost by keeping the missing voters away from the polls de jure or de facto. The scholarly consensus sees a partisan differential here, that current and former inmates, even if they don't vote much, are more likely to support Democrats. The data is far from conclusive (remember the Marshall Project/*Slate* survey), but there's general agreement that under certain circumstances ex-prisoners could help determine the outcome of statewide elections in favor of a Democratic candidate. Those conditions include a hotly contested race with substantial, if low, rates of ex-prisoner participation. Those are rare enough that Republican worries and Democratic hopes are not infrequently dismissed as partisans mistaking Matterhorns for molehills. I'm not so sure. Since 2000 presidential elections have, as often as not, been close-run affairs. Twice the Electoral College has put the loser of the popular vote in office. Swing states are routinely won by piddling margins that could easily swing the other way if even a relatively small group with a distinct partisan bias decided to show up to the polls. The population of ex-prisoners in many of those swing states fit that bill nicely. The issue is not whether they could tilt an election, but whether enough of them are motivated—or legally allowed—to cast a ballot. Is that possible? Could ex-prisoners as a constituency actually decide a presidential outcome? If their absence enters these counterfactual accounting exercises, the odds are that they already have.

Chapter 8

The Jailer's Reckoning

*In which we tally the price of mass incarceration
and ponder options to cut its costs.*

On April 29, 1966, Assistant Secretary of Commerce Eugene P. Foley released electrifying news about the Great Society project's next leap forward. To scribblers and scribes assembled for a presser in Oakland, California, Foley unveiled plans to drop roughly $30 million—real money in the mid-1960s[1]— to underwrite municipal infrastructure improvements, capital for local business loans, and a new health care center. Shoveling this sizable chunk of government cash into the city was expected to generate three thousand new jobs and a raft of new business development and improve social cohesion and harmony.

That last point loomed large. The federal government's brand-new Economic Development Agency (EDA) was giving Oakland special attention because of all-too-real fears about crime, social unrest, and racial inequality. The city's Black community—roughly a third of the population—disproportionately bore the burdens of the city's high unemployment and crime rates, and the community was frustrated and angry over long-standing official indifference to their plight. A particular sore point was the overwhelmingly white police department and its inequitable distribution of authoritarian backhanders.[2] Things were bad enough that the tang of incipient violence hung heavily in the air. The Watts race riots—thirty-four dead, tens of millions of dollars in property damage—had rocked Los Angeles only eight months before Foley's press conference. Seething resentments in Oakland looked to be teeing up a sequel. At Oakland's Merritt College, Huey Newton and Bobby Seale were busy founding the Black Panther Party.[3] Black community leaders openly expressed frustration and bitterness in increasingly blunt and scalding terms. Sample quote to a government official: "We hate Whitey because he hates us . . . If we don't get (justice), we'll have a Watts here, and kill and bomb."[4]

Unsurprisingly, addressing the spiral of social resentment, inequity, and dislocation in Oakland rocketed to the top of government's to-do list. It was a publicly acknowledged priority issue for municipal, state, and federal governments, local civic leaders committed to do their bit, and the community itself was demanding in no uncertain terms that action be taken. Resources were not going to be a problem. If it was possible for taxpayer cabbage to smother a social conflagration before it really took off then the EDA was going to make sure the necessary green was there.

If the gist of this fifty-year-old tale sounds disturbingly contemporary, the punch line gets worse. Despite genuine good intentions, herculean efforts to make good on them, and eye-watering expenditures, the EDA's Oakland project became notorious as a ginormous flop. The infrastructure projects— a marine terminal, aircraft hangars, access roads—failed to generate many jobs. Those that did materialize did not particularly benefit the minority community. Firms receiving government-backed loans went bust at an alarming rate. Paperwork, regulation, and a loss of focus as attention inevitably drifted to the next big thing combined to thwart and dishearten those trying to make a difference. The whole sorry tale is famously told in Jeffrey Pressman and Aaron Wildavsky's 1973 book *Implementation*, a classic familiar to generations of public policy students.[5] Their study contains an important lesson for all hubristic proto-policy wonks: effectively addressing complex social problems is incredibly hard. Good intentions, common sense, broad agreement, and bags of cash are not enough. And if policy solutions to difficult social problems can bomb when pretty much the entire system is straining to succeed, imagine what happens when bits and pieces of that system can't even agree on what the problem is, let alone how to address it.

Though a half-century old, Pressman and Wildavsky's lesson remains evergreen. The codas of investigations into big, complex social problems by wonky academics are typically reserved for laying out a case for a particular set of policy solutions. That will not happen here. I'm finishing not with flashy programmatic bangs, but with an explanation of why we should not be surprised when efforts to address the problem of mass incarceration and its social, economic, and political spillover effects end with EDA-style policy whimpers. There is hope here—important wins are possible. Failure, though, very much remains a possibility. Indeed, it may represent the default option.

FIRST, SOME GOOD NEWS

Is there nothing we can do to effectively address mass incarceration and its negative social, economic, and political effects? Quite the opposite. It is important to acknowledge there is considerable reformatory light beaming through the doom and gloom. For one thing, incarceration rates, at least as of this writing, *are* down—way down—from historical highs. There is, of course, lots of state-to-state variation but, generally speaking, incarceration rates reached a zenith between 2000 and 2010. Growth rates then either plateaued or dropped, in some cases dramatically. For example, incarceration rates in New York hit a historical high of 386 per 100,000 in 1999, ticked down for a year or two and then went into a ski slope descent. In 2019, New York's incarceration rate was 223 per 100,000, 42 percent less than its 1999 high. Reductions that large are hardly the norm, but even a state such as Texas—hardly known for its mollycoddling of criminals—clipped its prison population by more than 20 percent across the same time span. In 2020, Texas was closing prisons for lack of inmates.[6]

In part, incarceration rates are simply catching up to crime trends, particularly a sustained drop in the sort of violent crime that would-be officeholders grandstand about come election time. After marching relentlessly upward during the 1970s and 1980s, by the early to mid-1990s violent crime was trending down, a trend that largely continued for the next decade or two. At some point the fact that there are fewer violent criminals available to lock up had to start braking incarceration rates. Shrinking prison populations, though, cannot simply be chalked up to declining crime trends. Over the past couple of decades there has also been a growing movement deliberately pushing state governments to rely less on incarceration and more on rehabilitation, diversion, and alternate forms of punishment such as fines or electronic surveillance through ankle bracelets (sometimes called "e-carceration").

Such efforts are championed by programs like the Justice Reinvestment Initiative (JRI), a public-private initiative between the federal government's Bureau of Justice Assistance and the Pew Charitable Trusts. JRI's basic purpose is to help states use evidence-based strategies to improve their criminal justice systems, an effort that includes figuring out ways to reduce incarceration and recidivism.[7] JRI provides financial support and technical assistance to support a range of reform efforts along these lines, and it has seen some success. For example, eliminating mandatory minimum sentences, creating specialty courts and diversionary programs, conditional early release, and focused help on reentry are all examples of policies that actually seem to meaningfully move the needle on incarceration rates.[8]

At first blush those sorts of policies seem the sort of thing that might be greeted with deep skepticism by law-and-order conservatives. Yet a conservative case for reducing prison populations has steadily gained credibility. This is partly a question of ideology bumping into economics. State-level correctional expenditures quadrupled between 1980 and 2010.[9] Corrections now account for roughly a nickel of every dollar state governments spend, an outlay of more than $45 billion a year—roughly the annual budget of the US

Marine Corps.[10] It's not just expenditures attracting conservative interest. As the ranks of corrections employees grew, their unions became powerful political players. The purpose of state government from their perspective was to educate, medicate, and incarcerate, and not necessarily in that order.[11] Anyone committed to smaller government and reducing pressure on the public treasury—or reining in the power of public unions—has plenty of incentive to take a serious look at prison populations.

Bipartisan consensus on the need to curtail incarceration rates does not point to agreement on the means to achieve that goal but suggests there is plenty of policy bandwidth available for exploration. This is brought into sharp relief by comparing states to other countries, a comparison that immediately suggests the former may be over-reliant on incarceration as a response to criminal offending. In the Netherlands only 10 percent of criminal convictions result in a custodial sentence, and in Germany it's a barely-there 6 percent. The comparable figure in the United States is something like 70 percent. States also stand out for the length of custodial sentences. More than 90 percent of sentences in Germany are for less than two years, in the Netherlands 90 percent of sentences are for less than one year. And many of those are suspended. In contrast, the *average* prison sentence in, say, Georgia or Pennsylvania is three-and-a-half-years.[12] The average non-violent felony sentence in Washington clocks in at nearly two years.[13] Overall, for roughly similar crimes, the United States sends people to prison at twice the rate of Canada and six times the rate of the United Kingdom, and it sends them there for much longer—the average custodial sentence in the United States clocks in at four times the average in England and more than ten times the average in Canada. And those numbers exclude life without parole or death sentences because in other countries they are either extremely rare or entirely non-existent. Even when released, convicted criminals in the United States remain much more likely to have their freedom limited through supervision and monitoring by a criminal justice agency.[14] Compared to other liberal democracies, states appear to massively overuse incarceration, especially for non-violent offenses, and underuse alternatives like community-based sanctions or fines.

Those huge comparative differences suggest that, when it comes to reducing incarceration rates, there is a huge underexploited policy space available to state lawmakers. Yet there remain good reasons to suspect there are hard limits to what can be achieved in that space. Those limits might exist below—perhaps considerably below—historical highs, but they will persist at levels that maintain American exceptionalism. We might manage to stuff bits and pieces back into the jar. The genie's out, though, and plugging it back into a 1980 incarceration-level bottle is something a thousand EDA-like efforts will struggle to achieve. Why? It is what inevitably provides the boundaries for those policy spaces: politics.

IT'S POLITICS. IT'S ALWAYS POLITICS

Remember the big predictors of incarceration, the "tigers" that kept padding out of the statistical jungle regardless of what conditional and methodological fauna I populated it with? Those apex predictors included race and racial diversity, economic inequality, culture, institutional features of democracy, partisan control of government, and violent crime. If those predictors are indeed causal,[15] they suggest no obvious policy solution, no clear directions to a shutoff valve that will prevent the needless sluicing of millions into penitentiaries. Yep, the analyses told us why some states have (comparatively) lower incarceration rates. But, nope, the laboratories of democracy did not distill a policy at the bottom of some test tube that stands a realistic chance of (a) quick adoption and (b) universal effectiveness at lowering prison populations. Think of marijuana decriminalization—a swing at ending the war on drugs—which scuttled away from the predictive tigers like the mouse it proved to be. Exporting the predictive traits of lower incarceration states are either extremely hard (reduce levels of violent crime) or flat-out impossible (importing different demographic profiles and political beliefs). There are some actionable inferences, some policy adjustments or structural changes might help (stop electing judges). But good luck shifting culture or an electorate's partisan and ideological loyalties. And it is this—the primary features of the political environment—that determines the boundaries of legal or programmatic possibility.

Changing what's possible means moving those boundaries and that, well, that's going to be tough. It matters not who likes it, democratic governments will respond to majoritarian preferences, or at least to the preferences of influential constituencies. If the analyses reported in chapter 4 are even vaguely within the realm of reality, those constituencies frequently and consistently respond to higher levels of violent crime, and to perceived social and economic instability, by pushing their governments to make more aggressive use of prisons. In response to social instability (perceived or real) states get "tighter," becoming less tolerant and forgiving of deviance.[16] Those calls get particularly amplified in places where cultural beliefs and prevailing partisan loyalties attach high value on defending the status quo.

I want to be crystal clear about the main point here: this is absolutely not an argument for abandoning serious policy proposals with reasonable chances of making a dent in mass incarceration and its spillover effects. All the hopeful notes sounded in the previous section should continue to be sounded and nothing I've intentionally argued is a reason not to press on with these efforts. Quite the opposite. The point is not to pooh-pooh particular reforms but to put them into sobering context. The reality is that in many states the political nature of the problem means even modest proposals aimed carefully at non-violent offenders will face tough opposition. The going will get much tougher when those efforts make contact with the main, proximal reason that so many people are behind bars—being convicted of committing a violent crime. Evidence for this comes from some of the states successfully reducing prison populations by lifting mandatory minimums, experimenting with diversion, and putting more emphasis on rehabilitation. Many of those same states are also concurrently *increasing* penalties for violent crime. Why? The realities of the political environment demand a trade-off: experimental reforms can advance on the condition legislators can still demonstrate to important constituencies that they remain tough on crime. That trade-off bows to the reality of the political environment's boundaries . . . and rows directly against the reform tide, pushing prison populations up as much as down. As reforms also have a track record of overpromising and underperforming on projected cost savings, they harden skepticism among the same constituencies reluctant to do anything with convicted criminals other than treat them more punitively.[17]

The bottom line is that efforts to reduce prison populations tend to bog down the closer they get to the electoral system. Evidence for that can be found in the mixed record among states that made concentrated efforts to reduce their incarcerated populations in response to recession-associated budget problems in the early part of this century. Some states actually managed to pull this off. Others did not. What marked success from failure? It was whether decision-making authority for things like early parole and custodial sentencing resided in a relatively politically insulated bureaucracy or sat closer to legislative scrutiny and responsibility. The more like the latter, the less likely prison populations were going to be reduced.[18]

The politics of incarceration, in short, follows the iron laws of democracy, and criminals—especially violent criminals—exercise no real political power. Chapter 7 hints at the possibility that could change, that there is some latent electoral muscle lurking among the ranks of ex-prisoners. Those same analyses also suggest that possibility is likely to stay mostly latent. Until that happens those apex predictors—race and racial diversity, economic inequality, culture, partisan control of government, the institutional features of democracy, and violent crime—will continue to set limits on what is, and is not, possible.

The political nature of the problem bridges and connects arguments about what "really" caused the era of mass incarceration. The more you scratch at those arguments, the more you see what they have in common. What I termed the social order and social control arguments turned out not to be the competing explanatory vehicles described by their scrapping pit crews. They are not separate vehicles or even, metaphorically speaking, vehicles at all. If anything, they describe complementary navigators, both sitting in the same backseat giving very similar guidance to the same driver. That driver—the fifty state governments—dutifully follows the social order and/or social control directions issued by its democratic guides. Whether its policy GPS is powered by social order or social control justifications, it has pointed toward the same terminus for at least four decades. In a practical sense, it matters not whether the underlying guidance system orients toward a genuine desire to address crime or to disguise a true north that seeks to suppress groups that menace the guardians of the status quo. Influential constituencies across the ideological spectrum have pushed along both of these paths in different states at different times. Some states zigged while others zagged, but ultimately it mattered little. Journey's end plonked most down in more or less the same place, as polities characterized by levels of incarceration that are rare, or entirely unknown, currently or historically, in other liberal Western democracies.

Try to move from that point using fuel saturated by the abrasive grit of social dislocation—shifting demographics, economic inequality—the constant social misfires surrounding race, deeply rooted partisan loyalties, and cultural values, and the result is political gear grinding. That can take many forms. It can mean proposals that, prima facie, are infeasible and/or seriously misguided (defund the police!) or behavioral demands equally disconnected from social realities (just say no!). Such bumper sticker policy philosophies often burn hot, rallying predictable constituencies to their banner. They also rarely have any practical impact on the complex social problems they putatively address.[19] Like brushfires, they burn through political discourse consuming vast amounts of oxygen, leaving more practical and potentially effective solutions less room to breathe. Some of this sort of thing can feed straight into out-group ugliness, self-confirming attitudes on the racial biases of cops, say, or just flat-out old-fashioned racism. That hardening of suspicions makes it even harder for potentially effective responses to a massive social problem to make it through the democratic sausage-making machine. The gears grind on, pushing out the odd success here and there, but mostly throwing out grist for an inexhaustible number of Pressman and Wildavsky sequels.

Even if all the promising reform efforts get goosed along with generous portions of bipartisan backing and dollops of cash, sooner or later they will run smack into the realities of the political environment. It's not a question of if that wall gets hit, but where. If mass incarceration is a political phenomenon, and reducing prison populations is limited by politics, what is that limit?

How far will the political environment let prison populations fall? Here's a hint: barring some pretty radical changes to the political climate, not nearly as far as some reformers hope.

VIOLENCE

Most state prison inmates—roughly 60 percent—have been convicted of a violent crime.[20] A key implication of that fact is that releasing *everyone* locked up for a non-violent offense would still leave us with one of the highest incarceration rates in the world, and the highest among industrialized Western democracies.[21] If you flip back to figure 1.1 you can get a rough sense of what this would look like by eyeballing the bars in the middle of those boxes. That's approximately what incarceration rates would look like if we locked up only violent offenders.[22] That would get us back to something like the incarceration rates of the late 1980s and early 1990s, a time when academics and journalists were sounding ear-splitting alarms about runaway growth in prison populations.

Taking prison sentences off the table for all non-violent offenders, of course, is never going to happen. It would take a mighty brave politician to argue those who defraud others out of their life savings or expose themselves to minors should not face the risk of doing time. More realistic proposals may indeed substantively chip away at incarceration rates. Decriminalizing drug possession—or even entire classes of drugs—logically implies fewer people locked up. Allowing judges more leeway to take context and individual circumstances into account might help take more off the conveyer belt to prison. Placing better oversight and regulatory constraints on elected prosecutors might do the same. These are all serious policy proposals deserving of serious consideration. Yet if tomorrow we collectively gave jurists free rein to follow their bleeding hearts, released everyone convicted of a non-violent drug crime, and made all prosecutors long-term appointed positions, we'd still have exceptionally high incarceration rates. As currently constructed, the political system in most states is simply too committed to incarceration as the primary state response to violent crime.

Making a big impact on prison populations thus requires confronting the primary reason most people are in state prisons. And that means reducing violent crime and/or engineering a sea change in attitudes on how to best respond to violent crimes. That's a tall order because in most states the political system torques sympathy and policy away from anything that smacks of tolerance toward violent social predation. The optimal solution is, obviously, to reduce violent crime. There's universal agreement here; no one lauds the social benefits of a good mugging or the upsides of settling disagreements with extra-legal bloodshed. The problem is the preferred means to achieve that goal. The deterrence crowd argues tough sentences and the credible probability of serving them is the ticket to persuading rational agents not to commit violent crimes. Others argue violent crime is less a product of individual cost-benefit analyses than the inevitable outcome of stressed social environments. From that side of the fence prison is the part of the systemic problem, not the answer. Feed views from both ends—and all points in between—into state political systems as they exist and the result is pretty much what we have. The gears grind on.

The fundamental question then, boils down to this: what do we do about people who continue to commit violent crimes? That is a fundamentally political question. The decision of who ends up behind bars and why is ultimately made collectively, by state governments responsive to their constituents. That means the answers also have to be political, with all the negotiation, compromise, and trade-offs that implies. Fact is, America is a pretty violent place.[23] We've dealt with that massive social problem largely by concentrating on removing violent criminals from society, depriving them of their liberty, involuntarily confining them to penal institutions, limiting their freedoms on release, and permanently squeezing their social and economic opportunities. Want smaller prison populations? Then figure out an alternative response or a means to prevent violent crime from happening in the first place. Politically speaking, both are hard and complicated social objectives. Recognizing that these are political issues offers no solution. Pretending they are something other than political, though, is to ignore the key problem.

To make this point clear, consider the universal objective we all agree on: we want less violent crime. It's not as if we have no idea how to achieve that objective—social scientists have focused intense attention on the reasons violent crime started falling in the mid-1990s. While the halls of academia continue to ring with arguments over the causal veracity of this or that predictor, there is a rough consensus on what reduces crime: larger police forces, more aggressive law enforcement, and expanding the use of incarceration (discussed in chapter 2). These are all examples of a society getting "tighter," less tolerant and forgiving of deviance. Over the long-term, violent crime also decreases if abortion is legal and if the population is growing older.[24] Considered in the light of reducing mass incarceration these raise huge policy—read political—challenges. Getting tighter might reduce crime, and it will almost certainly be politically popular (among some constituents anyway), but by design it keeps incarceration rates high. Getting tight also has political knock-on effects given its fundamental reliance on the energetic vigilance of law enforcement. For one thing, it delegates the problem of dealing with violent crime to an institution external to the communities suffering from its effects. Members of that community might want lower levels of crime, but if the price is constant surveillance and what is seen as never-ending hassle from agents of an alien bureaucracy, it will breed distrust and resentment. This is hardly news. It's the same recipe for the social tinderbox in 1960s Oakland that so terrified government officials. For another thing, law enforcement agencies do not come cheap, and we're not just talking salaries. Those holding the thin blue line will, perfectly reasonably, not want to be outnumbered or outgunned. Supporters of law enforcement are an influential political constituency so they are likely to get at least some of what they ask for. The overall political dynamics thrown off here are all depressingly familiar. Pressure for more cops, fewer cops, spend more, spend less, be more aggressive and less aggressive. The oppositional battle lines define themselves not just by community or agency but also by ideological worldview and partisan preference. The political boundaries press in.

Political no-retreat battle lines are not just drawn around law enforcement. For example, the evidence that legalized abortion results in less violent crime downstream is fairly strong. John Donohue and Steven Levitt argued more than two decades ago that the legalization of abortion in the early 1970s resulted in a significant drop in the births of children with higher probabilities of growing up to commit violent crime. Needless to say, this generated a lot of controversy. Donohue and Levitt's predictions, though, were prescient, and in a follow-up study they estimated that legalized abortion reduced violent crime by nearly half between 1991 and 2014.[25] Regardless of the strength of evidence, however, I suspect it will do little to shift the politics of abortion, let alone the politics of incarceration.

It might be possible to duck some of the political entanglements accompanying traditional approaches to addressing violent crime by taking alternate routes to a solution. There are actually a whole range of options here, and, again, their effectiveness is backed by empirical evidence. Some of these are as simple as ensuring effective street lighting or making sure the physical environment does not signal abandonment and decay (for example, by tending to abandoned lots).[26] One of the best-known advocates of such alternate approaches is sociologist Patrick Sharkey, who has made one of the most thoughtful and sustained arguments for a new approach to dealing with violent crime. Sharkey's work shows that institutions internal to the communities suffering from high rates of violent crime can, given half a chance, have an outsized impact in improving public safety. A key insight from Sharkey's work is that it's not just aggressive law enforcement that reduces violence; reductions can also be predicted by the presence and growth of nonprofit groups. These can take any number of forms, but those addressing issues like drug addiction, mental health problems, finding people meaningful jobs, or providing services such as after-school programs for at-risk youth have shown themselves to be astonishingly effective at reducing violent crime.

One study by Sharkey and colleagues looked at 264 cities over a two-decade span and found that for every ten additional such organizations operating, the local murder rate declined by nearly 10 percent. This study, it should be noted, was not merely predictive, it was explicitly designed to tease out causality.[27]

Sharkey makes a persuasive case that even greater reductions could be achieved if we were willing to invest in an alternate model of addressing violent crime that gave community-based programs a starring role. Sharkey is not arguing to replace law enforcement, but to scale up these programs by giving them something approaching equal budgetary consideration to law enforcement.[28] And that's where the promise of programs that really do seem to work might start to hit political limits. Imagine a traditionalistic state with high rates of economic inequality, rapidly changing demographics, and a conservative-leaning electorate predisposed to social order and screw-it-down-tight responses to dealing with crime. Do you think that persuading a municipal government, let alone the state legislature, to put those nonprofits on an equal financial footing with police departments might be a struggle? I bet it would be a lot harder than persuading them to financially support law enforcement when violent crime goes up.

It's not even (just) a matter of money. A lesson that still echoes from Pressman and Wildavsky is that policy failures are as likely as successes, so addressing complex social problems requires mustering the political will to deal with failure—likely repeated failures—and keep pressing on. Another lesson is that the difference between success and failure often comes down to who has the authority to make decisions. Success often comes down not to finding people who know what *should* be done, but finding people who know *how* to get things done, then giving them the authority to do exactly that, and then getting the heck out of their way. The guardians of the public treasury, though, have little incentive to champion programs with small, localized decision chains and nontrivial probabilities of failure. One of the few behavioral certainties discovered by political scientists is that legislative behavior is driven primarily by electoral concerns.[29] A central implication is that in a legislature what can be done—and who can claim credit for it—inevitably is farther up the priority list than how things get done on the ground. As any programmatic failure is almost sure to bring blowback, a generous ration of courage is required of legislators to champion these efforts.

The point here is not to pessimistically grump that all efforts to reduce incarceration are doomed to die a death of a thousand political cuts. One more time: there is a lot of evidence that plenty of these efforts work. The point is that if you want to reduce incarceration, you have to address violent crime. And if you want to address violent crime, it's not enough to have a plan, even a plan that seems to work, that most people support, and can be amply resourced. To be successful, that plan has to be planted in the political environment and prove itself hardy enough to thrive there. Given the big determinants of the political environment as it relates to incarceration, that's no small challenge.

RACE

If violent crime defines one major boundary of the political possibilities for addressing incarceration, race defines another. This is partially due to race's perennial role as a fault line running through American society. The tectonic plates grinding underground and destabilizing Oakland in the 1960s continue to send tremors through the political system. The wave of civil disorder following the murder of George Floyd by a Minneapolis police officer in May 2020 stands as a disheartening reminder that, whatever progress has been made in addressing that basic fault line, the racially related social concerns motivating the EDA's Oakland efforts are far from resolved. The countless, ongoing other acts of violence where race seems to have been a factor and even the need for people to proclaim "black lives matter"—you would only feel the need to say this if you felt there was an overwhelming belief that those lives didn't matter—only belabor this point.

More specifically, though, race marks a hard boundary for the politics of incarceration because the costs exacted by a prison sentence are so disproportionately concentrated in a single demographic group: Black males. For many, that staggering demographic imbalance is the sine qua non issue linked to the era of mass incarceration. This is true not just because of racial imbalances in prison populations but also in the costs that a prison record exacts. Black males are more likely to have social and economic opportunities constrained because of a felony conviction, and in some states they are being disenfranchised at rates that are truly mind-boggling. In the last chapter Florida was held up as this phenomenon's exemplar, but it's far from the exception. A fifth of African Americans in Tennessee and Wyoming are disenfranchised. Given the huge gender disparities in criminal convictions, those averages almost certainly underestimate the proportion of Black males being consigned to second-class citizenship.

These huge racial disparities add another big, uncomfortable challenge to anyone trying to hopscotch across a political minefield already strewn with violence-related trip wires. The issues of race and violence are—whether anyone likes it or not—intertwined, and their combination exponentially adds to the explosive power of potential political detonations. There are very different perspectives on underlying causes here; feed those differences into a state's political system and the players often see themselves engaged in an existential, zero-sum contest. Advocates of social control explanations, especially those anchored in beliefs about systemic racism, see the imbalances as bequests of prejudices woven deeply into the warp and woof of society and the institutions that govern it. In an era where arguments for an overdue racial reckoning are ascendant, these arguments pack a powerful moral wallop in the political arena. Inevitably, though, these hit exhibit A of the social order riposte, which is another inarguable fact: the racial disparity in the commission of violent crimes.[30] The social control perspective views this as more symptom than cause, a byproduct of a long history of racial apartheid, of communities long treated with active hostility or, at best indifference, by a range of institutions—banks, schools, law enforcement, and legislatures. Yet there is an alternative explanation that retains considerable political muscle in environments where there are concerns about violent crime, worries about social instability, and deeply embedded values governing expectations on the treatment of rule breakers.

This explanation points not to the system as a whole but toward a specific community culture that fails to provide the values and social expectations that constrain predatory behavior. These arguments date back at least to Daniel Patrick Moynihan, who at roughly the same time the EDA was gearing up to invest in Oakland was preparing a report on Black poverty.[31] What's been known ever since as the Moynihan Report argued that a corrosion of Black family structure—rising births to unwed mothers, increasing single-parent households—and an increasing reliance on welfare over employment was feeding a negative social dynamic. More than anything, it was this that trapped many Black communities in geographically concentrated pockets of poverty and crime.

The Moynihan Report landed right before the Watts riots, triggering a bruising debate that has never fully subsided. The report's references to family dysfunction, social pathology, and a culture of poverty continue to outrage many who hear the unmistakable tones of racist dog whistles.[32] Others argue taking such offense requires willfully misreading the whole point of the analysis, that the core of these problems is less race than class. The report's underlying motivation, its defenders argue, is not to cast blame but to try to figure out some sort of effective set of social provisions capable of elevating struggling communities out of the mire of unemployment, poverty, crime, and social malaise. And effective provisions, the argument goes, requires being clear-eyed about the proximate causes of the problem. Whatever points got scored in the ensuing debate, Moynihan himself never pulled punches or backed down. He later argued any community that, "allows a large number of young men to grow up in broken families, dominated by women, never acquiring any stable relationship to male authority, never acquiring any set of rational expectations about the future—that community asks for and gets chaos." There was nothing coded about his meaning here. What all this led to was, "Crime, violence, unrest, disorder."[33] As a cogent and accurate analysis of what underlies the racial dimensions of crime and incarceration, that argument remains persuasive to many.[34]

Moynihan has been excoriated for victim-blaming racism and lauded for his prescience in roughly equal measure. Liberals continue to lambaste the report's conclusions, just as told-you-so conservatives argue for its timeless explanatory power. I seek to provide neither fear nor favor for either side but simply to point out the political problem inherent in this clash. Versions of these arguments have duked it out for decades, with both cycling through eras of wax and wane. What their sometimes-titanic clashes in the political arena have thrown off in terms of policies effectively reducing incarceration is mostly more of the same. Some successes, some failures. Masses of heat. The occasional lumen or two of light. The gears grind on.[35]

The fraught politics surrounding race and incarceration do, I think, provide yet more reasons to pay attention to the arguments of people like Patrick Sharkey. The community-anchored model of addressing violent crime he outlines will, assuming broad effectiveness, almost certainly have disproportionately positive effects on Black communities. These efforts, as discussed above, probably cannot do a complete end run on the political challenges of dealing with the racial dimension of incarceration, any more than they can end run those associated with the politics of violent crime. Still, their demonstrated effectiveness and decentralized nature may provide enough political cover to meaningfully move the needle.

THE JAILER'S RECKONING

Even with the significant contractions in prison populations over the past decade or two, we are in no real danger of relinquishing our position as the world's greatest jailer. There's no dodging the core underlying issues of violence and race, nor the state-level political context and constraints that place hard floors under any incarceration rate descents. The central message of the first half of this book is that mass incarceration is a fundamentally political problem, and as such, as most political problems are, it is going to be hard to address, let alone resolve.

Perhaps the big takeaway of the second half of the book can in some small way aid that task by helping to force a broader recognition of what's at stake. This is not just whether social order or social control arguments are correct, or what constitutes the "best" apportionment of blame, responsibility, and consequences between the individual, the system, or particular groups within it. The key lesson from the last three chapters is that mass incarceration exacts a significant social and economic toll not just on politically marginalized groups like criminals, the poor, and racial minorities. Those groups either have no real political power at all (criminals) or struggle to assert their interests when competing with more influential constituencies (the poor and racial minorities).

The jailer's reckoning, though, is not paid by these groups alone. The stakes—for all of us—are huge: corrosion of social capital, economic growth retarded by an underground labor market regulator. If the analyses those inferences rest on are even roughly accurate, the implications are staggering. Mass incarceration is feeding social dislocation and disassociation on a huge scale, and it's costing individual states billions in lost economic output. It is hard to imagine a hostile polity devising and successfully pursuing a more effective means for stealthily fracturing the social foundations of the republic. Maybe one way to give reform arguments better odds of advancing in the political arena is to launch them from this position. In other words, to frame the argument as an effort to save ourselves not from "them" but from, well, ourselves.

That sounds a tad hyperbolic, but these are not trifling social forces. Social scientists have long recognized that a healthy and functional society needs a set of broadly agreed-on norms and values to bind it together, an agreed-upon story about who we are and what we stand for. Mass incarceration has been quietly removing pages from that story for a very long time. Sociologists have a term for what happens to communities lacking collectively agreed-upon and enforced values and behavioral expectations: anomie. The term is attributed to Emile Durkheim, and it literally means "normlessness," the lack of shared social values and the absence of institutions to administer and defend them.[36] Anomic societies do not lack individual freedom, they lack shared values, a broadly held sense of who "we" are and what we're all about. Durkheim tells us that individuals in such societies have a hard time finding connection and meaning and that social life becomes characterized by a sense of drift and anxiety. The absence of these communally enforced constraints produces increases in antisocial behavior, notably crime.[37] This thumbnail of an anomic society sounds a lot like the social capital outcomes being predicted back in chapter 5. Mass incarceration is a social cohesion solvent. It atrophies the communal sinews that bind us all together. Not just because of the numbers behind bars, but because of the ever-larger numbers being socially and economically hobbled by their experience with the criminal justice system. This constitutes a threat that should resonate even in places where changes to the status quo are typically resisted—traditionalistic states, for example. Put this way, figuring out a way to reduce mass incarceration is an objective less anchored in the underlying philosophies of social order or social control and more of an appeal to social salvation.

If appeals to the commonweal are insufficient, overtures can also be made to economic self-interest. The potential for prison labor to profit public and private employers, and to provide a steady supply of cheap labor to a ravenous economy is, as chapter 6 detailed, an argument with deep historical roots. Its empirical foundations, though, are shaky, or at least they are if the analyses reported in that chapter are reasonably on target. At a minimum, anything that shaves billions off of a state's GSP hits everybody in the economic food chain, not just those trying to piece things together at its lower reaches. That means less is available to invest in communal and (small-d) democratic infrastructure—institutions like schools, law enforcement, and welfare, investments that might help push back anomic pressures.

If these appeals are to successfully gain any traction in the political arena, they need to keep front and center the key social consequence of mass incarceration. The big plot line of this forty-year-old morality tale is not simply how many people we shoveled through the front door of penitentiaries, but how many came gushing out the back. The latter get decanted back into society with more limited social and economic opportunities. As those numbers grow, a prison record—having one, knowing someone who has one—becomes normalized, and the consequences push closer to the mainstream. Arguably, those consequences have already paddled their way into the middle of the social current. In the United States a criminal record is a social and economic disadvantage that directly or indirectly touches a mind-bogglingly large proportion of adult citizens. As those numbers have grown, an anomic society inches closer and economic advances move further away. At some point—if indirect experience is included, a point we likely have already passed—there is going to be no "them" who bear the consequences of the jailer, it will simply be "us." The distinction between the jailer and the inmate has been blurring for decades, and it's getting more and more difficult to distinguish the boundary between who is in the cell and who is guarding it.

Take a random sample of adult males in 1980 and roughly two in a hundred could report some experience with incarceration, or at least detention. Take the same sample in 2010 and the number is one in twenty. For Black males it's one in six.[38] Expand this pool to include everyone with a felony conviction, and the total numbers are by now well north of twenty million.[39] If these folks were concentrated into a single geographic area, by population they would constitute the third largest state in America, below California and Texas and slightly above Florida.[40] The political power bequeathed to those states through their large populations is undisputed; indeed, it's a central fulcrum of the federal system. Felons, of course, do not have their own commonwealth, they are unevenly dispersed across state populations with varying degrees of access and interest to even the most basic rights of democratic citizenship.

Numbers on that order, though, matter, even in a place as large and as complex as the United States. If we take a conservative back-of-the-envelope guesstimate that for every person convicted, five others—partners, parents, siblings, children, employers, friends—are also affected, we're looking at a deeply embedded social phenomenon. Given those numbers and the spillover effects—social, economic, and political—that impact all of us, the stakes surely justify efforts to address mass incarceration even if we fail as much as we succeed.

CONCLUSION: IF ALL ELSE FAILS, TRY THE TUNA FISH SANDWICH TEST

Why did we become the world's most voracious jailer? The first four chapters of this book constitute an extended tour of the scholarly and journalistic investigations into that question. That culminated in an in-depth statistical examination of what are widely argued to be the key predictors of incarceration rates. The latter pitched up a reasonably clear answer: incarceration rates began seriously accelerating roughly a half-century ago as response to rising levels of violent crime. What was mostly a defensible social order reaction to a very real social problem drove smack into an era of accelerating social dislocations. These included increasing racial diversity, growing political polarization, and increasing economic inequity. Combined, this provided plenty of incentive for political actors to smuggle—and sometimes brazenly advocate—social control justifications for stuffing ever greater numbers into prisons. I freely admit that other scholars using different data and different methods might find points to disagree with, both in my findings on the causes of mass incarceration and its implications. As I made no small effort to underline back in chapter 4: my statistical models are wrong. But then again, so are everyone else's. My claim here is not to be right, but not to be importantly wrong.

If we can, at least for the purposes of argument, accept that I am not importantly wrong about what caused mass incarceration, then the big, open, and unanswered question is what are the consequences of that social phenomenon? What has being the planet's largest jailer done to us? That may be the more interesting and less fully explored question this book has tried to grapple with. What I found on the positive side of the ledger was a defensible argument that more aggressive use of incarceration did, perhaps, achieve one of its central social order objectives: it helped reduced crime, at least a little bit, and at least for a little while. Though even if we accept the argument that the social benefits from the aggressive use of incarceration are real, you still have to employ some pretty creative bookkeeping to get that measure to zero out a very long list of costs and liabilities. If the picture painted in the last half of the book is even halfway in touch with reality, the unintended consequences of locking up ever greater numbers of people are worrying and widespread. At a minimum, the era of mass incarceration has contributed to hollowing out communities, kneecapped economic opportunity for millions, and deprived millions more of the most basic right of democratic citizenship. If the inferences suggested by my analyses are within hailing distance of reality, it's also a good bet that mass incarceration has eroded social cohesion at the state level, served as a significant brake on state economies, discouraged even many who are eligible from politically participating, and perhaps even created an anonymous kingmaker for the most powerful office on the planet. Politics shaped mass incarceration, and mass incarceration may now be returning the favor. Regardless, the key point is that if you total up benefits and balance them against costs, what you find is that the jailer's reckoning is, by any accounting method, extraordinarily high.

Having answers in hand to the questions that motivated this book is, to say the least, a mixed blessing. These throw light onto the complicated nature of the problem and its broader social, economic, and political implications. The huge, negative effects of the latter are getting worse. Can states steer themselves beyond the era of mass incarceration and mitigate the jailer's reckoning? The short answer is probably yes. There are lots of people and organizations formulating and implementing ideas that, at least in theory, can shorten the circumference of the jailer's reach. These often have a hard time gaining purchase, though, because they have no choice but to navigate the fundamental *political* nature of the problem. The politics surrounding violence and race provide ample evidence of just how hard that can be. There's no easy solution, but framing these efforts in terms of the stakes—for everyone—might marginally increase their chances of success. Knowing the jailer's reckoning may not point toward clear and obvious solutions. What it can do is clarify the challenges any such response must overcome if it is to have any hope of success.

The condensed and intuitive version of this is what might be termed the tuna fish sandwich test. Think back to what happened to Larry Dayries, who was effectively sentenced to a life term following an act of nickel-and-dime larceny. Are we really all better off if he disappears behind bars for good? Is the million dollars well spent because it assures society it is never again troubled by his petty crimes? If so, what about the millions of Dayries who do get out only to face limited social, economic, and political options, perhaps while dealing with unaddressed mental health challenges and substance addictions? This is not a cheap appeal to empathy, but to hard-nosed self-interest—the sheer numbers we're talking about mean social, economic, and political costs for everyone, including *you*. If the tuna fish sandwich just ain't worth it, maybe we should think of something else—perhaps by granting more political oomph to arguments by the likes of Patrick Sharkey, Peter Enns, John Pfaff, Marie Gottschalk, and the myriad others whose work is foundational to this entire book.[41] If we—the collective we—do not want to do that, then the politics of incarceration will grind on, and the jailer's reckoning calculated over the last half of this book is just going to come due in ever larger amounts. And the jailer's reckoning comes for us all.

Notes

PREFACE

1. Enns, P. K. 2016. *Incarceration Nation*. Cambridge, UK: Cambridge University Press.

2. These estimates are based on Shannon et al. As those estimates are dated—they only go through 2010—I'm rounding up rather than down. See:

Shannon, S. K., C. Uggen, J. Schnittker, M. Thompson, S. Wakefield, and M. Massoglia. 2017. The Growth, Scope, and Spatial Distribution of People with Felony Records in the United States, 1948–2010. *Demography*, *54*(5), 1795–1818.

3. The study in question is cited below. Last time I checked Google Scholar, it had 265 citations and was still racking up ten or a dozen cites a year. Not exactly Steven Pinker territory, but not bad by average social science standards.

Smith, K. B. 2004. The Politics of Punishment: Evaluating Political Explanations of Incarceration Rates. *Journal of Politics*, *66*(3), 925–38.

CHAPTER 1

1. The details of Larry Dayries crime, arrest, and sentencing are drawn from multiple sources. See, especially: Hannaford, Alex. "No Exit." *Texas Observer*, October 3, 2016, https://www.texasobserver.org/three-strikes-law-no-exit/, and Larry Dayries, Appellant v. The State of Texas, Appellee, NO. 03-10-100704-CR (August 30, 2011), https://law.justia.com/cases/texas/third-court-of-appeals/2011/20503.html. At the time of writing, the Texas Department of Criminal Justice projected his release date as February 6, 2080, and his earliest parole eligibility date as February 7, 2040, https://offender.tdcj.texas.gov/OffenderSearch/start.action.

2. Bureau of Justice Statistics. 2020. "Correctional Populations in the United States, 2017–2018." US Department of Justice, https://www.bjs.gov/content/pub/pdf/cpus1718.pdf. The 200,000 number quoted in the text refers to adults in prison or local jails, which in Texas in 2018 was reported as 218,000. The total number being supervised by the Texas system, that is, including people on probation or parole, is much higher—672,400 in 2018.

3. The Vera Institute. "The Price of Prisons: Prison Spending in 2015," https://www.vera.org/publications/price-of-prisons-2015-state-spending-trends/price-of-prisons-2015-state-spending-trends/price-of-prisons-2015-state-spending-trends-prison-spending.

4. Hannaford, "No Exit."

5. NIDA. June 1, 2020. Criminal Justice Drug Facts, https://www.drugabuse.gov/publications/drugfacts/criminal-justice.

6. Steadman, H. J., F. C. Osher, P. C. Robbins et al. 2009. Prevalence of Serious Mental Illness among Jail Inmates. *Psychiatric Services, 60*, 761–65.

7. Texas Department of Criminal Justice FY 2017 Statistical Report, https://www.tdcj.texas.gov/documents/Statistical_Report_FY2017.pdf, page 1.

8. Bonczar, Thomas, and Allen Beck. 1997. "Lifetime Likelihood of Going to State or Federal Prison." *Bureau of Justice Statistics Special Report*, NCJ-160092.

9. Shannon, S. K., C. Uggen, J. Schnittker, M. Thompson, S. Wakefield, and M. Massoglia. 2017. The Growth, Scope, and Spatial Distribution of People with Felony Records in the United States, 1948–2010. *Demography, 54*(5), 1795–1818.

10. World Prison Brief, Institute for Crime and Justice Policy Research. 2020. "Highest to Lowest—Prison Population Rate," https://www.prisonstudies.org/highest-to-lowest/prison_population_rate?field_region_taxonomy_tid=All.

11. Bureau of Justice Statistics, Key Statistics. "Estimated Number of Inmates Held in Local Jails or Under the Jurisdiction of State or Federal Prisons and Incarceration Rate, 1980–2016," https://www.bjs.gov/index.cfm?ty=kfdetail&iid=493.

12. Carson, E. Ann. 2020. "Prisoners in 2019." Bureau of Justice Statistics, October 22, 2020, https://www.bjs.gov/index.cfm?ty=pbdetail&iid=7106.

13. Carson, "Prisoners in 2019."

14. Sawyer, Wendy, and Peter Wagner. "Mass Incarceration: The Whole Pie 2020." Prison Policy Initiative, https://www.prisonpolicy.org/reports/pie2020.html.

Technically Washington, D.C. may count as a small fourth bucket. It runs what are the equivalent of local jails, but its prison population has effectively been integrated into the Federal Bureau of Prisons since 2001.

15. Throughout the book I've tried to cite specific sources for data and draw heavily from official sources such as the federal government's Bureau of Justice Statistics. In terms of state incarceration rates, I specifically focus on inmates serving sentences of more than twelve months who are under the jurisdiction of state governments. See methodological appendix on the book's website for details: rowman.com/ISBN/9781538192382.

16. Carson, E. Ann, and Joseph Mulako-Wangota. Bureau of Justice Statistics. "Imprisonment Rates of Total Jurisdiction." Generated using the Corrections Statistical Analysis Tool (CSAT). Data was generated for 1978 to 2018, using total population under jurisdiction of state institutions at year-end.

17. Schneider, A. L. 2012. Punishment Policy in the American States from 1890 to 2008: Convergence, Divergence, Synchronous Change, and Feed-Forward Effects. *Policy Studies Journal, 40*(2), 193–210.

18. Crime and incarceration are most definitely related—after all, to be incarcerated you first have to be convicted of a crime. The issue has more to do with whether

the massive increase in state-level incarceration was driven by some equally massive crime wave that occurred between the late 1970s and mid-1990s. Scholars have generally argued that the answer to that seems to be no. While the research literature is not definitive, a general takeaway is that crime—especially violent crime—is predictive of incarceration levels, changes in crime during that period can at best account for only a small portion—perhaps as little as 12 percent—of the huge growth in state prison populations from 1980 to the mid-1990s. A good review of the relevant literature can be found in Pfaff, J. F. 2007. "The Empirics of Prison Growth: A Critical Review and Path Forward." *J. Crim. L. & Criminology*, *98*, 547.

19. According to Wikipedia, 166 of the 193 member states of the United Nations have unitary systems of government: https://en.wikipedia.org/wiki/Unitary_state.

20. In comparison Brazil has 26 states, India 29, Mexico 32, and Canada 10.

21. For a book-length treatment of these issues, see: Tarr, Alan. 1998. *Understanding State Constitutions*. Princeton, NJ: Princeton University Press.

22. In all its full civics class glory, the Tenth Amendment states that, "The powers not delegated to the United States by the Constitution, nor prohibited by it to the States, are reserved to the States respectively, or to the people."

23. For examples see:

Hawkins, Darrell, and Kenneth Hardy. 1989. "Black-White Imprisonment Rates: A State-by-State Analysis." *Social Justice*, *16*(4) (38), 75–94.

Enns, Peter K. 2014. "The Public's Increasing Punitiveness and Its Influence on Mass Incarceration in the United States." *American Journal of Political Science*, *58*(4), 857–72.

Beckett, Katherine, and Bruce Western. 2001. "Governing Social Marginality: Welfare, Incarceration, and the Transformation of State Policy." *Punishment & Society*, *3*, 43–59.

24. Elazar, Daniel. 1966. *American Federalism: A View from the States*. New York: Cromwell.

25. A more recent but very similar sort of argument to Elazar's can be found in David Hacker's work. See, Hacker, David. 1989. *Albion's Seed*. New York: Oxford University Press. The political scientist who has done the most to advance and update the Elazar/Sharkansky culture argument is Joel Lieske, who has drilled down to the county level to examine regional subcultures anchored in race, ethnicity, and religious affiliation. Lieske's updated measures of political culture, at least in some areas, outperform Elazar's (see Lieske, Joel. 2012. "American State Cultures: Testing a New Measure and Theory." *Publius: The Journal of Federalism*, *42*, 108–33). Others seem to have stumbled on the same basic concept of state culture without realizing its deep academic roots. An article, in of all places, the *Proceedings of the National Academy of Sciences*, presents a measure of "tight" state cultures characterized by strongly enforced rules and norms and "loose" cultures with higher levels of tolerance. Their quantitative measure is impressive for the sheer number of inputs it is built from, but statistically speaking it turns out to be something very close to Sharkansky's fifty-year-old measure (Harrington, Jesse, and Michele Gelfand. 2014. "Tightness-Looseness across the 50 United States." *Proceeding of the National*

Academy of Sciences, *111*(22), 7990–95). Neither Elazar, Sharkansky, nor Lieske are cited in this study.

26. Sharkansky, Ira. 1969. The Utility of Elazar's Political Culture: A Research Note. *Polity*, *2*(1), 66–83.

27. See Lieske, "American State Cultures: Testing a New Measure and Theory."

28. The bivariate correlation between incarceration rates and state culture in 2010 is .67, in other words, the R2 or explained variance = .67 X .67 ~45%.

29. For example, Greenberg and West undertook a widely cited review of the range of explanations of growth in state prison populations and explicitly considered culture as an important explanatory variable. Yet their cultural focus is mostly about the South being different (a reasonable enough argument). Elazar and Sharkansky are not cited at all in their review. See: Greenberg, D. F., and V. West. 2001. State Prison Populations and Their Growth, 1971–1991. *Criminology*, *39*(3), 615–54. Similarly, the National Research Council's 2014 doorstopper of a review on the causes of incarceration growth never really addresses the concept of state culture, let alone cites Elazar or Sharkansky. See: Travis, J., B. Western, and F. S. Redburn (eds.). 2014. *The Growth of Incarceration in the United States: Exploring Causes and Consequences*. Washington, DC: National Academies Press.

CHAPTER 2

1. Tocqueville, Alexis de. 2000. *Democracy in America*. Chicago: University of Chicago Press.

2. Dickens, Charles. 1850. *American Notes for General Circulation*. London: Chapman and Hall.

3. Though well known in his day, de Beaumont is largely (and unjustifiably) forgotten today. Though his work on prisons brought a measure of international recognition, his intellectual light was simply eclipsed by the philosophical and literary achievements of de Tocqueville. I could not locate a biography of de Beaumont—at least according to his Wikipedia page he and de Tocqueville had at least a couple of major falling outs over political matters. There is an illuminating book of de Tocqueville and de Beaumont's correspondence in an English translation: Zunz, Oliver (ed.). 2011. *Alexis de Tocqueville and Gustave de Beaumont in America: Their Friendship and Their Travels*. Charlottesville: University of Virginia Press. Translation is by Arthur Goldhammer.

4. The Charles Dickens Page. "Charles Dickens in America," https://www .charlesdickenspage.com/charles-dickens-in-america.html.

5. Grass, Sean C. 2000. "Narrating the Cell: Dickens on the American Prisons." *The Journal of English and Germanic Philology*, *99*, 50–70.

6. Making a point to visit prisons while on a grand tour of America is not quite as strange as it sounds. During the nineteenth century there was something of a fad for institutional tourism centered on visiting prisons and asylums in Canada and America. Dickens was just one of thousands who were ducking in and out of these places to

have a look around. See: Miron, Janet. 2011. *Prisons, Asylums and the Public: Institutional Visiting in the Nineteenth Century*. Toronto: University of Toronto Press.

7. Earle, Alice Morse. 1896. *Curious Punishments of Bygone Days*. Chicago: H. S. Stone & Co.

De Beaumont and de Tocqueville specifically mention branding and mutilation as punishments on offer in various states and note that in Massachusetts burglary could be a capital crime. See De Beaumont, Gustave, and Alexis de Tocqueville. 1833. *On the Penitentiary System in the United States and Its Application in France*. Philadelphia: Carey, Lea and Blanchard. Translation by Francis Lieber. Page 16.

8. Meskell, Matthew. 1999. "An American Revolution: The History of Prisons in the United States from 1777 to 1877." *Stanford Law Review*, *51*, 839–66.

9. Meskell, "An American Revolution."

10. Meskell, "An American Revolution."

11. Meskell, "An American Revolution."

12. On the upside, inmates in the Pennsylvania System at Cherry Hill had running water and even flush toilets—luxuries that even the White House lacked. See: "General Historic Overview: Eastern State Penitentiary," https://www.easternstatc.org/sites/easternstate/files/inline-files/ESPHistoryOverviewrev5.2019v2.pdf.

13. De Beaumont and de Tocqueville, *On the Penitentiary System in the United States and Its Application in France*, 11.

14. De Beaumont and de Tocqueville, *On the Penitentiary System in the United States and Its Application in France*, 13.

15. De Beaumont and de Tocqueville, *On the Penitentiary System in the United States and Its Application in France*, 15.

16. Lewis, Orlando Faukland. 1922. *The Development of American Prisons and Prison Customs, 1776–1845*. Albany, NY: J. B. Lyon Company.

17. De Beaumont and de Tocqueville, *On the Penitentiary System in the United States and Its Application in France*, 24.

18. Lewis, *Development of American Prisons and Prison Customs*, 50.

19. Lewis, *Development of American Prisons and Prison Customs*, 55.

20. See Blumstein, Alfred. 1998. "U.S. Criminal Justice Conundrum: Rising Prison Populations and Stable Crime Rates." *Crime & Delinquency*, *44*, 127–35.

21. Wozniak, Kevin H. 2014. "American Public Opinion about Prisons." *Criminal Justice Review*, *39*(3), 305–24.

Cullen, Francis, and Bonnie Fisher. 2000. "Public Opinion about Punishment and Corrections." *Crime and Justices*, *27*, 1–79.

22. O'Hear, Michale M. 2016. "Public Attitudes toward Punishment, Rehabilitation, and Reform: Lessons from the Marquette Law School Poll." Faculty Publications. Paper 678, http://scholarship.law.marquette.edu/facpub/678.

23. Princeton Survey Research Associates International for National Center for State Courts. 2007. The NCSC Sentencing Attitudes Survey: A Report on the Findings. *Indiana Law Journal*, *82*(I), 1319.

24. These estimates are based on straightforward OLS regression analysis where incarceration rate is the dependent variable and crime rate is the independent variable. Here is the full table of results:

	1980	1990	2000	2010
Violent Crime Rate	0.133***	0.241***	0.421***	0.459***
	-0.029	-0.037	-0.099	-0.135
Constant	59.390***	117.558***	199.526***	237.108***
	-14.844	-22.286	-45.81	-52.843
Observations	50	50	50	50
R^2	0.302	0.47	0.273	0.195
Adjusted R^2	0.287	0.459	0.257	0.178
Residual Std. Error (df = 48)	47.052	73.404	131.316	134.489
F Statistic (df = 1; 48)	20.757***	42.511***	17.989***	11.633***

Note: *p**p***p<0.01

25. Travis, Jeremy, Bruce Western, and Steven Redburn (eds.). 2014. *The Growth of Incarceration in the United States: Exploring Causes and Consequences.* Washington, DC: National Academies Press, 104–56.

26. This is a large and evolving academic literature and while I've tried to give an honest, succinct takeaway, there's no getting around the fact that there's a lot of room for disagreement. Here are some examples of the studies I've drawn from to make these claims (these include several review pieces):

Stemen, D. 2006. Reconsidering Incarceration: New Directions for Reducing Crime. *Fed. Sent. R.*, *19*, 221.

Liedka, R. V., A. M. Piehl, and B. Useem. 2006. The Crime-Control Effect of Incarceration: Does Scale Matter? *Criminology & Public Policy*, *5*(2), 245–76.

Chalfin, Aaron, and Justin McCrary. 2017. "Criminal Deterrence: A Review of the Literature." *Journal of Economic Literature*, *55*(1), 5–48.

Durlauf, S. N., and D. S. Nagin. 2010. "The Deterrent Effect of Imprisonment." In *Controlling Crime: Strategies and Tradeoffs*. Chicago: University of Chicago Press, 43–94.

27. Fazel, S., and A. Wolf. 2015. A Systematic Review of Criminal Recidivism Rates Worldwide: Current Difficulties and Recommendations for Best Practice. *PloS one*, *10*(6), e0130390.

28. Alper, M., M. R. Durose, and J. Markman. 2018. *2018 Update on Prisoner Recidivism: A 9-Year Follow-up Period (2005–2014).* Washington, DC: US Department of Justice, Office of Justice Programs, Bureau of Justice Statistics.

29. World Population Review. 2020. "Recidivism Rates by State 2020," https://worldpopulationreview.com/state-rankings/recidivism-rates-by-state. Their numbers were sourced from a report compiled by the Virginia Department of Corrections: Virginia Department of Corrections. 2018. "State Recidivism Comparison," https://vadoc.virginia.gov/media/1363/vadoc-state-recidivism-comparison-report-2018-12.pdf.

30. Though far from the only one. Correctional education programs, for example, seem to do a pretty good job of helping lower the probability of reoffending, and

the effect seems to be positive whether it is secondary (e.g., focused on completing high school or getting a GED), postsecondary (college courses), or vocational. A 2013 meta-study by the RAND Corporation estimated these sorts of programs could help lower recidivism rates by 30 to 40 percent, or even higher, compared to inmates who were not enrolled in these programs. Political support for such programs, though, almost predictably seems to be fairly shallow. See David, Lois, Robert Bozick, Jennifer Steele, Jessica Saunders, and Jeremy Miles. *Evaluating the Effectiveness of Correctional Education*. RAND Corporation.

31. Steffensmeier, D. J., and M. D. Harer. 1987. Is the Crime Rate Really Falling? An "Aging" US Population and Its Impact on the Nation's Crime Rate, 1980–1984. *Journal of Research in Crime and Delinquency*, *24*(1), 23–48.

CHAPTER 3

1. Foucault, M. 2012. *Discipline and Punish: The Birth of the Prison*. New York: Vintage.

2. My own humble opinion is that *Discipline and Punish* is actually a fairly clear read if it's compared to the larger canon of postmodernist writing. That still makes it pretty heavy going. Speaking as someone who has at various times in their career been forced to engage with the output of various of postmodern/poststructural/post insert-big-whoop-sounding-adjective-here authors, my advice for interested general readers on how to approach this sort of material is pretty simple: Don't. I mostly wish I hadn't.

3. Alford, C. F. 2000. What Would It Matter If Everything Foucault Said about Prison Were Wrong? "Discipline and Punish" after Twenty Years. *Theory and Society*, *29*(1), 125–46.

4. This argument is backed by empirical evidence. For example, Duxbury links a huge number of changes in state sentencing policies to public opinion between 1975 and 2012. His key conclusion is that these changes in sentencing policy, which almost certainly led to higher incarceration levels, were linked to specifically white public opinion, which in turn was responsive to the size of minority populations. See: Scott W. Duxbury. 2021. "Who Controls Criminal Law? Racial Threat and the Adoption of State Sentencing Law, 1975–2012." *American Sociological Review* *86*(1), 123–53.

5. Smith, Kevin. 2004. "The Politics of Punishment: Evaluating Political Explanations of Incarceration Rates." *The Journal of Politics*, *66*(3), 925–38.

6. Key, V. O. 1949. *Southern Politics in State and Nation*. Knoxville: University of Tennessee Press.

7. Blalock, H. M. 1967. Toward a Theory of Minority-Group Relations. New York: Wiley.

8. I examined the proportion of a state population that is Black and male with state incarceration rates for each year between 1996 and 2010 and the results were a steady correlation of ~.65. This did drop to ~.60 in the later years, but even if we except that as the more realistic contemporary number, it means race alone accounts for roughly

a third of the variation in incarceration rates. For comparison, total crime rates during the same time period correlated with incarceration rates at ~.50, meaning they account for about a quarter of incarceration rates.

9. For example, see: Hawkins, Darrell, and Kenneth Hardy. 1989. "Black-White Imprisonment Rates: A State-by-State Analysis." *Social Justice*, *16*(4) (38), 75–94.

Beckett, Katherine, and Bruce Western. 2001. "Governing Social Marginality: Welfare, Incarceration, and the Transformation of State Policy." *Punishment & Society*, *3*, 43–59.

Yates, Jeff. 1997. Racial Incarceration Disparity among States. *Social Science Quarterly*, *78*, 1001–10.

Phelps, Michelle S., and Devah Pager. 2016. Inequality and Punishment: A Turning Point for Mass Incarceration? *The ANNALS of the American Academy of Political and Social Science*, *663*(1), 185–203.

10. Yates, Jeff, and Richard Fording. 2005. "Politics and State Punitiveness in Black and White." *The Journal of Politics*, *64*, 1099–1121.

11. Alexander, M. 2020. *The New Jim Crow: Mass Incarceration in the Age of Colorblindness*. New York: The New Press.

12. Alexander, *The New Jim Crow*, 2.

13. For example, see: Peffley, M., and J. Hurwitz. 2002. The Racial Components of "Race-Neutral" Crime Policy Attitudes. *Political Psychology*, *23*(1), 59–75.

Peffley, Mark, Jon Hurwitz, and Jeffery Mondak. 2017. "Racial Attributions in the Justice System and Support for Punitive Crime Policies." *American Politics Research*, *45*(6), 1032–58.

Smith, K. B. 2004. The Politics of Punishment: Evaluating Political Explanations of Incarceration Rates. *The Journal of Politics*, *66*(3), 925–38.

14. For example, see: Fellner, J. 2009. *Decades of Disparity: Drug Arrests and Race in the United States*. Human Rights Watch.

Mitchell, O. 2005. A Meta-Analysis of Race and Sentencing Research: Explaining the Inconsistencies. *Journal of Quantitative Criminology*, *21*(4), 439–66.

15. Shannon, Sarah, Christopher Uggen, Jason Schnittker, Melissa Thompson, Sara Wakefield, and Michael Massoglia. 2017. The Growth, Scope, and Spatial Distribution of People with Felony Records in the United States, 1948–2010. *Demography*, *54*, 1795–1818.

16. Schoenfeld, Heather. 2018. *Building the Prison State: Race and the Politics of Mass Incarceration*. Chicago: University of Chicago Press.

17. In March 2021, the exact figure was 46.4 percent of people serving time in federal prisons were there because of drug offenses. Federal Bureau of Prisons. "Inmate Statistics: Offenses," https://www.bop.gov/about/statistics/statistics_inmate_offenses .jsp.

18. These figures come from analyses conducted by John Pfaff:

Pfaff, J. F. 2014. Escaping from the Standard Story: Why the Conventional Wisdom on Prison Growth Is Wrong, and Where We Can Go from Here. *Federal Sentencing Reporter*, *26*(4), 265–70.

Pfaff, J. F. 2015. The War on Drugs and Prison Growth: Limited Importance, Limited Legislative Options. *Harv. J. on Legis.*, *52*, 173.

19. Murakawa, N. 2011. Toothless: The Methamphetamine "Epidemic," "Meth Mouth," and the Racial Construction of Drug Scares. *Du Bois Review: Social Science Research on Race*, *8*(1), 219–28.

20. Mauer, M. 2009. *The Changing Racial Dynamics of the War on Drugs*. Washington, DC: Sentencing Project.

21. In 2018, of the roughly 1.2 million sentenced prisoners under state jurisdiction, roughly 394,000 were white, 410,000 were Black, and 274,000 were Hispanic. See: Carson, E. Ann. "Prisoners in 2019." Bureau of Justice Statistics, https://www.bjs.gov/index.cfm?ty=pbdetail&iid=7106.

22. Forman J. Jr. 2017. *Locking Up Our Own: Crime and Punishment in Black America*. New York: Farrar, Straus and Giroux. The basic argument that Black voters and their elected officials became more punitive and thus helped drive up incarceration rates is also backed by academic studies, for example, Clegg, John, and Adaner Usmani. 2017. "The Racial Politics of Mass Incarceration." *SSRN Electronic Journal*, 1–40.

23. Spohn, Cassia. 2000. U.S. National Institute of Justice, ed, Criminal Justice 2000, v. 3. Washington, DC: National Institute of Justice, 427–501, esp. p. 481.

24. King, Ryan, and Michael Light. 2019. "Have Racial and Ethnic Disparities in Sentencing Declined?" *Crime and Justice*, *48*(1), 365–437.

25. Carson, "Prisoners in 2019"; Pfaff, Escaping from the Standard Story.

26. For a description of the two data sources and their similarities and differences, see: "The Nation's Two Crime Measures." 2004. Department of Justice, https://bjs.ojp.gov/content/pub/pdf/ntcm.pdf.

As discussed in the text, and like many others who have spent time surfing through this data, my reading is that both sources clearly support the general argument of racial disparities in criminal offending described in the text, even though they do not always agree on specifics. Whatever the flaws of these two data sources—and they are not trivial—they seem to triangulate and arrive at the same conclusions about differences about arrests and offenses committed by race and ethnicity.

27. Beck, Allen. 2021. "Race and Ethnicity of Violent Crime Offenders and Arrestees, 2018." Bureau of Justice Statistics, https://www.bjs.gov/index.cfm?ty=pbdetail&iid=7226.

28. For example, see: Sampson, R. J., and J. L. Lauritsen. 1997. Racial and Ethnic Disparities in Crime and Criminal Justice in the United States. *Crime and Justice*, *21*, 311–74. Correlations between violent crime and percent Black male ranged from ~.40 to ~.60 for the fifty states between 1980 and 2014. The correlation represented in figure 3.2 is fairly representative of this range, r=.46.

29. This might undersell the war on drugs argument somewhat. Violence is much more likely to be used as an enforcement or regulatory mechanism in markets for illegal substances like drugs, thus it is a good bet that some of those listed as being in prison for violent offenses were committing that violence as part of the drug trade.

30. Morgan, Rachel, and Jennifer Truman. 2020. "Criminal Victimization, 2019." Bureau of Justice Statistics, https://www.bjs.gov/index.cfm?ty=pbdetail&iid=7046. See esp. table 16.

31. The differences in crime across racially divided communities is truly eye-opening. See: Peterson, R. D., and L. J. Krivo. 2010. *Divergent Social Worlds: Neighborhood Crime and the Racial-Spatial Divide.* New York: Russell Sage Foundation.

32. In 2017 the Centers for Disease Control estimated that homicide was the fourth overall leading cause for Black males but the number one cause of death for Black males under the age of forty-four. See: Centers for Disease Control and Prevention. 2019. "Leading Causes of Death—Males-Non-Hispanic Black—United States, 2017," https://www.cdc.gov/healthequity/lcod/men/2017/nonhispanic-black/index.htm. Medical and public health authorities have been red-flagging these alarming numbers and urging more aggressive attempts to address the underlying problems for years. For example, see: Hennekens, C. H., J. Drowos, and R. S. Levine. 2013. Mortality from Homicide among Young Black Men: A New American Tragedy. *American Journal of Medicine, 126*(4), 282–83.

33. Frase, R. S. 2009. What Explains Persistent Racial Disproportionality in Minnesota's Prison and Jail Populations? *Crime and Justice, 38*(1), 201–80.

34. Though the criminal justice system is routinely charged with systemic racial bias by champions of the social control explanation of mass incarceration, it bears repeating that there's plenty of evidence to challenge that claim on empirical grounds. For example, some longitudinal studies find no evidence that the criminal justice system treats Black males systematically differently than whites after accounting for (especially violent) criminal behavior. A meta-analysis of more than fifty studies also concludes there is little evidence for systematic racial bias and specifically suggests that contradictory evidence is most likely anchored in "overinterpretation of statistically significant 'noise' from large sample studies." As I argue explicitly in the text, I'm not taking these sorts of studies as empirically and definitively ending any debate over systemic racial bias in the criminal justice system. My point is that any honest and genuine inquiry into the merits of the social order and social control arguments cannot, and should not, ignore this evidence and its implications. See:

Beaver, K. M., M. DeLisi, J. P. Wright, B. B. Boutwell, J. C. Barnes, and M. G. Vaughn. 2013. No Evidence of Racial Discrimination in Criminal Justice Processing: Results from the National Longitudinal Study of Adolescent Health. *Personality and Individual Differences, 55*(1), 29–34.

Ferguson, C. J., and S. Smith. 2023. Race, Class, and Criminal Adjudication: Is the US Criminal Justice System as Biased as Is Often Assumed? A Meta-Analytic Review. *Aggression and Violent Behavior*, 101905.

35. Quoted in *The Economist*, "A Modern Murder Mystery," March 27, 2021, p. 23.

36. Rabuy, Bernadette, and Danial Kopf. 2015. "Prisons of Poverty." Prison Policy Initiative, https://www.prisonpolicy.org/reports/income.html.

37. Harlow, Caroline Wolf. 2002. "Education and Correctional Populations." Bureau of Justice Statistics, https://www.bjs.gov/content/pub/pdf/ecp.pdf.

38. The classic study of legislative behavior is David Mayhew's *Congress: The Electoral Connection*, and his central finding—that the primary influence on office-holder behavior is a calculation of the electoral implications of any choice or

action—seems to apply to virtually all democratically elected offices and all levels of government.

39. Bennett, W. J., J. J. Dilulio Jr., and J. P. Walters. 1996. *Body Count: Moral Poverty . . . and How to Win America's War against Crime and Drugs*. New York: Simon and Schuster, 27.

40. Gottschalk, Marie. 2006. *The Prison and the Gallows: The Politics of Mass Incarceration in America*. New York: Cambridge University Press.

41. This point is reinforced in Forman's work discussed early in the chapter, that is, Black municipal leaders enthusiastically championing punitive approaches to dealing with urban crime problems. The 2014 National Academies report also highlights the fact that liberals in general were slow to push back on conservative drives to crack down on crime, even when those agendas had distinct racial undertones. See: Travis, Jeremy, Bruce Western, and F. Steven Redburn (eds.). 2014. *The Growth of Incarceration in the United States: Exploring Causes and Consequences*. Washington, DC: National Academies Press, 113–15.

42. Gottschalk, *The Prison and the Gallows*, 11. It's also worth noting that progressive political leaders were sometimes not just half-hearted in their opposition to conservative-led efforts but actually at the forefront of the sort of initiatives that Alexander takes to task in *The New Jim Crow*. Nelson Rockefeller, for example, was a progressive Republican with a history of treating drugs as a social problem rather than a criminal problem. As governor of New York in the 1970s, however, he successfully pushed for the adoption of some of the most criminally punitive drug laws in the nation. This was widely interpreted as a way to build tough-on-crime cred as a preliminary to a presidential run. In short, even moderates like Rockefeller saw tough on crime as an electoral winner and a reputation for being compassionate to offenders as an electoral liability.

43. A review of ten of the most widely cited state-level statistical analyses of incarceration found that all ten examined partisan control of the legislature as an explanatory variable and six examined partisan control of the governor's office. See: Smith, Kevin B., and Clarisse Warren. Nd. "Lock 'Em Up Democracy: A Test of the Democracy-in-Action Hypothesis of Mass Incarceration."

44. In Kansas City, Missouri, public defenders routinely handle 100 cases a week. In New Orleans, 60 public defenders handle 20,000 cases a year. The case/defender ratio is so bad public defenders have sued states. States are often more interested in cutting their budgets than expanding them. See: Wiltz, Teresa. 2017. "Public Defenders Fight Back against Budget Cuts, Growing Caseloads." Pew Trusts, https://www.pewtrusts.org/en/research-and-analysis/blogs/stateline/2017/11/21/public-defenders-fight-back-against-budget-cuts-growing-caseloads.

45. Pfaff, John. 2017. *Locked In*. New York: Basic Books, 127–59.

46. Coppole, George. 2003. "States That Elect Their Chief Prosecutors." Office of Legislative Research, Connecticut General Assembly, https://www.cga.ct.gov/2003/rpt/2003-R-0231.htm.

47. For examples see: Bandyopadhyay, S., and B. C. McCannon. 2014. The Effect of the Election of Prosecutors on Criminal Trials. *Public Choice*, *161*(1–2), 141–56.

Nadel, Melissa, Samuel Scaggs, and William Bales. 2017. "Politics in Punishment: The Effect of the State Attorney Election Cycle on Convictions and Sentencing Outcomes in Florida." *American Journal of Criminal Justice*, *42*, 845–62.

48. Melinda Gann Hall did the groundbreaking work on the electoral connection and state-level judicial behavior back in the 1990s. As a grad student I served as her research assistant and helped with the data collection for some of her work—this is what originally sparked my interest in state-level criminal justice questions. See:

Hall, Melinda Gann. 1992. "Electoral Politics and Strategic Voting in State Supreme Courts." *The Journal of Politics*, *54*(2), 427–46.

Hall, Melinda Gann. 1995. "Justices as Representatives: Elections and Judicial Politics in the American States." *American Politics Quarterly*, *23*(4), 485–503.

The claim that judicial decision making is responsive to electoral considerations is by now widely demonstrated and has been approached from a number of different angles. For more recent examples see:

Dippel, Christian, and Michael Poyker. 2020. "How Common Are Electoral Cycles in Criminal Sentencing?" NBER Working Paper No. 25716. (DOI): 10.3386/w25716.

Lim, Claire. 2013. "Preferences and Incentives of Appointed and Elected Public Officials: Evidence from State Trial Court Judges." *American Economic Review*, *103*(4), 1360–97.

49. Probably the best known of these is Berry et al.'s measure of citizen and government ideology. See: Berry, William, Evan Ringquist, Richard Fording, and Russell Hanson. 1998. "Measuring Citizen and Government Ideology in the American States, 1960–93." *American Journal of Political Science*, *42*, 327–48.

50. The specific technique is called multilevel regression and postratification, or MRP. This basically means fitting survey responses to demographic and geographic traits using multilevel regression and then using state-level census data to weight the results. This can seem a complicated and technical process to the non-expert, but the results are recognized as likely the best estimates of state-level public opinion we are going to get in the absence of independent, identical polls conducted simultaneously in all fifty states. For technical presentations of the approach see:

Park, David, Andrew Gelman, and Joseph Bafumi. 2004. "Bayesian Multilevel Estimation with Postratification: Sate-Level Estimates from National Polls." *Political Analysis*, *12*, 375–85.

Lax, Jeffrey, and Justin Phillips. 2009. "How Should We Estimate Public Opinion in the States?" *American Journal of Political Science*, *53*, 107–21.

51. For a full treatment of the state-level ideology measure, see: Enns, Peter K., and Julianna Koch. 2013. "Public Opinion in the US States: 1956 to 2010." *State Politics & Policy Quarterly*, *13*(3), 349–72.

There is a full discussion of his measure of public opinion punitiveness at the state level in his book: Enns, Peter. 2016. *Incarceration Nation*. New York: Cambridge University Press, 133–35.

Other scholars have also found a strong link between public opinion, especially fear of crime, and incarceration rates. Duxbury uses a similar approach to measuring state-level opinion and reports similar relationships. See: Scott W. Duxbury. 2021.

"Fear or Loathing in the United States? Public Opinion and the Rise of Racial Dispar-ity in Mass Incarceration, 1978–2015." *Social Forces, 100*(2), 427–453.

52. Enns, *Incarceration Nation.*

53. Pickett, Justin. 2019. "Public Opinion and Criminal Justice Policy: Theory and Research." *Annual Review of Criminology*, *2*, 405–28.

54. To be clear, little attention does not mean no attention. Enns, for example, acknowledges that chief prosecutors have a "direct incentive" to respond to public opinion, as well as judges, legislators, and even police officers. What I'm referring to here is less about an acknowledgment that public opinion is translated into action by democratic mechanisms, which as far as I know is not contested by anyone I'm citing in the section. In empirical analyses, though, one or the other tends to be focused on rather than the other.

55. See Duxbury, "Who Controls Criminal Law? Racial Threat and the Adoption of State Sentencing Law, 1975–2012."

CHAPTER 4

1. Box, George E. P. 2010. "An Accidental Statistician," http://pages.stat.wisc.edu /~yandell/stat/50-year/Box_George.html.

2. Smith, A. F. M. 2015. "George Edward Pelham Box. 10 October 1919–28 March 2013." *Biographical Memoirs of Fellows of the Royal Society*, *61*, 23–37. doi:10.1098/ rsbm.2015.001.

3. Box, George E. P. 1976. "Science and Statistics." *Journal of the American Sta-tistical Association*, *71*, 791–99, esp. p. 792.

4. The 40 to 50 is a subjective estimate, but it is based on reading a lot of such studies. Hawes (2017) and Jacobs and Carmichael (2001) are more or less random examples of what I see as good, conscientious scholars doing studies with carefully thought through statistical models of state-level mass incarceration. The former includes 20 variables, the latter 12, and by my count there are at least a dozen vari-ables that are included in one of these models but not the other. Smith and Warren (nd) identified more than 30 variables employed in ten of the most cited studies using statistical models of incarceration, and only 2—crime rates and partisan/ideological control of the state legislature—were employed in all ten. Purdy (2013) lists at least a dozen categories of variables variously employed to predict incarceration rates, each category containing multiple potential variables. If anything, I think the 40 to 50 is probably a lowball guess.

Hawes, D. P. 2017. Social Capital, Racial Context, and Incarcerations in the Ameri-can States. *State Politics & Policy Quarterly*, *17*(4), 393–417.

Jacobs, D., and J. T. Carmichael. 2001. The Politics of Punishment across Time and Space: A Pooled Time-Series Analysis of Imprisonment Rates. *Social Forces*, *80*(1), 61–89.

Smith, Kevin B., and Clarisse Warren. Nd. "Lock 'Em Up Democracy: A Test of the Democracy-in-Action Hypothesis of Mass Incarceration."

Purdy, A. Nd. "Mass Incarceration: A Review of the Literature on Structural Racism within the US Criminal Justice System."

5. Including lots of variables in a regression model (the form of statistical model used here) is not the worst statistical sin, but the downsides are important: it eats up degrees of freedom and almost certainly will result in redundant variables. Those both inflate standard errors. In technical terms, the estimators generated by the model will not be biased, but they will be less stable (more likely to change depending on what mix of variables is added or subtracted from the model). An over-specified model is also simply harder to interpret.

6. In technical terms, a regression model assumes that the dependent variable (that which is predicted) is a function of the predictor variables included in the model plus error. The error is assumed to be random. Excluding a variable with a strong, causal relationship to the dependent variable effectively means the error assumption is violated, and the model's estimates are suspect. The error assumption is violated to some extent in all statistical models, the real issue is question of degree. Excluding a few variables with minor relationships to the dependent variable is no big deal, the resulting estimates will still be pretty robust. Exclude a variable that is a primary causal driver of the dependent variable, though, and the estimates are, in technical terms, doo-doo.

7. To methodologist types shocked at this shallow and not wholly accurate explanation of ordinary least squares regression, I say *thpppt*. Feel free to bore anyone reading this book with all the mathematical details. I think George Box would be okay with this, and that's good enough for me.

8. Gory details, plus information on how to access the data set as well as all the code used for the analysis, can be found in the methodological appendix.

9. Actually, in reality it's not like this at all. It usually involves months of trying to dig up data, weeks of coding in some statistical programming language, checking lots of assumptions, and much wailing and gnashing of teeth to get the code to run properly and produce output that meets all minimal standards of good statistical practice.

10. This process, as summarized later in this chapter, is known as an extreme bounds analysis.

11. This example is taken from: Rushton, Michael. 2008. "A Note on the Use and Misuse of the Racial Diversity Index." *Policy Studies Journal*, *36*(3), 445–59. See esp. p. 456.

12. For example, people who live in more diverse places tend to perceive fewer differences between groups. Paradoxically, being immersed in an environment where there are lot of differences seems to make people appear more similar. See: Bai, Xuechunzi, Miguel Ramos, and Ssuan Fiske. 2020. "As Diversity Increases, People Paradoxically Perceive Social Groups as More Similar." *PNAS*, *177*(23), 12741–49.

13. There are hundreds, likely thousands, of published academic studies on race/ethnic groups and social conflict/harmony. While drawing definitive inferences from all this should be approached with extreme caution, it's fair to say that ethnic group conflict is broadly accepted as a primary driving force of civil wars, and, less dramatically, that increasing ethnic (and religious) diversity has created social

conflicts, or at least declines in social trust, that many Western liberal democracies have struggled to deal with. For reviews/overviews see:

Denny, E. K., and B. F. Walter. 2014. "Ethnicity and Civil War." *Journal of Peace Research, 51*(2), 199–212.

Dinesen, P. T., M. Schaeffer, and K. M. Sønderskov. 2020. Ethnic Diversity and Social Trust: A Narrative and Meta-analytical Review. *Annual Review of Political Science, 23*(1), 441–65.

14. Goodhart, D. 2017. *The Road to Somewhere: The Populist Revolt and the Future of Politics.* Oxford, UK: Oxford University Press.

Kaufmann, E. 2018. *Whiteshift: Populism, Immigration and the Future of White Majorities.* Penguin UK.

15. Hochschild, A. R. 2018. *Strangers in Their Own Land: Anger and Mourning on the American Right.* New York: The New Press.

16. These sorts of arguments have been applied to incarceration for a long time. For example, increasingly punitive attitudes toward punishment, that is, greater support for get-tough approaches to incarcerations, have been linked to declining confidence in social values and cohesion for at least forty years. See: Allen, F. A. 1981. *The Decline of the Rehabilitative Ideal: Penal Policy and Social Purpose.* New Haven, CT: Yale University Press, 14.

17. Technically what I am using for cutoff points are the proportion of the cumulative distribution function of the betas from a Sala-i-Martin's Extreme Bounds Analysis where those beta coefficients are assumed to be normally distributed. Beta coefficients that have a CDF>=.90 or <=.10 (i.e., 90 percent of the distribution is on one side of zero) are considered consistent—I'm using the term "90 percent consistent" for ease of exposition. Percent conservative had a mean CDF of 89.25 of beta coefficients greater than zero, in that case I rounded up to 90.

18. This is part of the reason crime was the only variable deliberately included in all of the statistical models run—instability doesn't make it a mouse.

19. Yes, I do realize I'm running cross-sectional models. These, though, should be picking up long-term relationships. The fact some coefficients seem to be systematically moving around seems to hint, at least to me, that some long-term relationships changed over this three-decade period. The time element I specifically model in the panel analyses, but the discussion around table 4.1 is mostly about trying to identify the best (in a Boxian sense) group of variables to include in a full-blown analysis.

20. Most notably in the work of Peter Enns (see Enns, *Incarceration Nation.* New York: Cambridge University Press, 2016), but see also Duxbury, Scott W. 2021. "Fear or Loathing in the United States? Public Opinion and the Rise of Racial Disparity in Mass Incarceration, 1978–2015." *Social Forces, 100*(2), 427–453.

21. A standard technical overview of panel analysis that covers all these issues is: Baltagi, Badi. 2008. *Econometric Analysis of Panel Data.* Hoboken, NJ: John Wiley & Sons.

22. Duxbury, Scott W. 2021. "A General Panel Model for Unobserved Time Heterogeneity with Application to the Politics of Mass Incarceration." *Sociological Methodology*, 00811750211016033. This article also contains a good explanation of various approaches to panel analysis estimators.

23. For example, care needs to be taken in comparing results from one model to another. Different estimation approaches are mostly based on executing different underlying data transformations to meet particular modelling assumptions. Those transformations have implications for inference—for example the level of a crime rate is not the same thing as the difference in the crime rate.

24. This is a model of first differences, that is, it analyzes the differences from one year to the next rather than the levels in separate years. In other words, rather than analyzing diversity in year 1 and year 2 it analyzes the difference of year 2 minus year 1. The estimated coefficient here is huge (the standard error is orders of magnitude larger than the estimated coefficient). Basically, this just tells us that incarceration rates do not instantaneously respond to changes in racial/ethnic diversity, which is hardly surprising. See methodological appendix.

25. These estimates are, somewhat arbitrarily, based on the results of the random effects model, which I chose simply because those results seemed reasonably representative of the results generally, it includes all predictors, it uses a tried-and-true estimation approach, and it meets minimum statistical thresholds for trustworthiness (see methodological appendix for details).

26. This actually understates things a little. To increase by 1 percentage point means the total number of Black males would have to increase by 21 percent. This is because 1 is 21 percent of 4.8, so 5.8 represents a 1 percentage *point* increase but a 21 percent *overall* increase.

27. Duxbury reports a similar common trend estimate in his analysis, finding that "A 1 percent mean increase in the percentage black population increases the mean state incarceration rate by 85 people per 100,000 people." Duxbury's between and within estimates were also similar to those reported in the methodological appendix. The fact that I'm finding a slightly higher impact in the common trend estimate I attribute in part to his use of percent Black population while I'm using Black male population. Regardless, the fact that two analyses independently landed on similarly high estimates reinforces the need to take this finding seriously. See Duxbury, "A General Panel Model for Unobserved Time Heterogeneity with Application to the Politics of Mass Incarceration," 20.

28. Just in case there's any confusion: By "brave" I actually mean "deluded."

29. The emphasis here is on violence and violent crime. Though cross-national comparisons are fraught with difficulties (data collection, measurement, and definitions can vary considerably), property crime rates for the United States do not seem to be particularly anomalous. Where the United States stands out is in its higher rates of lethal violence. Homicide rates in the United States are estimated to be seven times higher than other high-income countries; gun homicides are twenty-five times higher. See:

Zimring, F. E., and G. Hawkins. 1999. *Crime Is Not the Problem: Lethal Violence in America*. Oxford, UK: Oxford University Press.

Grinshteyn, E., and D. Hemenway. 2016. "Violent Death Rates: The US Compared with Other High-Income OECD Countries, 2010." *American Journal of Medicine*, *129*(3), 266–73.

30. Minnesota is the big exception here; it elects judges for courts of original jurisdiction.

31. The most diverse state on this list is Massachusetts, a state with a 2010 population that was 76.1 percent non-Hispanic white.

32. The top five incarceration states in 1980 were Louisiana, Georgia, Nevada, South Carolina, and North Carolina. In 2010 the top five list was Alabama, Oklahoma, Texas, Mississippi, and Louisiana.

CHAPTER 5

1. Lewis's comment, the mission of the *Enola Gay*, and its aftermath are well known and documented (Little Boy, *Enola Gay*, the bomber's individual crew members, and the atomic bombings of Hiroshima and Nagasaki all have their own well-sourced Wikipedia pages). Lewis was asked about the mission post-war on the TV show *This Is Your Life*, which makes for painful watching—he clearly was still struggling emotionally with the devastation he helped unleash. These comments are included in the 2007 documentary *White Light/Black Rain*, and a clip of the interview is available on YouTube: https://www.youtube.com/watch?v=c_58byuLBu0&t=120s.

2. Estimates of prison records are from Shannon et al. (The Growth, Scope, and Spatial Distribution of People with Felony Records in the United States, 1948–2010. *Demography, 54*(5), 1795–1818), estimates on eye/hair color come from Healthline (https://www.healthline.com/health/red-hair-blue-eyes), the left-handed estimate is an overall population estimate reported in the *Washington Post* (https://www.washingtonpost.com/news/wonk/wp/2015/09/22/the-surprising-geography-of -american-left-handedness/).

3. Enns, P. K., Y. Yi, M. Comfort, A. W. Goldman, H. Lee, C. Muller et al. 2019. "What Percentage of Americans Have Ever Had a Family Member Incarcerated?: Evidence from the Family History of Incarceration Survey (FamHIS)." *Socius, 5*, 2378023119829332.

4. Kaeble, Danielle. 2021 (March). "Time Served in State Prison, 2018." Bureau of Justice Statistics, https://www.ojp.gov/library/publications/time-served-state-prison -2018. Non-violent offenders are more likely to get released early, but even those serving time for the most violent offenses often do not serve their full sentences. In 2018 those being released after serving time for rape completed, on average, 68 percent of their sentence, and those being released after murder convictions served an average of 58 percent of their sentence. The average time served in state prisons for all offenders is a little less than three years.

5. Shannon et al., The Growth, Scope, and Spatial Distribution of People with Felony Records in the United States, 1948–2010.

6. Calculations by author using Shannon et al. (The Growth, Scope, and Spatial Distribution of People with Felony Records in the United States, 1948–2010) data.

7. An estimated 16 percent of consumers shop at Whole Foods, 15 percent report using online dating sites or mobile dating apps. See:

Schmidt, Sarah. 2016. "New Survey Reveals Where Consumers Shop for Groceries." MarketResearch.com, https://blog.marketresearch.com/new-survey-reveals-where-consumers-shop-for-groceries.

Smith, Aaron. 2016. "15% of American Adults Have Used Online Dating Sites or Mobile Dating Apps." Pew Research Center, https://www.pewresearch.org/internet/2016/02/11/15-percent-of-american-adults-have-used-online-dating-sites-or-mobile-dating-apps/.

8. As of 2021, there were an estimated 7.8 million veterans who had served in the Gulf War era. While there are no estimates I am aware of that report the total numbers with prison records in 2021, the estimate from Shannon et al. (The Growth, Scope, and Spatial Distribution of People with Felony Records in the United States, 1948–2010) was 7.3 million in 2010. That figure was almost certainly higher in 2021. It jumped by 2 million between 2000 and 2010 according to Shannon et al.'s estimates. If we are assuming something comparable between 2010 and 2020 (which is probably conservative), there was likely something like more than 1 to 2 million more people with prison experience than Gulf-era veterans. Of course, these are not independent populations—like all demographic groups, some of those vets are also people who have served time in prisons. Veteran population estimates taken from: Shaeffer, Katherine. 2021. "The Changing Face of America's Veteran Population." Pew Research Center, https://www.pewresearch.org/fact-tank/2021/04/05/the-changing-face-of-americas-veteran-population/.

9. If you do need an academic study, a good place to start is with Bruce Western's book: Western, Bruce. 2007. *Punishment and Inequality in America*. New York: Russell Sage Foundation.

10. Hagan, John, and Ronit Dinovitzer. 1999. "Collateral Consequences of Imprisonment for Children, Communities, and Prisoners." In *Prisons*, Michael Tonry and Joan Petersilia (eds.). Chicago: University of Chicago Press.

11. Giordano, Peggy C. et al. 2019. "Linking Parental Incarceration and Family Dynamics Associated with Intergenerational Transmission: A Life-Course Perspective." *Criminology*, *57*(3), 395–423, esp. p. 397.

While the impact of incarceration on family stability generally is clearly negative, those negative effects are particularly sharp when mothers are incarcerated. While the incarcerated population is overwhelmingly male, the number of women incarcerated—including mothers—has also increased dramatically. Generally speaking, the resulting impact on family and child development has been devastating. See for example:

Myers, B. J., T. M. Smarsh, K. Amlund-Hagen, and S. Kennon. 1999. "Children of Incarcerated Mothers." *Journal of Child and Family Studies*, *8*(1), 11–25.

Turney, K., and C. Wildeman. 2018. "Maternal Incarceration and the Transformation of Urban Family Life." *Social Forces*, *96*(3), 1155–82.

Johnston, D. 1995. "Jailed Mothers." In K. Gabel and D. Johnston (eds.). *Children of Incarcerated Parents*. New York: Lexington Books, 41–55.

12. See for example:

Rose, Dina R., Todd R. Clear, and Judith A. Ryder. 2000. *Drugs, Incarceration and Neighborhood Life: The Impact of Reintegrating Offenders into the Community*. Final Report to the National Institute of Justice. John Jay College (September).

Sampson, Robert J., Stephen Raudenbush, and Felton Earls. 1997. "Neighborhoods and Violent Crime: A Multilevel Study of Collective Efficacy." *Science* 277, 918–24.

13. A central puzzle at the heart of *Making Democracy Work* is the long-standing differences between Northern and Southern Italy, the former having a long-standing historical reputation for better and more effective governance.

Putnam, R. D., R. Leonardi, and R. Y. Nanetti. 1994. *Making Democracy Work*. Princeton, NJ: Princeton University Press.

14. The title refers to the decline in membership and participation in social groups like bowling leagues.

Putnam, R. D. 2000. *Bowling Alone: The Collapse and Revival of American Community*. New York: Simon and Schuster.

15. Sampson, Robert J., Stephen Raudenbush, and Felton Earls. 1997. "Neighborhoods and Violent Crime: A Multilevel Study of Collective Efficacy." *Science* 277, 918–24, esp. p. 918.

16. A good overview of this general argument and a fairly comprehensive, if by now somewhat dated, literature review can be found in: Rose, D. R., and T. R. Clear. 2003. "Incarceration, Reentry, and Social Capital: Social Networks in the Balance." In Travis, Jeremy, and Michelle Waul. *Prisoners Once Removed: The Impact of Incarceration and Reentry on Children, Families, and Communities*. Washington, DC: Urban Institute Press, 2004, 313–41.

17. Fukuyama, Francis. "Social Capital and Civil Society." IMF Conference on Second Generation Reforms, October 1, 1999, https://www.imf.org/external/pubs/ft/seminar/1999/reforms/fukuyama.htmma.

18. It's not even clear that social capital is always socially beneficial. There's a fascinating exchange in political science surrounding this issue. Putnam indicates that social capital and social/racial equity are, or at least can, be positively related. Rodney Hero argues that they are negatively related, essentially that higher levels of social capital can be used by a dominant group to better mobilize and advance its interests at the expense of a minority group. At the risk of gross oversimplification, Hero's argument is that at the aggregate level, the benefits of social capital are not evenly distributed across racial groups, and that the key factor to achieving greater social equality is not higher levels of social capital but greater levels of racial diversity. Daniel Hawes and Rene Rocha published a really insightful study that tackled these differences in light of some of the measurement issues I refer to in the main text. One of their key takeaways was that social capital and racial diversity are inversely related, that is, as social capital decreases racial diversity tends to increase. The upshot to this research agenda—which is still ongoing—seems to be that high stocks of social capital are good for some and decidedly not so good for others. For a good overview of the relevant arguments see: Hawes, Daniel P., and Rene R. Rocha. 2011. "Social Capital, Racial Diversity, and Equity: Evaluating the Determinants of Equity in the United States." *Political Research Quarterly*, *64*, 924–37.

19. A table listing these definitions along with original sources can be found in: Bjørnskov, C., and K. M. Sønderskov. 2013. "Is Social Capital a Good Concept?" *Social Indicators Research, 114*(3), 1225–42. Bjørnskov and Sønderskov's table lists eighteen separate definitions, though there are undoubtedly more.

20. Putnam used this approach in *Bowling Alone*. He created a state-level index of capital using fourteen different variables sourced from a variety of sources, including survey data from Roper, the General Social Survey and the DDB Needham Life Style archive, as well as state-level statistical sources such as the US Census Bureau and the Department of Commerce. For a full list of sources see Putnam, *Bowling Alone*, page 435, and for correlations of these variables with his full social capital index, see page 291.

21. Bjørnskov and Sønderskov, "Is Social Capital a Good Concept?"

22. In 2018 Republicans on the US Senate Joint Economic Committee put out an earnest and well-executed report on how to best measure social capital. The idea was that social capital was really important, critical even, to states being able to meet a range of challenges (including the erosion of associational life) and that policymakers needed a quality state (and county) measure of this concept. The report works through the literature on social capital measures and attempts to triangulate on a big set of aggregate level measures to create one overall social capital index and seven sub-dimensional indexes. One of those sub-dimensions was collective efficacy and it consisted of a single variable: violent crime rates. How exactly this captures communal agency is not fully explained, but if collective efficacy is affected by violent crime rates—a reasonable hypothesis—it becomes impossible to test using this measure. In essence that would mean testing whether violent crime is systematically associated with violent crime (hint: it is). See: *The Geography of Social Capital in America*, SCP Report No. 1–18, April 2018, https://www.jec.senate.gov/public/index .cfm/republicans/2018/4/the-geography-of-social-capital-in-america.

23. Specifically in the Penn State measure of social capital. This actually is a county-level measure that can be aggregated to the state level. See: Rupasingha, A., S. J. Goetz, and D. Freshwater. 2006, with updates. "The Production of Social Capital in US Counties." Journal of Socio-Economics, *35*, 83–101. The data and updates are publicly available: https://aese.psu.edu/nercrd/community/social-capital-resources.

I am genuinely not trying to be overly critical of this or any other measure of social capital—the Penn State team has performed an invaluable service in trying to piece together a valid county- and state-level index over time. This is a hugely challenging task, and what I'm hoping doesn't get lost here is that those who have taken on that challenge deserve a massive thanks from the scholarly community, not least from me. The point I'm trying to make is not that people have been going about measuring social capital all wrong, but that measuring social capital is really, really hard.

24. One of the astonishing things about the scholarly literature on social capital at the state level is the relative inattention paid to political culture as conceptualized and operationalized by Elazar, Sharkansky, and intellectual heirs such as Joel Lieske. I am avoiding the whole question of the social capital/political culture relationship here primarily because it would require a big, time-consuming digression from the main objectives of the chapter. Given political culture's fifty-year-plus predictive record

at the state level, there's surely a dissertation's worth of a deep dive into how that concept relates to state-level social capital.

25. The correlation between Putnam's social capital index and political culture is .77. This is another example of why the work of comparative state scholars—which for reasons that baffle me continue to remain relatively anonymous to vast swaths of academia—should be paid more attention to.

26. See note 18. Putnam argues social capital is a positive contributor to social tolerance and equity, Hero raises doubts because of the inequitable distribution of social capital across racial groups. I'm not taking a side here, just stating a fairly common claim made in this literature.

27. Arguably there are two. The measure created by Rupasingha, Goetz, and Freshwater has been periodically updated and as of this writing is available for the years 1990, 1997, 2005, and 2009 (see link in note 23 for source link). For the purposes of this chapter, this represents a clear advantage over purely cross-sectional indexes such as those compiled by Putnam of the SJC's Social Capital Project (see note 22). The problem with this measure is twofold. First it is available for only a very limited number of years, and the years it is available for the most part post-date the huge leap in incarceration rates of the 1980s and early 1990s. Second, the variables used to compile the index change somewhat depending on version/year. That raises questions about comparability across time if not between states.

28. Hawes, D., R. Rocha, and K. Meier. 2013. Social Capital in the 50 States: Measuring State-Level Social Capital, 1986–2004. *State Politics & Policy Quarterly*, *13*(1), 121–38.

Hawes, D. 2017. "Social Capital, Racial Context, and Incarcerations in the American States." *State Politics & Policy Quarterly*, 17, 393–417.

In any given year, the cross-sectional (fifty states, single year) correlation between the Hawes, Rocha, and Meier measure and the Putnam measure is ~.80. That's large enough to defend an argument they are probably measuring the same thing, but the big difference being that the Hawes et al. measure captures temporal change and the Putnam measure does not.

29. Technically, these are factor scores. See Hawes, Rocha, and Meier, Social Capital in the 50 States, for details.

30. Economist Clive Granger first proposed his causality test in 1969, and it has been adopted to be used with panel data. In the text I'm glossing over a lot of important detail, and I freely confess to favoring expository clarity over the technical precision in my description of the technique. For full details see:

Granger, C. W. J. 1969. "Investigating Causal Relations by Econometric Models and Cross-spectral Methods." Econometrica, 37(3), 424–38;

Dumitrescu E., and C. Hurlin. 2012. "Testing for Granger Non-Causality in Heterogeneous Panels." *Economic Modelling*, *29*(4), 1450–60;

Lopez L., and S. Weber. 2017. "Testing for Granger Causality in Panel Data." *Stata Journal*, *17*(4), 972–84.

As discussed in the text, the causal logic underlying the test is straightforward—causality is based on establishing three criteria: co-variation, temporal precedence, and the elimination of spuriousness. It should also be noted that this definition of causality has its critics. There's been something of a new dawn in causal reasoning of the past couple of decades driven by the work of computer scientist and philosopher Judea Pearl. His framework has been enthusiastically adopted by a broad swath of social scientists. This is for good reason. Some of his insights are pretty eye popping, for example, the notion that interpreting all coefficients in a regression model as causal—a pretty standard approach for generations of scholars who use that tool—is probably not a good idea. And the whole issue of what a confound is and how to deal with it is laid out better in Pearl's framework than any other approach I'm familiar with. I'm not fully sold, though. For one thing the basic approach to laying out the causal logic of an analysis in a Pearlian framework is to use what's known as a directed acyclic graph (DAGs). These don't permit reciprocal causation—they are acyclic—or at least they don't without drawing up some pretty dang complicated graphs. They also aren't super great at dealing with repeated measures, that is, measuring the same unit analysis across time. Those are pretty significant drawbacks for investigating reciprocal causation in a panel data set. I'm a fan of the Pearl approach, I just think in this case good old-fashioned Granger causality is a more straightforward and defensible—and certainly easier to explain—means to get at the question at hand. For a comprehensive overview of the Pearl system see:

Pearl, J. 2009. *Causality*. Cambridge, UK: Cambridge University Press.

As a complete digression, I can't resist noting that academics have had a lot of fun with Granger causality tests. For example, they have answered the age-old question of whether the chicken or the egg comes first (answer: the egg). See:

Thurman, Walter, and Mark Fisher. 1988. "Chickens, Eggs, and Causality, or Which Came First?" *American Journal of Agricultural Economics*, 70(2), 237–38.

31. The hypothesis of incarceration Granger causing social capital was supported at $p < .10$ in all seven cases, it was supported five out of seven at $p < .05$ (the second lag was $p < .06$, the fourth $p < .08$). The hypothesis of social capital Granger causing incarceration was supported five times at $p < .05$, and rejected twice at $p > .20$. See methodological appendix for details.

32. See methodological appendix for details.

33. Eight states have positive correlations between incarceration rates and social capital scores across the twenty-seven years available: Connecticut, Delaware, New Jersey, New York, Rhode Island, South Carolina, Virginia, and West Virginia. The confidence intervals of two—New York and Delaware—are not bounded by zero, indicating these variables are bouncing around so much in relation to each other that it brings into question the overall inference of positive relations. All other states have negative correlations.

CHAPTER 6

1. Stiles, Matt, Ryan Menezes, and John Schluess. "Malibu's Wildfire History." *Los Angeles Times*, December 12, 2018, https://www.latimes.com/projects/la-me-malibu -wildfire-history/.

2. Cornhusker State Industries, https://csi.nebraska.gov/.

Corcraft Products (Department of Correctional Services, Division of Industries), https://www.ny.gov/agencies/corcraft-products-department-correctional-services-division-industries.

3. The Economist. "Prison Labour Is a Billion-Dollar Industry, with Uncertain Returns for Inmates." March 18, 2017, https://www.economist.com/united-states/2017/03/16/prison-labour-is-a-billion-dollar-industry-with-uncertain-returns-for-inmates.

It's important to note that the 60,000 number is just an estimate for those working in correctional industries. Roughly a million inmates have assigned jobs, though the big majority of these involve institutional operation, such as jobs in food service, laundry, cleaning, and so on. See: Gottschalk, Marie. 2015. *Caught: The Prison State and the Lockdown of American Politics*. Princeton, NJ: Princeton University Press, 57.

4. Lowe, Jaime. 2021. *Breathing Fire*. New York: Farrar, Straus, and Giroux, 56.

5. Lowe, *Breathing Fire*, 4.

6. Sawyer, Wendy. "How Much Do Incarcerated People Earn in Each State?" Prison Policy Initiative, April 10, 2017, https://www.prisonpolicy.org/blog/2017/04/10/wages/.

7. Jobs like those on Crew 13–3 are filled by volunteers, but even here there's an element of coercion. See Lowe, *Breathing Fire*.

8. Jaime Lowe's book (*Breathing Fire*) tells some of their stories. I can't recommend Lowe's book highly enough—it's brilliantly reported and written and tells the story of a group of women who perform a tough and dangerous job and not infrequently gain a wholly justifiable sense of pride in what they've accomplished. Their thanks is minimal. After release they often struggle with the constraints and stigma that accompany a prison record, even if that record is defined by a huge community service contribution.

9. Armstrong, A. C. 2011. Slavery Revisited in Penal Plantation Labor. *Seattle UL Rev.*, *35*, 869.

10. Gottschalk, *Caught: The Prison State and the Lockdown of American Politics*, 58.

11. California Legislative Analyst's Office. 2019. "How Much Does It Cost to Incarcerate an Inmate?" https://lao.ca.gov/policyareas/cj/6_cj_inmatecost.

12. Lowe, *Breathing Fire*, 56.

13. US Bureau of Labor Statistics. "How the Government Measures Unemployment," https://www.bls.gov/cps/cps_htgm.htm.

14. Ansari, Ammara. "For Accurate Unemployment Numbers, Incarcerated Individuals Should Be Counted." *Daily Kos*, October 2, 2019, https://www.dailykos.com/stories/2019/10/2/1889124/-For-accurate-unemployment-numbers-incarcerated-individuals-should-be-counted.

15. For fuller discussions of the impact of prison populations on unemployment rates see:

Beckett, K., and B. Western. 1997. "The Penal System as Labor Market Institution: Jobs and Jails, 1980–95." *Overcrowded Times*, *8*(6).

Western, B., and K. Beckett. 1999. How Unregulated Is the US Labor Market? The Penal System as a Labor Market Institution. *American Journal of Sociology*, *104*(4), 1030–60.

Downes, D. 2001. The Macho Penal Economy: Mass Incarceration in the United States—A European Perspective. *Punishment & Society*, *3*(1), 61–80.

16. According to the data platform Statista, an estimated 147,000 full-time workers were employed by Apple in 2020, 58,000 for Facebook, and 135,000 for Alphabet (Google). The Census Bureau estimates that full-time state employment in corrections in 2020 was approximately 430,000. See:

US Census Bureau. "State Government: Employment and Payroll Data by State and by Function: May 2020," https://www.census.gov/programs-surveys/apes/data/datasetstables/2020.html.

Statista. "Number of Full-Time Facebook Employees from 2004 to 2020," https://www.statista.com/statistics/273563/number-of-facebook-employees/.

Statista. "Number of Full-Time Alphabet Employees from 2007 to 2020," https://www.statista.com/statistics/273744/number-of-full-time-google-employees/.

Statista. "Apple's Number of Employees in the Fiscal Years 2005 to 2020," https://www.statista.com/statistics/273439/number-of-employees-of-apple-since-2005/.

17. Though widely touted as sources of good jobs that can provide a boost to local economies, the evidence backing those beliefs is, to put it mildly, mixed. See: Genter, S., G. Hooks, and C. Mosher. (2013). Prisons, Jobs and Privatization: The Impact of Prisons on Employment Growth in Rural US Counties, 1997–2004. *Social Science Research*, *42*(3), 596–610.

18. King, R. S., M. Mauer, and T. Huling. 2003. *Big Prisons, Small Towns: Prison Economics in Rural America*. Washington, DC: Sentencing Project, 1.

19. Wray, L. Randall. 2000. "A New Economic Reality: Penal Keynesianism." *Challenge*, *43*(5), 31–59.

20. Western, B., J. Kling, and D. Weiman. 2000. "The Labor Market Consequences of Incarceration." *Crime & Delinquency*, *47*(3), 410–27.

21. See, for example:

Western and Beckett, How Unregulated Is the US Labor Market?

Beckett and Western, "The Penal System as Labor Market Institution."

Pager, D., B. Bonikowski, and B. Western. 2009. Discrimination in a Low-Wage Labor Market: A Field Experiment. *American Sociological Review*, *74*(5), 777–99, https://doi.org/10.1177/000312240907400505.

Western, B. 2002. The Impact of Incarceration on Wage Mobility and Inequality. *American Sociological Review*, *67*(4), 526–46, https://doi.org/10.2307/3088944.

22. Schmitt, John, and Jori Kandara. 2021. "The Carceral State and the Labor Market." Economic Policy Institute, https://www.epi.org/blog/the-carceral-state-and-the-labor-market/.

23. Nationally, roughly 2 percent of the population of the United States has a PhD and about 13 percent has an advanced degree of some kind. The average proportion of a state population that has served time in prison is 1.25 percent, but ranges from .15 to 4.37 percent over the entire time span covered by the Shannon et al. (The Growth,

Scope, and Spatial Distribution of People with Felony Records in the United States, 1948–2010) data.

24. The correlation isn't big, r~.27. Delaware is clearly a big outlier, though, and the rest of the states are much more tightly grouped around the regression line in figure 6.1.

25. Important caveat—the 1980 to 2010 data spans the discontinuity in how GSP was calculated. I avoid that discontinuity in the larger analyses reported later in the chapter because this could clearly have implications for inference. I'm okay using the full data range here simply because this is for expository purposes. I'm not making any claims about what relationship does or doesn't exist, with figures 6.1 and 6.2. I'm just trying to illustrate the key possibilities using real data.

26. Shannon et al. (The Growth, Scope, and Spatial Distribution of People with Felony Records in the United States, 1948–2010) are the source of all such estimates used here. See methodological appendix.

27. There is a fairly rich literature on the independence, or lack thereof, of state-level economies. For examples, see:

Wibbels, Erik. 2000. "Federalism and the Politics of Macroeconomic Policy and Performance."

American Journal of Political Science, 44(4), 687–702.

Miller, Stephen M., and Frank S. Russek. 1997. "Fiscal Structures and Economic Growth at the State and Local Level." *Public Finance Review, 25*(2), 213–37.

Super, David A. 2005. "Rethinking Fiscal Federalism." *Harvard Law Review, 118*(8), 2546–52.

28. Brace, Paul, and Aubrey Jewett. 1995. "The State of State Politics Research." *Political Research Quarterly, 48*(3), 643–81, esp. p. 662.

29. Smith, K. B., and J. S. Rademacker. 1999. Expensive Lessons: Education and the Political Economy of the American State. *Political Research Quarterly, 52*(4), 709–27, esp. p. 710.

The pioneering work on state political economy, especially in the sense of state governments as important economic policymakers, was done by Paul Brace. See:

Brace, P. 1994. *State Government and Economic Performance*. Baltimore: John Hopkins University Press.

30. Rickman and Wang review dozens of studies that are broadly consistent with these claims. See:

Rickman, D., and H. Wang. 2020. US State and Local Fiscal Policy and Economic Activity: Do We Know More Now? *Journal of Economic Surveys, 34*(2), 424–65.

A good review of the relevant literature can also be found in Baldwin et al. See:

Baldwin, J. N., S. A. Borrelli, and M. J. New. 2011. State Educational Investments and Economic Growth in the United States: A Path Analysis. *Social Science Quarterly, 92*(1), 226–45.

The studies already cited in notes 25, 26, and 27 (see above) are broadly supportive of the argument being made in the text. That said, I fully recognized there is a *lot* of variation in this literature, not just in model specification and methodological approach, but theoretical setup and inferential claims.

31. The big drawback to using GSP is that, annoyingly, the BEA switched its accounting methods in 1998 (the same is true of GDP). In other words, about halfway through the time period I'm targeting—roughly 1980 to 2010—there's a pretty significant change in how GSP is summed up. This discontinuity could raise big issues for inference so I'm only analyzing data up to 1997. I'm using the years under the old system of calculated GSP simply because I have more of them available to analyze. Nebraska gets excluded from most of the analyses I ran because one of the controls included in my models was partisan control of government, which excludes Nebraska's non-partisan unicameral system. See methodological appendix for more details.

32. A random effects model was used to generate these estimates—it includes all variables, it is a tried-and-true estimator, and it kicks out pretty similar numbers to the fixed effects model. All monetary variables, including per capita GSP, are inflation adjusted. See methodological appendix for further details.

33. The five million estimate is from Shannon et al. (The Growth, Scope, and Spatial Distribution of People with Felony Records in the United States, 1948–2010). That estimate is for 2010, and a decade plus later it is a safe bet that the number has risen significantly, the only question is by how much.

CHAPTER 7

1. Caston was convicted as a teenager and served twenty-six years, being released in late 2021, roughly six months after his election. His election received a fair amount of media coverage. See:

Austermuhle, Martin. "My Voice Still Matters: Resident at D.C. Jail Wins Local Election." National Public Radio, https://www.npr.org/local/305/2021/06/17/1007604505/my-voice-still-matters-resident-at-d-c-jail-wins-local-election.

Fieldstadt, Elisha. "Washington, D.C., Inmate Becomes First Incarcerated Person in City to Win Elected Office." NBC News, https://www.nbcnews.com/news/us-news/washington-d-c-inmate-becomes-first-incarcerated-person-city-win-n1271033.

2. Only two states, Maine and Vermont, allow felons to vote while incarcerated. The District of Columbia also allows inmates to vote, which explains how Caston stitched together his majority. State laws vary considerably on the rights of those convicted of a felony to vote or run for public office. Texas bars anyone with a felony record from running for public office. In Connecticut a former felon can not only cast a ballot, but also run for state legislature.

3. The estimates for Shannon et al. (The Growth, Scope, and Spatial Distribution of People with Felony Records in the United States, 1948–2010) data I'm using only go through 2010, and that year these data estimate ~304,000 ex-prisoners in those three states. What those numbers looked like a decade later I don't know, but it's a pretty safe bet that they were higher.

4. Chan, Tara Francis. 2019. "Do Felons Vote Democrat? Why Bernie Sanders' Idea to Let Felons Vote Probably Wouldn't Change Election Results." *Newsweek*, https://www.newsweek.com/felons-vote-democrat-bernie-sanders-1404728.

5. Estimates of voter turnout among those incarcerated (where eligible) or with prison records tend to fall between 10 percent on the low end and 35 percent on the high end. The weight of the evidence suggests the low estimates are more accurate. Few ex-prisoners bother to register, let alone vote. See:

White, A. R., and A. Nguyen. 2021. How Often Do People Vote While Incarcerated? Evidence from Maine and Vermont. *Journal of Politics*, https://www.journals .uchicago.edu/doi/pdf/10.1086/714927.

Gerber, A. S., G. A. Huber, M. Meredith, D. R. Biggers, and D. J. Hendry. 2015. Can Incarcerated Felons Be (Re) Integrated into the Political System? Results from a Field Experiment. *American Journal of Political Science, 59*(4), 912–26.

Uggen, C., and J. Manza. 2002. Democratic Contraction? Political Consequences of Felon Disenfranchisement in the United States. *American Sociological Review*, 777–803.

6. Studies suggest that even minor contact with the criminal justice system—even just being questioned by police—correlates with lower political engagement. See:

Burch, T. 2011. Turnout and Party Registration among Criminal Offenders in the 2008 General Election. *Law & Society Review, 45*(3), 699–730.

Haselswerdt, M. V. 2009. Con Job: An Estimate of Ex-Felon Voter Turnout Using Document-Based Data. *Social Science Quarterly, 90*(2), 262–73.

Weaver, V. M., and A. E. Lerman. 2010. Political Consequences of the Carceral State. *American Political Science Review, 104*(4), 817–33.

7. That law was ruled unconstitutional by a federal judge but then restored by an appeals court consisting of mostly Republican-appointed judges in 2020. As of this writing, most felons in Florida still cannot vote. See:

Mazzei, Patricia, and Michael Wines. 2021. "How Republicans Undermined Ex-Felon Voting Rights in Florida." *New York Times*, https://www.nytimes.com/2020 /09/17/us/florida-felons-voting.html.

8. For a description of the survey project and its results, see:

Lewis, Nicole, Aviva Shen, and Anna Flagg. 2020. "What 8,000 Prisoners Think about American Politics." *Slate*, https://slate.com/news-and-politics/2020/03/prisoner -survey-politics-2020.html.

The survey data and associated codebooks are publicly accessible. See:

Flagg, Anna. "Survey of the Incarcerated." 2020. Github, https://github.com/ themarshallproject/incarcerated_survey/blob/master/readme.md.

9. The survey did ask a question about state location, but the vast majority of respondents (>60 percent) did not respond. Only six states were specifically identified by respondents—Arkansas, California, Illinois, Kansas, Maine, and Montana. Arkansas (N=1124) and Kansas (N=1439) were, by far, the most represented states where data was available.

10. The Democratic choices and their support in the survey were Amy Klobuchar (1.8 percent), Andrew Yank (1.8 percent), Bernie Sanders (12.3 percent), Cory Booker (1.6 percent), Elizabeth Warren (3.7 percent), Joe Biden (9.7 percent), Julian Castro (1.2 percent), Kamala Harris (2.9 percent), Pete Buttigieg (1.8 percent), and Tom Steyer (2.5 percent).

11. Manza, J., and C. Uggen. 2008. *Locked Out: Felon Disenfranchisement and American Democracy*. Oxford, UK: Oxford University Press.

Uggen, C., and J. Manza. 2002. Democratic Contraction? Political Consequences of Felon Disenfranchisement in the United States. *American Sociological Review*, 777–803.

Manza, J., and C. Uggen. 2004. Punishment and Democracy: Disenfranchisement of Nonincarcerated Felons in the United States. *Perspectives on Politics*, 2(3), 491–505.

12. Thirty-five percent of 1,500,000 is 525,000, 73 percent of 525,000 is 383,250, and that would be the estimated number of votes the Democratic nominee gains. If we assume all remaining 141,750 of the 525,000 votes go to the Republican candidate, then the net gain to the Democrat is 383,250 minus 141,750 (Democratic votes gained minus Republican voted gained) = 241,500. The actual estimate of felons disenfranchised in Florida in the immediate wake of the ballot initiative was a bit more than 1.41 million. I'm rounding to 1.5 just to make the math easier to follow, and the net effect of this is I'm probably very slightly exaggerating impacts, but nowhere near enough to raise doubts about the substantive arguments made in the text.

13. Hjalmarsson, R., and M. Lopez. 2010. The Voting Behavior of Young Disenfranchised Felons: Would They Vote If They Could? *American Law and Economics Review*, 12(2), 356–93.

14. White, A. R., and A. Nguyen. 2021. How Often Do People Vote While Incarcerated? Evidence from Maine and Vermont. *Journal of Politics*, https://www.journals.uchicago.edu/doi/pdf/10.1086/714927.

15. Gerber, Huber, Meredith, Biggers, and Hendry, Can Incarcerated Felons Be (Re) Integrated into the Political System? 912–26.

16. Meredith, M., and M. Morse. 2014. Do Voting Rights Notification Laws Increase Ex-Felon Turnout? *ANNALS of the American Academy of Political and Social Science*, 651(1), 220–49.

17. Fifteen percent of 1,500,000 is 225,000. If 55 percent of the latter vote Democratic and 15 percent Republican, that's 123,750 more votes for the Democratic candidate and 33,750 for the Republican candidate (the rest of the 225,000 are assumed to vote third party). Subtract those two numbers and you end up with a net gain of 90,000 for the Democratic candidate. I want to be absolutely clear: these estimates are purely for expository purposes. I am not claiming that they are realistic. The 90,000 Democratic advantage that my back-of-the-envelope sums totted up to is double the estimate Marc Meredith and Michael Morse—political scientists with way more expertise in this area than I have—came up with while running through a similar exercise for *Vox*. See:

Meridith, Marc, and Michael Morse. 2018. Why Letting Ex-Felons Vote Probably Won't Swing Florida. *Vox*, https://www.vox.com/the-big-idea/2018/11/2/18049510/felon-voting-rights-amendment-4-florida.

18. According to BallotPedia the average margin of victory in US Senate seats tends to fluctuate between 15 and 20 percentage points. For the 2020 analysis see:

BallotPedia. Election Results, 2020: Congressional Margin of Victory Analysis, https://ballotpedia.org/Election_results,_2020:_Congressional_margin_of_victory_analysis.

19. Each state's Electoral College vote is equal to the size of its congressional delegation, so effectively each state gets two votes for its senators plus one for each of its representatives. Maine and Nebraska award two electoral votes—that is, its Senate votes—to the winner of the statewide popular vote and apportion the rest on the basis of the popular vote winner in each congressional district. In other states, the winner of the statewide popular vote gets all the Electoral College votes. It's actually more complicated than that: what presidential candidates actually get when they win a state are their preferred set of electors appointed to the Electoral College. These are typically chosen on the basis of party loyalty and expected to vote for their party's candidate, but there have been historical examples of unfaithful electors who didn't vote as expected. As I hint at in the text, the Electoral College is kind of a weird and complicated way to elect the leader of the world's major democracy. For one thing, it's not strictly democratic. People can and do become president even though most voters cast a ballot supporting their opponent.

20. As opposed to the between-state relationship. In other words, I'm interested in what happens to the Democratic vote share in, say, Michigan when its ex-prison population goes up over time, as opposed to looking at the differences in Democratic vote share and the size of ex-prisoner populations between Michigan and, say, Texas at a particular point in time.

21. The evidence for household or community spillover effects on voting behavior is mixed, and as far as I'm aware there's not much of a research literature on those effects at the state level. Still, there's certainly enough in the existing scholarly work to defend this as a reasonable hypothesis. For a review of the relevant literature see:

White, A. R. 2022. Political Participation Amid Mass Incarceration. *Annual Review of Political Science, 25.*

22. The nine states with negative correlations are Alabama, Arkansas, Georgia, Kentucky, Louisiana, Mississippi, Tennessee, West Virginia, and Wyoming. Roughly half of these states (Mississippi, Alabama, Tennessee, and Wyoming) have pretty strict felony disenfranchisement laws, but the rest for the most part allow convicted felons to vote once they have served their sentence.

23. A complete summary of the 2016 prediction forecasts can be found here:

Campbell, J. E., H. Norpoth, A. I. Abramowitz, M. S. Lewis-Beck, C. Tien, R. S. Erikson et al. 2017. A Recap of the 2016 Election Forecasts. *PS: Political Science & Politics, 50*(2), 331–38.

A summary of the 2020 models can be found here:

Abramowitz, Alan. 2020. "How Did the Political Science Forecasters Do?" Sabato's Crystal Ball, University of Virginia Center for Politics, https://centerforpolitics.org/crystalball/articles/how-did-the-political-science-forecasters-do/.

24. DeSart, J. A. 2021. A Long-Range State-Level Forecast of the 2020 Presidential Election. *PS: Political Science & Politics, 54*(1), 73–76.

25. Shannon et al.'s data (The Growth, Scope, and Spatial Distribution of People with Felony Records in the United States, 1948–2010) indicate that the mean percent

of state population with a prison record was 0.62 in 1980, and an increase of 1 percentage point in that number did not occur until 2008 (mean that year = 1.66).

26. I'm calculating these numbers using data included in a report published by the Sentencing Project, an advocacy center that seeks to reduce the use of incarceration and has been tracking these sorts of numbers for a long time: "Locked Out 2020: Estimates of People Denied Voting Rights Due to A Felony Conviction," https://www.sentencingproject.org/wp-content/uploads/2020/10/Locked-Out-2020.pdf#page=17.

If you look at Florida's numbers in table 3 of that report, it provides the total proportion of disenfranchised. I calculated the post-sentence proportion by simply dividing that number (column 6) into the voting-age number reported (column 8). The national numbers are reported in the last row of table 3.

27. Again, these numbers come from the Sentencing Project report.

28. If we take the estimated 2.25 million disenfranchised nationally from the Sentencing Project report and assume the low-end turnout rate of 10 percent used earlier, that's 225,000 missing voters. That almost certainly is a conservative, low-end estimate.

29. McDonald, M. P., and S. L. Popkin. 2001. The Myth of the Vanishing Voter. *American Political Science Review*, *95*(4), 963–74.

30. McDonald & Popkin, The Myth of the Vanishing Voter, 963.

31. At the state level, VAP and VEP measures are highly correlated ($r \sim .95$), and if you substitute one for the other in a statistical model, the inferences from a typically standard set of predictors—education levels, competitiveness of race, and so on—just don't change that much. The basic story of turnout decline, though, does change and pretty dramatically in some states, and some of the key findings from a long turnout literature using VAP as the target variable are brought into question when VEP is used. For example, using VAP California has a very low turnout rate—it ranks forty-fourth among the fifty states. Switch to VEP, that is, throw out non-citizens and inmates, and it rockets to twenty-ninth. See:

Holbrook, T., and B. Heidbreder. 2010. Does Measurement Matter? The Case of VAP and VEP in Models of Voter Turnout in the United States. *State Politics & Policy Quarterly*, *10*(2), 157–79.

32. US Census Bureau. 2021. Voting and Registration in the Election of November 2020, table 1, https://www.census.gov/data/tables/time-series/demo/voting-and-registration/p20-585.html.

33. For example, see:

King, J. D. 1994. Political Culture, Registration Laws, and Voter Turnout among the American States. *Publius: The Journal of Federalism*, *24*(4), 115–27.

Geys, B. 2006. Explaining Voter Turnout: A Review of Aggregate-Level Research. *Electoral Studies*, *25*(4), 637–63.

Li, Q., M. J. Pomante, and S. Schraufnagel. 2018. Cost of Voting in the American States. *Election Law Journal: Rules, Politics, and Policy*, *17*(3), 234–47.

Neiheisel, J. R., and B. C. Burden. 2012. The Impact of Election Day Registration on Voter Turnout and Election Outcomes. *American Politics Research*, *40*(4), 636–64.

34. This is the within, or fixed effect, model—see methodological appendix for details.

35. Vermont, Texas, South Dakota, Ohio, Mississippi, Montana, Kentucky, Indiana, Arkansas, and Alaska. These were all calculated from Shannon et al.'s (The Growth, Scope, and Spatial Distribution of People with Felony Records in the United States, 1948–2010) data.

CHAPTER 8

1. $30 million in 1966 is roughly $267 million in 2022 dollars. The EDA was proposing spending the equivalent of approximately $750 in contemporary money for every resident of Oakland. On a per capita basis, that's more than Los Angeles spends on police protection. See:
Bureau of Justice Statistics. 2020. State and Local Government Expenditures on Politic Protection in the U.S., 2000–2017, Table 2, https://bjs.ojp.gov/content/pub/pdf /slgeppus0017.pdf.

2. Bay Area Census data puts the Black population at 23 percent of Oakland's population in 1960 and 34 percent in 1970, and what I'm using here is a midpoint of those two estimates. See: Bay Area Census, http://www.bayareacensus.ca.gov/cities /Oakland50.htm.

3. Austin, C. J. 2006. *Up against the Wall: Violence in the Making and Unmaking of the Black Panther Party*. Fayetteville: University of Arkansas Press, 30–47.

4. Bradford, A. 1968. *Oakland's Not for Burning*. Philadelphia: D. McKay Company, 4.

5. Pressman, J., and A. Wildavsky. 1979. *Implementation: How Great Expectations in Washington Are Dashed in Oakland*. Berkeley: University of California Press. Much of my description of the Oakland program is sourced from Pressman and Wildavsky.

6. Texas Department of Criminal Justice. 2020. The Texas Department of Criminal Justice to Close Two Prison Units in 2020, https://www.tdcj.texas.gov/news/TDCJ_to _close_two_units_2020.html.

7. Bureau of Justice Assistance. Justice Reinvestment Initiative (JRI). US Department of Justice, https://bja.ojp.gov/program/justice-reinvestment-initiative/overview.

8. Schrantz, D., S. T. DeBor, and M. Mauer. 2018. Decarceration Strategies: How 5 States Achieved Substantial Prison Population Reductions. The Sentencing Project, https://www.sentencingproject.org/app/uploads/2022/08/Decarceration-Strategies .pdf.

9. Between 1986 and 2001 correctional spending was one of the fastest growing areas of state expenditures. In 1986 states spent $11.7 billion on prisons. By 2001 it was $29.5 billion. In 2010 it was $48.5 billion. In 2001 California alone was spending nearly $3 billion a year on salaries and benefits for correctional employees, $720 million on inmate health care, and $140 million on prison food service. The bill for all this worked out to nearly $120 for every one of 2001 California's 34.5 million residents. See:
Kyckelhahn, T. 2012. State Corrections Expenditures, FY 1982–2010. *Bureau of Justice Statistics, 2012*, 1–14.

Stephan, J. J. 2004. *State Prison Expenditures, 2001*. Washington, DC: US Department of Justice, Office of Justice Programs, Bureau of Justice Statistics.

10. National Conference of State Legislatures. Reducing Spending, Preserving Public Safety in Criminal Justice Budgets, https://www.ncsl.org/research/civil-and-criminal-justice/reducing-spending-preserving-public-safety-in-criminal-justice-budgets.aspx.

Athey, P. 2021. Marine Corps Continues to Get Smaller under Latest Budget Proposal, https://www.marinecorpstimes.com/news/your-marine-corps/2021/05/28/marine-corps-continues-to-get-smaller-under-latest-budget-proposal/.

11. The California Correctional Peace Officers Association, for example, pours millions into high-profile state races and historically has not been shy about locking horns with political leaders. It once paid for a truck with a huge unflattering photo of then governor Arnold Schwarzenegger to circle around the state capitol.

Myers, John. 2018. Once an Electoral Juggernaut, California's Prison-Guard Union Steps Back into the Spotlight. *Los Angeles Times*, https://www.latimes.com/politics/la-pol-ca-road-map-prison-guards-union-20180923-story.html.

12. Subramanian, R., and A. Shames. 2013. *Sentencing and Prison Practices in Germany and the Netherlands: Implications for the United States*. New York: Vera Institute of Justice.

13. Caseload Forecast Council. 2020. Statistical Summary of Adult Felony Sentencing, Fiscal Year 2020, Washington State, https://www.cfc.wa.gov/PublicationSentencing/StatisticalSummary/Adult_Stat_Sum_FY2020.pdf.

14. Petteruti, A., and J. Fenster. 2011. *Finding Direction: Expanding Criminal Justice Options by Considering Policies of Other Nations*. Justice Policy Institute, https://justicepolicy.org/research/finding-direction-expanding-criminal-justice-options-by-considering-policies-of-other-nations/.

15. Once again: interpreting parameters from regression models applied to observational data needs to be done with conscious caution, a point I've made repeatedly when discussing inferences from my analyses. I'm giving myself a little more interpretational rope here because conclusions are where empirical scholars are traditionally allowed some speculative leeway to describe the story they believe the data is telling.

16. This argument is made in more depth here:

Harrington, J. R., and M. J. Gelfand. 2014. Tightness–Looseness across the 50 United States. *Proceedings of the National Academy of Sciences*, *111*(22), 7990–95.

17. See Schrantz, D., S. T. DeBor, and M. Mauer, Decarceration Strategies: How 5 States Achieved Substantial Prison Population Reductions.

18. Heather Scheonfeld and Michael Campbell's case studies of New Jersey, Pennsylvania, Illinois, and Michigan provide a compelling case for this argument. What they find is that prison population reductions were more likely to be successful if this could be accomplished in what they called "back-end correctional processes." If reductions hinged on front-end processes—read got closer to the legislature—they were much less likely to happen. See:

Schoenfeld, H., and M. C. Campbell. 2023. Early 21st Century Penal Reform: A Comparative Analysis of Four States' Responses to the Problems of Mass Incarceration. *Law & Policy*, *45*(4), 482–506.

19. They may even have a negative impact. There has been a fierce debate about the impact of intense focus on police/minority community relations and the need for police reform initiated by the Black Lives Movement (BLM). One study suggests that cities where there were BLM protests tended to see a reduction in police killings but an increase in homicides. The estimates suggest roughly 300 fewer police killings but an increase of 1,000 to as much as 6,000 homicides. This seems consistent with a broader narrative that when the police retreat from socially stressed, high-crime neighborhoods they are involved in fewer violent confrontations but violence itself actually increases.

See: Campbell, Travis. Black Lives Matter's Effect on Police Lethal Use-of-Force (May 13, 2021), SSRN: https://ssrn.com/abstract=3767097.

20. Sawyer, Wendy, and Peter Wagner. "Mass Incarceration: The Whole Pie 2020." Prison Policy Initiative, https://www.prisonpolicy.org/reports/pie2020.html.

21. A quick back-of-the-envelope way to buttress this claim is to revisit the "World Prison League" numbers discussed in chapter 1. If you look at the prison population rate listed in the World Prison Brief for 2020, the United States is ranked first out of 223 countries listed. If you knocked 40 percent off the rate of 629 per 100,000 listed, the adjusted US figure would be 377.4. That would drop the United States to seventeenth place on this list. The nearest comparable democracy would be Australia, which comes in at ninety-third with a rate of 165. You could make a case for Israel, which is forty-ninth with a rate of 234. Even accepting that, though, leaves the United States as the mass incarceration champ by a long, long way. See:

World Prison Brief, Institute for Crime and Justice Policy Research, 2020. "Highest to Lowest—Prison Population Rate," https://www.prisonstudies.org/highest-to -lowest/prison_population_rate?field_region_taxonomy_tid=All.

22. This is meant as an approximate way to visualize these numbers, it's not an exact calculation. Those bars represent the median incarceration rate within a state between 1978 and 2019. The highest rates are not in 2019, but they are all to the right of that median figure. Looking at the median tells you what incarceration rates would look like if they were half of the highest number logged in that time window.

23. International comparisons of crime rates need to be taken with a pinch of salt, but according to the United Nations Office on Drugs and Crime, the United States has a homicide rate of 4.96 per 1,000 people, which puts it in the company of Cuba, Kazakhstan, Kenya, and Angola. Canada, our immediate neighbor and arguably closest social and cultural analog, has a homicide rate of 1.76. So by that measure, the United States is nearly three times as violent as Canada. Mass shootings in the United States far outstrip comparable other Western democracies. Violent crime rates, of course, vary enormously between and within states. Generally speaking, Southern states have higher rates of violent crime, as do larger cities. Independent collectors of crime statistics at the city level provide some eye-popping numbers on localized levels of violence. The long-running "HeyJackass!" website (mission: to illustrate Chicago values) keeps a running "shot clock" for the city. In 2021 it reported a person

was shot in Chicago roughly once every two hours. In 2019 Chicago had 521 homicides. To put that into context, London, United Kingdom, with roughly three times the population of Chicago, recorded 149 homicides that same year. See:

World Population Review. Violent Crime Rates by Country 2022, https://worldpopulationreview.com/country-rankings/violent-crime-rates-by-countrym.

Federal Bureau of Investigation. Crime in the United States, 2019, https://ucr.fbi.gov/crime-in-the-u.s/2019/crime-in-the-u.s.-2019/topic-pages/violent-crime.

HeyJackass! 2022. https://heyjackass.com/category/chicago-crime-2021/.

Action on Armed Violence. 2021. London 2019: A Year of Violent Deaths Examined, https://aoav.org.uk/2021/london-murder-capital-a-year-of-violent-deaths-examined/.

24. There's a huge amount of literature on what does or does not influence violent crime, and the sort of brief summary I'm providing here is skipping over important variables and undoubtedly glossing over a mountain of important detail. The basic causal variables I am mentioning, though, are backed up by research done by some of the best in the business. For good examples and overviews see:

Zimring, W. D. S. F. E. 2006. *The Great American Crime Decline*. New York: Oxford University Press.

Zimring, F. E. 2011. *The City That Became Safe: New York's Lessons for Urban Crime and Its Control*. New York: Oxford University Press.

Donohue, J. J., and S. Levitt. 2020. The Impact of Legalized Abortion on Crime over the Last Two Decades. *American Law and Economics Review*, *22*(2), 241–302.

25. Donohue and Levitt, The Impact of Legalized Abortion on Crime over the Last Two Decades, 241–302.

26. The evidence for improved street lighting is strong; the evidence for "greening" abandoned lots is more mixed, but untended abandoned lots are pretty consistently correlated with more crime. See:

Welsh, B. C., and D. P. Farrington. 2008. Effects of Improved Street Lighting on Crime. *Campbell Systematic Reviews*, *4*(1), 1–51.

Sivak, C. J., A. L. Pearson, and P. Hurlburt. 2021. Effects of Vacant Lots on Human Health: A Systematic Review of the Evidence. *Landscape and Urban Planning*, *208*, 104020.

27. Sharkey, P., G. Torrats-Espinosa, and D. Takyar. 2017. Community and the Crime Decline: The Causal Effect of Local Nonprofits on Violent Crime. *American Sociological Review*, *82*(6), 1214–40.

28. The thumbnail description I'm giving of Sharkey's arguments do not do them proper justice. They are more fully developed here: Sharkey, P. 2018. *Uneasy Peace: The Great Crime Decline, the Renewal of City Life, and the Next War on Violence*. New York: W.W. Norton and Company.

29. Mayhew, D. R. 2004. *Congress: The Electoral Connection*. New Haven, CT: Yale University Press.

30. One report by the Bureau of Justice statistics looked at firearm homicides by race over a nearly two-decade period, 1993–2010. They found the rate of firearm homicide for white Americans was 1.9 per 100,000 population. The comparable rate for Black Americans was more than seven times higher, 14.6. The latter number was

a big improvement—in the early 1990s it was 30. See: Planty, M., and J. L. Truman. Firearm Violence, 1993–2011. Washington, DC: Bureau of Justice Statistics, US Department of Justice. Figure 5.

31. The report was released in 1965. Though its formal title was "The Negro Family: The Case for National Action," it has always colloquially been called the Moynihan Report. See:

Moynihan, D. P. 1965. *The Negro Family: The Case for National Action* (No. 3). Washington, DC: US Government Printing Office.

32. Moynihan's arguments were not just condemned as racist but also sexist. Its traditional, patriarchal conception of family drew the ire of contemporary feminists, and read through modern eyes, it seems, at a minimum, to rely heavily on old-fashioned conceptions of gender roles.

33. Rustin, B., and D. P. Moynihan. 1966. *Which Way? A Discussion of Racial Tensions*. Lake Charles, LA: The America Press, 23–24.

34. For example, consistent with Moynihan's arguments, children (particularly males) raised in single-parent (especially fatherless) homes have been repeatedly found to be at higher risk of criminal behavior. For a review of the relevant literature see:

Kroese, J., W. Bernasco, A. C. Liefbroer, and J. Rouwendal. 2021. Growing Up in Single-Parent Families and the Criminal Involvement of Adolescents: A Systematic Review. *Psychology, Crime & Law*, *27*(1), 61–75.

The relationship between fatherless homes and juvenile delinquency, though, is more complex than presented in arguments such as the Moynihan Report. For example, nonresident fathers often increase contact with their biological children when the latter start to exhibit troubling behavior. See:

Coley, R. L., and B. L. Medeiros. 2007. Reciprocal Longitudinal Relations between Nonresident Father Involvement and Adolescent Delinquency. *Child Development*, *78*(1), 132–47.

35. There's an interesting study that looks in-depth at how the New Jersey legislature addressed a range of penal reform laws over more than a decade during the early part of the century. They find some change, some continuity, and a lot of what they term "crime control theater." The Manhattan Institute (a conservative think tank) responded to a raft of decarceration proposals advanced by 2020 contenders for Democratic presidential candidate with a study suggesting that because most people serving time have been convicted of a violent crime the main effect of decarceration will be an increase in violent crimes. See:

Campbell, M., H. Schoenfeld, and P. Vaughn. 2020. Same Old Song and Dance? An Analysis of Legislative Activity in a Period of Penal Reform. *Punishment & Society*, *22*(4), 389–412.

Mangual, R. A. 2019. Issues 2020: Mass Decarceration Will Increase Violent Crime. The Manhattan Institute, https://www.manhattan-institute.org/issues2020 -mass-decarceration-will-increase-violent-crime.

36. Durkheim, E. 2018. The Division of Labor in Society. In *Social Stratification*. UK: Routledge, 217–22. The concept of anomie was introduced in the original 1893 edition of this work.

37. Jonathan Haidt provides a good description of an anomic society. See:

Haidt, J. 2006. *The Happiness Hypothesis: Finding Modern Truth in Ancient Wisdom*. New York: Basic Books, 175–77.

38. These numbers are based on estimates presented in table 1 of Shannon et al. (The Growth, Scope, and Spatial Distribution of People with Felony Records in the United States, 1948–2010, p. 1805).

39. See figure 2, panel B in Shannon et al. (The Growth, Scope, and Spatial Distribution of People with Felony Records in the United States, 1948–2010). That estimate is slightly under twenty million in 2010. That number has certainly increased significantly since then.

40. Given I'm working from 2010 estimates provided by Shannon et al. (The Growth, Scope, and Spatial Distribution of People with Felony Records in the United States, 1948–2010), this ranking is contestable. Florida's population in 2020 was roughly 21 to 22 million. I'm making a guess that the population with a felony conviction in 2022 was higher than that, which seems a reasonable bet given the number was 20 million more than ten years previously. At a minimum, considered as a state population, felons would rank no lower than fourth below Florida, but above New York.

41. These are all successful academics whose work is well-known and broadly cited. In my own humble opinion, though, they should be even better recognized than they are.

Index